Diversity of Patchwork Capitalism in Central and Eastern Europe

This book is a comparative study which sheds a new empirical and theoretical light on the nature of post-communist capitalism in 11 EU new member countries of Central and Eastern Europe, or CEE11.

Extending and modifying a well-established conceptual framework for comparative capitalism rooted in new institutional economics and economic sociology, it offers a better explanation for transition-specific and path-dependent factors inherent to systemic transformation. Based on a vast dataset, the book therefore illuminates the (dis)similarities among the institutional architectures in the EU countries. Thus, the book argues that the evolving capitalism in Central and Eastern Europe exhibits strong symptoms of institutional ambiguity or a "patchwork" nature which makes it a distinct category from any of the co-existing models of Western European capitalism.

This book will be of key interest to scholars and students of comparative political economy, Eastern European politics, post-communist studies and more broadly to researchers in the fields of economics, European politics and the wider social sciences. It will also be of significance to journalists, policymakers, members of international organizations and consultancies with an interest in Central and Eastern Europe and in European integration.

Ryszard Rapacki is Full Professor and former Head of the Department of Economics at SGH Warsaw School of Economics, Poland.

Routledge Advances in European Politics

Italy from Crisis to Crisis
Political Economy, Security, and Society in the 21st Century
Matthew Evangelista

Lobbying Success in the European Union
The Role of Information and Frames
Daniel Rasch

Muslim Attitudes Towards the European Union
Bernd Schlipphak and Mujtaba Isani

The Populist Radical Left in Europe
Edited by Giorgos Katsambekis and Alexandros Kioupkiolis

External Energy Security in the European Union
Small Member States' Perspective
Matúš Mišík

The Balkans on Trial
Justice vs. Realpolitik
Carole Hodge

Greece and Turkey in Conflict and Cooperation
From Europeanization to De-Europeanization
Edited by Alexis Heraclides and Gizem Alioğlu Çakmak

Diversity of Patchwork Capitalism in Central and Eastern Europe
Edited by Ryszard Rapacki

For more information about this series, please visit: www.routledge.com/Routledge-Advances-in-European-Politics/book-series/AEP

Diversity of Patchwork Capitalism in Central and Eastern Europe

Edited by Ryszard Rapacki

In collaboration with Adam Czerniak

Routledge
Taylor & Francis Group
LONDON AND NEW YORK

First published 2019
by Routledge
2 Park Square, Milton Park, Abingdon, Oxon OX14 4RN

and by Routledge
605 Third Avenue, New York, NY 10017

First issued in paperback 2020

Routledge is an imprint of the Taylor & Francis Group, an informa business

The publishing of this book has been funded by a grant no. 2014/13/B/HS4/00549 from the National Science Centre, Poland.

British Library Cataloguing-in-Publication Data
A catalogue record for this book is available from the British Library

Library of Congress Cataloging-in-Publication Data
Names: Rapacki, Ryszard, editor.
Title: Diversity of patchwork capitalism in Central and Eastern Europe/ edited by Ryszard Rapacki.
Description: Abingdon, Oxon; New York, NY: Routledge, 2019. | Series: Routledge advances in European politics | Includes bibliographical references and index.
Identifiers: LCCN 2019004022 | ISBN 9780367174590 (hardback) | ISBN 9780429616198 (web pdf) | ISBN 9780429614989 (epub) | ISBN 9780429613777 (mobipocket/kindle)
Subjects: LCSH: Capitalism—Europe, Central. | Capitalism—Europe, Eastern. | Capitalism—Former communist countries.
Classification: LCC HC244. D54 2019 | DDC 330.943—dc23
LC record available at https://lccn.loc.gov/2019004022

ISBN 13: 978-0-367-72720-8 (pbk)
ISBN 13: 978-0-367-17459-0 (hbk)
ISBN 13: 978-0-429-05690-1 (ebk)

DOI: 10.4324/9780429056901

Contents

Maps

Tables

Contributors

Book editor

Ryszard Rapacki (Ph.D., Habilitation and Professor national academic title in Economics) is Full Professor and former Head of Department of Economics II at SGH Warsaw School of Economics. Principal Investigator and leader of the research team working on the project: "Diversity of the Emerging Capitalism in Poland and New EU Member Countries from Central and Eastern Europe" funded by a grant from the Polish National Science Center. Published over 200 journal articles, books, book chapters and conference papers in Poland and abroad (US, UK, Austria, Belgium, Estonia, Germany, Mexico, Taiwan) on diversity of contemporary capitalism, economic growth and real income convergence, privatization and international technology transfer. Co-edited (with George Blazyca) two books published in the UK (Pinter, 1991 and Edward Elgar, 2001) and contributed several chapters to edited volumes published by Routledge between 1995 and 2017 (eds. V. V. Ramanadham, M. Myant and T. Cox, and A. Grimmel). His most recent publications include three articles and three book chapters (published by Nomos in Germany, Nova Science in the US and the Polish Academy of Sciences) on the emerging diversity of post-communist capitalism in Central and Eastern Europe.

Chapter authors

Adam Czerniak (Ph.D. in Economics) is Assistant Professor, Department of Economics II at SGH Warsaw School of Economics. Member of a team working on the research project on the "Diversity of the Emerging Capitalism in Poland and New EU Member Countries from Central and Eastern Europe" funded by a grant from the Polish National Science Center. He is also a chief economist at the Center for Policy Analysis "Polityka Insight". Until 2012 he was a banking economist, before that he had worked with the World Bank and the FOR Foundation and also held a fellowship from the Ronald Coase Institute. He authored academic publications on functioning of the real estate market, institutional economics, economic sociology, philosophy of economics and economic policy. His most recent publications include four articles and a book chapter (published by the Polish Academy of Sciences) on the emerging diversity of post-communist capitalism in Central and Eastern Europe, with special focus on the varieties of residential capitalism.

Juliusz Gardawski (Ph.D., Habilitation and Professor national academic title in Sociology) is Full Professor and former Head of the Institute of Philosophy, Sociology and Economic Sociology at SGH Warsaw School of Economics, and Editor-in-Chief of the *Warsaw Forum of Economic Sociology*. Member of a team working on the research project on the "Diversity of the Emerging Capitalism in Poland and New EU Member Countries from Central and Eastern Europe" funded by a grant from the Polish National Science Center. His research interests cover the labor market and industrial relations and social dialogue in Poland and East Central Europe, the working-class attitudes toward the market and democracy, and workers' consciousness and economic mentality in a broad international perspective. His recent publications include three articles and a book chapter (published by the Polish Academy of Sciences) on the emerging diversity of post-communist capitalism in Central and Eastern Europe.

Bożena Horbaczewska (Ph.D. in Economics) is Assistant Professor, Department of Economics II at SGH Warsaw School of Economics. Member of a team working on the research project: "Diversity of the Emerging Capitalism in Poland and New EU Member Countries from Central and Eastern Europe" funded by a grant from the Polish National Science Center. Her research interests include financial markets with special reference to stock markets, dividend policies and corporate governance. Most recent publications include three articles and a book chapter (published by the Polish Academy of Sciences) on the emerging diversity of post-communist capitalism in Central and Eastern Europe.

Adam Karbowski (Ph.D. in Economics, M.A. in Psychology, P.G. Dip. in Philosophy) is Assistant Professor, Department of Business Economics at SGH Warsaw School of Economics. Member of a team working on the research project on the "Diversity of the Emerging Capitalism in Poland and New EU Member Countries from Central and Eastern Europe" funded by a grant from the Polish National Science Center. His research is interdisciplinary and combines recent advances in economics, psychology and sociology. He published his papers in journals including *Personality and Individual Differences*, *Behavioural Processes*, *Frontiers in Psychology*, *PLOS ONE*, *Economics and Sociology*, *Polish Psychological Bulletin*, *Warsaw Forum of Economic Sociology* and *Ekonomista*. His most recent publications include three articles and a book chapter (published by the Polish Academy of Sciences) on the emerging diversity of post-communist capitalism in Central and Eastern Europe.

Piotr Maszczyk (Ph.D. in Economics) is Assistant Professor at the Department of Economics II, and Head of the Research Centre on Institutions and Diversity of Capitalism at SGH Warsaw School of Economics. Member of a team working on the research project on the "Diversity of the Emerging Capitalism in Poland

and New EU Member Countries from Central and Eastern Europe" funded by a grant from the Polish National Science Center. His research interests cover, inter alia, institutional economics, comparative economic studies and diversity of modern capitalism. Author and co-author of over 30 scholarly articles and books. Most recent publications include three articles and two book chapters (published by Nomos in Germany and the Polish Academy of Sciences) on the emerging diversity of post-communist capitalism in Central and Eastern Europe.

Mariusz Próchniak (Ph.D. and Habilitation in Economics) is Associate Professor and Head of the Department of Economics II, SGH Warsaw School of Economics. Member of a team working on the research project on the "Diversity of the Emerging Capitalism in Poland and New EU Member Countries from Central and Eastern Europe" funded by a grant from the Polish National Science Center. His research interests focus on macroeconomics, and in particular on economic growth and real convergence, and diversity of contemporary capitalism. He (co)authored some 150 articles, books and book chapters published in *Economic Modelling*, *Eastern European Economics*, *Post-Communist Economies* and *Empirica*. Most recent publications include four articles (in Poland and the UK) and a book chapter (published by the Polish Academy of Sciences) on the emerging diversity of post-communist capitalism in Central and Eastern Europe.

Rafał Towalski (Ph.D. in Economics) is Assistant Professor at the Institute of Philosophy, Sociology and Economic Sociology at the Warsaw School of Economics. Collaborator of the research team working on the "Diversity of the Emerging Capitalism in Poland and New EU Member Countries from Central and Eastern Europe" project funded by a grant from the Polish National Science Center. His research interests encompass, inter alia, industrial relations and social dialogue, transformation in the public sector, social effects of privatization, human resource management practices and working conditions. He authored some 50 articles and book chapters, published in Belgium, France, Poland and the UK. Most recent publications include two articles and a book chapter (published by the Polish Academy of Sciences) on the emerging diversity of post-communist capitalism in Central and Eastern Europe.

Preface

The present book provides the results of an interdisciplinary research project on "comparative capitalism", carried out by the authors between 2015 and 2018. The research was funded by a grant from the National Science Center in Poland.[1] Its main aim was to shed new empirical and theoretical light on the nature and the most salient features of the emerging post-communist capitalism in 11 EU new member countries in Central and Eastern Europe, or CEE11 (Bulgaria, Croatia, Czech Republic, Estonia, Hungary, Latvia, Lithuania, Poland, Romania, Slovakia and Slovenia), against a broader backdrop of Western-type models of capitalism co-existing in the European Union (EU14). Altogether, the research sample involved encompassed 25 EU member states.

Adopting the theoretical and conceptual framework already well established in state-of-the-art literature and rooted in the paradigms of new institutional economics and new economic sociology the authors substantially amended and extended the original framework to better fit the specific conditions of former socialist countries and to take proper account of the peculiarities of their institutional endowment. Simultaneously, they used sophisticated machine-learning methods to capture the similarities among the EU countries, and to come up with a new typology of their clusters, using a vast dataset of over 130 institutional indicators, to an extent that has not been conducted in "comparative capitalism" studies ever before. Moreover, unlike in most other studies on the subject, the indicators applied in the book show both the input (i.e. institutional determinants) and output (i.e. economic performance) sides of diverse models of capitalism and their changes between 2005 and 2014, that is the initial and the final years of the study. Furthermore, the book provides a thorough explanation of the process and mechanisms that shaped the peculiar "institutional matrix" of capitalism in CEE11 countries, including an in-depth analysis of the coherence and complementarities among six dimensions or areas of their institutional architecture: (1) product market competition, (2) labor market and industrial relations, (3) financial intermediation, (4) social protection, (5) knowledge system and (6) housing market.

Based on their findings, the authors argue that – notwithstanding some seeming similarities to the Mediterranean model of capitalism – the most salient features of the evolving capitalism in CEE11 countries comprise, inter alia, the institutional ambiguity and a clear deficit of complementarity within its institutional architecture which justify dubbing it a "patchwork capitalism" as a new research category, distinct from any of the models of Western European capitalism in the European Union. At the same time, the patchwork capitalism in individual CEE11 countries exhibits essential institutional discrepancies vis-à-vis their peers which implies a considerable scope of diversity within this category.

The book is divided into ten chapters allocated to two parts. Part I provides the theoretical background for the study concerned and consists of three chapters. Chapter 1, authored by Juliusz Gardawski and Ryszard Rapacki, outlines the conceptual framework and a general theoretical background of the research on comparative capitalism. The authors emphasize close links of this line of research with the tradition of new institutional economics (NIE) and new economic sociology (NES), and explain the core concepts inherent to NIE and NES (such as institutions, institutional change and institutional complementarity) which are instrumental for the present research. In the "historical" part of the chapter they highlight the intellectual inspirations of Max Weber and the early pioneers of comparative capitalism, and overview the contributions of the contemporary antecedents of this current in the second half of the 20th century. In Chapter 2 the authors (Ryszard Rapacki, Adam Czerniak, Juliusz Gardawski, Bożena Horbaczewska, Adam Karbowski, Piotr Maszczyk, Mariusz Próchniak and Rafał Towalski) carry out a critical survey of the most representative theoretical and empirical studies on the emerging post-communist capitalism, with special reference to Central and Eastern Europe. In their overview they distinguish between (1) standard conceptual and methodological frameworks applied in the pertinent research, (2) straightforward applications or extensions of these frameworks, and (3) non-standard approaches. In Chapter 3 Adam Czerniak and Piotr Maszczyk bridge the theoretical and empirical parts of the book discussing the major methodological challenges facing the comparative studies on post-communist capitalism and outlining the research method and approach adopted in the present study. The authors pay special attention to a detailed substantiation of the amendments and extensions made to the original DoC methodology (i.e. the Diversity of Capitalism developed by Bruno Amable), which was the starting point for this research, aimed at adjusting it to the specific conditions of former socialist countries from the CEE region. Simultaneously, Czerniak and Maszczyk thoroughly explain the intricacies of the main research tool employed in this study, that is the subspace clustering machine-learning method (ORCLUS algorithm).

Part II of the book is devoted to the presentation and discussion of the empirical results. Chapters 4 through 9 show and interpret the major findings of the present study, broken down into six institutional areas, mentioned above. In Chapter 4 Mariusz Próchniak discusses the empirical results of the subspace clustering exercise in the area of product market competition. He also explains the reasons behind a limited number of clusters (only two) identified in the European Union in this institutional domain and tries to answer the question why the CEE11 economies have not formed their own cluster there. The authors of Chapter 5, Juliusz Gardawski and Rafał Towalski take up the issue of the co-existence of various labor market and industrial relations regimes in the European Union, with special regard to the 11 new EU member countries from the CEE region. They point to some ambiguities in the picture of the four clusters co-existing in the EU in this institutional area, identified by the ORCLUS algorithm. Gardawski and Towalski also provide some clue to comprehend why the CEE11 economies were found in two distinct clusters in the labor market and industrial relations area. In the concluding part of the chapter, they outline the most recent trends that have emerged in this area in CEE11 countries since 2014. In turn, Bożena Horbaczewska in Chapter 6 gives account of the most important empirical findings of the study in the area of financial intermediation and explains why the CEE11 countries have not formed their own, distinct model of capitalism and why only two clusters, i.e. a "bank-based" and a "market-based" models of financial intermediation were identified in the European Union. She also points to the key changes in financial intermediation that occurred between 2005 and 2014 in the CEE region resulting in – in varying proportions – both the convergence and divergence trends of individual CEE11 countries toward the "bank-based" and "market-based" models. In Chapter 7, Piotr Maszczyk sheds new empirical light on the three models of social protection system identified in the EU24 economies by 2014 and their evolution in the 2005–2014 period and highlights the role of "path dependence" as a key determinant of the institutional architecture in this particular domain. He also delves into the main underlying reasons that might explain the diverging evolutionary paths of the social protection systems in two CEE countries, i.e. Croatia and Slovenia which were found to be outliers from a separate CEE cluster in this area. In Chapter 8 that follows Adam Karbowski discusses the intricacies of the knowledge system and its evolution in the sample countries between 2005 and 2014. Based on the results of subspace clustering, he also carries out a comparative analysis of the most salient similarities and differences between four clusters identified in the European Union, with special reference to the CEE cluster. The central theme of Chapter 9 is the housing market. Adam Czerniak outlines the main institutional traits of four models of residential capitalism in the European Union identified by the ORCLUS algorithm. The author pays special attention to the "non-commodified" model in this institutional area found in the CEE11 economies. He also embarks on an in-depth analysis of the directions, strength and most plausible causalities involved in the changes in the institutional distance between individual CEE countries and the remaining clusters existing in the housing market in the 2005–2014 period. In the last chapter in this part (Chapter 10) Adam Czerniak and Ryszard Rapacki provide a summary of the empirical results of the whole study and justify the use of the term "patchwork capitalism" as the most adequate notion reflecting the nature and most important peculiarities of the evolving capitalism in Central and Eastern Europe. The book closes with "Concluding remarks" which are aimed at summarizing the research results and putting them in a broader perspective of new trends that emerged in both the CEE11 countries and in the European Union at large after 2014 (final year of the present study) and at outlining new challenges for the future research agenda in the field of comparative capitalism in the CEE region in particular and in the European Union in general.

Handing over the present book to the readers, the editor and the authors hope that it will induce an in-depth and critical reflection while at the same time inspiring new questions that mark out successive intellectual challenges and open up new territories in the study of comparative capitalism.

Ryszard Rapacki
Warsaw, December 2018

Note

1 Diversity of the Emerging Capitalism in Poland and New EU Member Countries from Central and Eastern Europe – an Attempt at Institutional Comparative Analysis", grant no. 2014/13/B/HS4/00549.

Acknowledgments

This book, as always, represents the efforts of a collective that goes beyond the team of authors. But first the editor must thank the authors for their patience in responding to the many requests we made with the assistant editor for several rounds of revisions and clarifications aimed to make the contributions clearer for the largely Western audience at which it is targeted. Special thanks go to Adam Czerniak who volunteered to act as assistant editor and whose invaluable help tremendously raised the quality standards of the edited book.

I am also grateful for the funding from the National Science Center in Poland which made the research project on the diversity of post-communist capitalism in Central and Eastern Europe feasible. I acknowledge with thanks the support from the management team of SGH Warsaw School of Economics, and in particular the Rectors and Provosts of SGH, and the Deans of the Collegium of World Economy at SGH.

I appreciate very much, similar to other research team members, fruitful discussions and encouragement from the colleagues in the Department of Economics II at SGH. Thanks also go to Aleksandra Bardadyn from this department who was extremely helpful to the editor and the team of authors with her initiative and high secretarial and organizational skills over the whole life cycle of our research project and book preparations.

On behalf of the research team, I would also like to express our gratitude to Martyna Kobus who suggested the application of the subspace clustering machine-learning method to our analytical problem.

Finally, very special thanks go to my wife and daughter, Anna Rapacka and Urszula Rapacka for their forbearance, support and encouragement as well as for their intellectual and linguistic inspirations during this time-consuming three-year book project.

Part I

Theoretical background

1 Comparative capitalism

Conceptual framework and theoretical background

Juliusz Gardawski and Ryszard Rapacki

Introduction

As spelled out in the preface, the overriding objective of the present book is to shed new empirical and theoretical light on the nature and most salient features of the emerging post-communist capitalism in Central and Eastern Europe (CEE) against the broader backdrop of Western-type models of capitalism co-existing in the European Union, with a view to better understand the peculiarities of institutional development in the CEE economies. In our approach, we subscribe to the research tradition dubbed "comparative capitalism" or "comparative political economy". In particular, in terms of its conceptual and methodological framework, the book draws considerably from two major contributions to the field: the trailblazing works on the diversity of contemporary capitalism in the Western Hemisphere by Bruno Amable (2003) and – to a lesser extent – Peter Hall and David Soskice (2001), respectively. Simultaneously, as the studies on comparative capitalism represent a broad, multidisciplinary perspective and are deeply rooted in the major currents of social sciences, in more general terms we also refer to most relevant theories in this scholarly area.

As a starting premise in our research, we discard the presumption regarding the incomparability of developed capitalist political economies in Western Europe and post-communist capitalism emerging in Central and Eastern Europe – a presumption which was popular in the early 1990s. Instead, we will argue that notwithstanding substantial dissimilarities in the institutional endowment between the former and the latter, the standard analytical frameworks developed in the West can be applied – though with some important extensions and amendments – to former socialist countries in Central and Eastern Europe, even more so with the fast economic and institutional catching-up process underway in CEE countries. At the same time, we will endeavor to highlight the most salient peculiarities of the evolving capitalism in the CEE region as a new research category. These peculiarities provide a strong premise for singling out a new, distinct type of European capitalism and justify the term "patchwork capitalism"[1] as the most adequate descriptor in our view of the essence of post-communist political economies that have evolved in Central and Eastern Europe since the outset of systemic transformation.

DOI: 10.4324/9780429056901-2

The specificity of the rebirth process of capitalism in the countries of Central and Eastern Europe and the multiplicity of institutional orders co-existing in the European Union requires conducting both economic analyses constituting the core reference framework of our research (new institutional economics) and sociological, anthropological and cultural studies (new economic sociology and related disciplines). Economic sociology can be roughly divided into the sociology of rational choice (James Coleman, Gary Becker) and humanistic-oriented sociology (Mark Granovetter). In our research, we will capitalize mostly on the latter trend, with sociological concepts playing (generally) a significant yet auxiliary role.

In essence, the study of comparative capitalism constitutes an important thread in a broad and heterogeneous research stream in contemporary social sciences. The key idea underlying the comparative capitalism approach is that different capitalist countries can survive and thrive with somewhat different sets of social arrangements or institutions aimed at coordinating production in particular and decisions made by social, economic and political agents in general. It highlights the co-existence of various models of capitalism or diverse forms of institutional architecture in particular countries or their groups. However, it should be emphasized that the institutional divergence or diversity of capitalism approach has faced opposition from the "convergence school", typical for the orthodox economic theory, which assumes the existence of one optimal pattern of institutional arrangements for a given historical period. At different times such convergence benchmarks were believed to be the institutional systems of the United States, Japan or Germany. Currently in the EU, the German institutional order serves as a reference model for the policymaking by the European Commission, which seems to be a challenge for the study of the multiplicity of capitalism (Johnston and Regan, 2018).

The research perspective emphasizing the diversity of capitalism has gained increasing popularity in social sciences in the last 50 years, especially since the (re)emergence of new institutional economics (NIE) in the United States (North, Williamson, Coase)[2] and new economic sociology (NES) and related disciplines of social sciences (Swedberg and Granovetter, 1992). NIE draws substantially from the scholarship of game theory and rational choice theory as well as cognitive psychology, while contemporary sociological sciences derive their inspiration from diverse sources that include the legacy of classical sociology: Durkheim's theory (he defined sociology as the science of institutions), Max Weber's *Wirtschaftssoziologie* tradition, the embeddedness idea of Karl Polanyi and the current lines of research such as interpretative sociology and constructivism developed by Berger and Luckman. The basic methodological premise of new institutionalists is that "institutions matter" as a key explanatory variable of socio-economic development and human behavior in a society. Over time this assumption has proliferated and started to become widely accepted and incorporated into the research agenda of a growing number of social science disciplines, including in particular economic sociology, political sciences, social psychology, organizational theory, management science, public choice theory, international relations, law and economics and cultural anthropology (Jasiecki, 2013).

The difference between old institutionalism (OI) and new institutionalism (NI) can be described as follows. The former is represented primarily by the American economic institutionalism of the late 19th and early 20th centuries, but the interest in institutionalism also arose in other disciplines of social sciences: "therefore, old and new institutionalism are different orientations and appearing in social sciences for the good 120 years. As part of almost every discipline (e.g. economics, political science or sociology), different variants of OI and NI can be distinguished" (Chmielewski, 2011). OI corresponds to the classical phase in the development of economic sociology (Marx, Durkheim, Weber, Sombart). Despite the differences regarding the role of individuals and institutions, the OI concepts emphasized the dependence of social activities on principles, norms, traditions, and institutional and cultural structure. Compared with neoclassical economics, the importance of intentional actions in the name of pursuing individual interests decreased while the interest in institutional and cultural factors increased. A separate mention should be devoted to Max Weber, whose oeuvre enjoyed a special status in this current and who developed his own concept of historical factors as well as his own version of "methodological individualism" (for a more comprehensive discussion, see Section 1.2).

In the first half of the 20th century, institutionalism almost completely vanished from the social sciences (the only exception being sociology) and was replaced by a non-institutional behavioral paradigm. The new paradigm was in essence reductionist (as it demanded to perceive social phenomena as outcomes of individual social activities, and only to a lesser extent as a result of institutional and cultural influences); utilitarian (postulating the interpretation of human actions as an effect of focusing on individual benefits rather than social obligations); instrumentalist (putting emphasis on the allocation of resources in the name of interest, ignoring the influence of symbols, rituals and ceremonies); and functionalist (focused on the study of social phenomena in terms of moving toward their equilibrium positions and assuming a single optimum) (March and Olsen, 1989).

The end of the 1970s and the 1980s witnessed a renaissance of institutionalism in many fields of social sciences, most often however not in the form of OI, but rather as a blend integrating OI with some important elements of non-institutional trend and neoclassical economics. OI downsized the role of "methodological individualism", which is a key factor for the mainstream or orthodox economic theory. The new institutionalism accepted this assumption, which enabled the application of the rational choice theory, building formal models, the use of game theory and combining institutional constraints (rules of the game) with the interests of players (Chmielewski, 2011). Williamson pointed out that in the mainstream economics, the new institutionalism should be seen as complementary and not substituting the traditional economic analysis (Williamson, 1975, p. 1; Swedberg and Granovetter, 1992, p. 14). Still, not all the directions of new institutionalism amalgamated the OI with the economic methodology. These include, among others, Granovetter's economic sociology (1985), Etzioni's socio-economics (1988) and Hodgson's evolutionary economics (1988), distancing themselves to some degree from the sociology of rational choice of James Coleman or Gary Becker.

As the research on comparative capitalism has been deeply embedded in the new institutional economics paradigm, the core element of its conceptual and methodological framework is the notion of "institutions". Hence, before outlining the theoretical background of contemporary research on comparative capitalism, we will first embark on a brief discussion of key concepts and definitions which are inextricably linked to the very institutionalist approach.

1.1 Key concepts and definitions

The rebirth and development of new institutional economics, as part of new institutionalism (NI), may be to some extent interpreted as a response to the revival of market fundamentalism and the neoclassical orthodoxy with their unrealistic assumptions regarding the operation of private markets and human behavior, after the first oil shock in 1973.[3]

NIE abandons the standard neoclassical assumption that individuals have perfect information and unbounded rationality and that transactions are costless and instantaneous. Instead, it assumes that individuals have incomplete information and limited mental capacity;[4] because of this they face uncertainty about unforeseen events and outcomes and incur transaction costs to acquire missing information. With a view to reduce risk and transaction costs, members of society create formal and informal institutions: constitutions, laws, contracts and regulations as well as norms of conduct, beliefs and habits of thought and behavior (Ménard and Shirley, 2005).

On the other hand, however, unlike "old" institutional (or OI) economics (Veblen, Commons, Mitchell), NIE does not completely abandon the neoclassical economic theory. While the new institutionalists reject the neoclassical belief in perfect information and instrumental rationality, they simultaneously accept the orthodox assumptions of scarcity and competition (Arrow, 1987; Williamson, 2000).

However, what gives NIE a distinct identity and rising intellectual recognition is the fact that it tries to raise and answer questions which neoclassical economics has never addressed. In particular, as indicated by North (2004), neoclassical economics was not created to explain the process of economic change, let alone the political and social change. New institutionalists in contrast aim to understand change through understanding human incentives and intentions as well as the beliefs, norms and rules they create in pursuit of their goals.

Notwithstanding the heterogeneity of the research program and diversity of approaches inherent to NIE institutional economists share a number of key assumptions and methodological premises or a fundamental set of statements about the world and the research program concerned. Following the Lakatosian definition, these may be interpreted as the "hard core", "positive heuristic" and "protective belt" (Lakatos, 1978) of new institutional economics. The most salient shared beliefs in NIE encompass in particular the following:

- Institutions have important effects on economic performance.
- Institutions may be analyzed using the same tools which have been developed in neoclassical tradition supported by additional research methods, such as case studies and experiments.

- An important methodological premise of any NIE research program is the interrelatedness of theory and empirical studies.
- The scope of NIE research programs ought to be interdisciplinary drawing from the scholarship of many disciplines of social and natural science (including history, cognitive science, law, psychology, sociology, political science, anthropology and evolutionary biology).
- While studying the role of institutions in economic performance, focus should be placed on long-term dynamic considerations of change, with special emphasis on the key role of innovation.
- Another important trait of the NIE approach is a specific understanding of the core building block of new institutional economics – the very notion of institutions. Unlike in the management science or mainstream economics where institutions are often understood as constructs synonymous to organizations, NIE conceives this term in a different manner (see the subsequent part of this section).

Apart from the key paradigm adopted in this study, which is NIE, we also make use of the humanistic paradigm of the new economic sociology (NES). Notwithstanding the differences, both paradigms are part of the new institutionalism (NI) and – seen from the angle of our research – are complementary. The differences involved boil down to a large extent, though not exclusively, to the scope of using the rational choice theory research apparatus. Anticipating the empirical results of our study presented in Chapters 4 through 10, we can hint at this stage that NIE allowed to build a tentative typology of political economies in Central and Eastern Europe against a broader backdrop of the co-existing models of capitalism in the European Union. It turned out, however, that the interpretation of some institutional differences requires the extension of the cognitive perspective to NES, to include certain cultural archetypes, which cannot in principle be explained by the rational choice theory. NES grows primarily from the opposition to "economic imperialism" whose main representative is Gary Becker. NES does not underestimate either the neoclassical tools or the rational choice theory, but rather builds a "sociological perspective upon economic phenomena" (Smelser and Swedberg, 2005, p. 3), pointing out that the economic phenomena, "[w]hile they use different emphases, theories, and methodologies, all economic sociologists argue that economic phenomena have to be understood in relation to the social mechanisms that facilitate, form, and maintain them" (Guillén et al., 2005 after Talmud, 2013, p. 1). NES focuses on contextual analysis. From Beckert and Streeck's point of view:

> markets and economic action can only be understood if they are conceived as social structures and social action, respectively – that is, embedded in social relations not originally created for economic purposes, and connected to a regime of collective values and interests of which economic efficiency is just one among others.
>
> (Beckert and Streeck, 2008, p. 12)

Three central propositions were adopted in the initial period of NES development: (1) economic action is a form of social action; (2) economic action is socially situated; and (3) economic institutions are social construction (Swedberg and Granovetter, 1992). In this respect, an economy is a "relational social space created by cultures, moral communities, arenas of political action, institutional practices, and shared and often reinforced cognitions and frames. [. . .] Economic sociology focuses on four dimensions shaping the economic structure and behavior: networks, power, institutions, and cognitions" (Beckert, 2007).

Among the NES research categories, the key role has been played by the notion of embeddedness, taken from Karl Polanyi. Seen from the angle of our research problem, the concept of embeddedness is particularly useful. This category was initially criticized, mostly due to its metaphorical character and the resulting difficulties with its operationalization, but later Zukin and DiMaggio managed to distinguish its additional dimensions (apart from the structural dimension being highlighted by Granovetter, they added cultural, political and cognitive dimensions; Zukin and DiMaggio, 1990).

The humanistic trend within the NES provides a significant enrichment of the concept of human motivation. The neoclassical economic theory defines human being as a *homo oeconomicus* making rational decisions and striving to realize his/her own interest. NES agrees to a certain extent with this simplification, since idealizations are necessary for building formal scientific models. However, it treats with great reserve the proposition that all altruistic behaviors stem logically from selfish interest. NES and behavioral economics have revealed the existence of altruistic motives that are independent of interest, and which sometimes may even hinder the realization of one's own interest (Kahneman, Knetsch and Thaler, 1986).

Institutions

The best-known and most followed definition of institutions within NIE is that put forward by Douglass North, who described them as "rules of the game". In North's wording:

> institutions are the rules of the game – both formal rules, informal norms and their enforcement characteristics. Together they define the way the game is played. Organizations are the players. They are made up of groups of individuals held together by some common objectives.
>
> (North, 2005, p. 22)

Noteworthy is his distinction between institutions as rules of the game which are not the same as players that play that game (organizations and individuals).

In his other work, North not only provided an answer to the question "what" are institutions but also explained "why" institutions are designed and implemented. In his view, "institutions are the product of intentional human efforts to give structure to an uncertain world and are congruent with a society's dominant belief system of how the world operates" (North, 2004).

Another prominent economist who contributed to the development of the NIE conceptual framework was Masahiko Aoki (2001, 2007), whose research made him a pioneer in comparative institutional analysis. In his studies he concentrated on institutions as pillars of collectively recognized rules and symbols as well as behavioral beliefs (expectations) of agents about other players' choices and intentions. According to Aoki, players base their own behavior (strategies, actions, etc.) on these beliefs. He argued that institutions are self-sustaining, salient patterns of social interactions. He defined institutions as "rules cum shared beliefs" (Aoki, 2001, 2007).

The foregoing definitions are more comprehensive than the conception of institutions adopted in old institutional economics (Veblen, Commons, Mitchell) as a commonly accepted way of thinking in a particular social group and the resulting rules and norms of behavior (e.g. ownership, income distribution and division of labor in a society).

North's proposition inspired other scholars to go along similar lines. For example, Bruno Amable defines institutions as follows: "Institutions are endogenously determined rules of the game [*in a society – authors' comment*]. Once the rules have been agreed upon, they are taken as parts of the environment by agents who devise their strategies within the constraints defined by these rules" (Amable, 2003, p. 10). In yet another part of his book Amable describes institutions in terms of political economy equilibria (Amable, 2003, p. 11).

Both definitions do not seem fully operational from the angle of the research objectives of this study and call for some particularization. That is why for the purpose of the present book we decided to adopt – as a core concept – the definition of institutions put forward by Ménard and Shirley, further amended with three important extensions.

> Institutions are written and unwritten rules, norms and constraints that humans devise to reduce uncertainty and control their environment. These include (i) written rules and agreements that govern contractual relations and corporate governance, (ii) constitutions, laws and rules that govern politics, government, finance, and society more broadly, and (iii) unwritten codes of conduct, norms of behavior and beliefs.
>
> (Ménard and Shirley, 2005, p. 1)

It has to be added, as the first amendment to our core definition, that in studying institutions and their interactions with specific arrangements, new institutionalists have become increasingly concerned with *mental models and other aspects of cognition* that determine how humans interpret reality, which in turn shape the institutional environment they build (North, 1991; Williamson, 2000; Tversky and Kahneman, 1981; Kahneman, Slovic and Tversky, 1982).

The second extension, or a complement to the core definition, emphasizes three more crucial aspects in defining institutions: their anonymity, time stability and repeated game nature. According to Phil Hanson:

> Economic institutions [. . .] are social arrangements that regulate economic behavior in ways that may not coincide with short-run individual preferences; they are based on shared expectations derived from custom, trust and law; they are best understood if economic activity is seen as a repeated game. Effective institutions [. . .] require that the rules of the game are not constantly amended to fit particular individuals, in other words, that they entail anonymity.
>
> (Hanson, 2007, p. 2)

Finally, the third extension is related to new economic sociology. It broadens the NIE perspective and consists in taking into account the emergence of institutions as a process in which various activities and interests clash, while at the same time various social networks, social structure, political influences, rootedness in tradition, social values and aspirations and so forth are subject to updating. Furthermore, NES emphasizes that the institutional arrangement which was ultimately adopted does not need be more efficient than the rejected solution at the time of its implementation. In this perspective, there is a room for many potential optima.[5]

This dimension is also present in NIE, but the sociological and cultural approach is more subtle and better fitted to the analysis of activities that are motivated not only by economic and political interest, but also by values and tradition, social and cultural resources (social capital) and so forth. We believe that such extension can be particularly useful in the study of the origins and fate of some institutions in countries undergoing systemic transformation from state socialism to capitalism. Here we have in mind particularly those institutions that are the result of imitation and exhibit a low level of institutionalization. Such situations should be examined not only through the lens of the rational choice theory and codified psychological models, but also by means of the idiographic methods of interpretative sociology (i.e. the "thick description" inspired by the ideas of classical sociology).

Institutional change

In most general terms institutional change, seen from the new institutionalist (NI) perspective, may be defined as a deliberate process shaped by the perceptions of the players, that is individuals and organizations, about the consequences of their actions. The key to the choices and decisions they make is the perception of their expected payoffs (North, 2005).

According to North, under normal circumstances an institutional change tends to be incremental as there is a crucial factor of path dependence involved which constrains the room of maneuver or the scope of choices made by individuals and policymakers (North, 2005). This general statement, however, should be subject to two important amendments. First, in some special historical moments (e.g. wars, natural disasters, revolutions, spectacular acts of terrorism, eruptions of social discontent or implosions of empires, with a special case of the collapse of the Soviet Union which paved the way to systemic transformation in former imperial clusters or satellite countries), institutions may be subject to more radical or abrupt changes. Second, the speed and frequency of institutional changes may also depend on the type of institutions involved. This is illustrated in Table 1.1 which reproduces the distinction made by Oliver Williamson (2000), who argued that institutional analysis (or more broadly, social science research) should be conducted at four interconnected levels, as there are four different types of institutions with the frequency of changes ranging between 100 to 1,000 years and continuous.

Bearing in mind our core definition of institutions, we can conclude from Table 1.1 that informal institutions (e.g. customs, traditions, norms of behavior, religions) are located at the first, highest level of Williamson's scheme, as well as at the second level, and thus tend to be the slowest to change. In turn, management practices regarding resource allocation are the fastest to alter. The Williamson's diagram implies the necessity of using two methodological paradigms: on the one hand, the method established in mainstream economics (second level), and on the other hand, the one applied in sociology (the first level related to embeddedness). This is particularly true when examining the economic mentality – researchers must take account of the extremely long duration of certain archetypal social norms and cognitive schemes. As a matter of example, in the case of Poland,

Table 1.1 Time frames for institutional change

Level	*Underlying theory*	*Frequency of change (years)*	*Purpose*
Embeddedness, informal institutions	(Economic) sociology	100–1000	Spontaneous, often non-calculative
Institutional environment – formal institutions, especially property rights	Economics of property rights/ political economy	10–100	Designing and engineering the institutional environment
(Corporate) governance – especially contracting (aligning governance structures with transactions)	Transaction costs economics	1–10	Designing and adjusting the governance structures
Resource allocation, demand management, production and employment decisions (prices and quantities, incentive alignment)	Neoclassical economics/agency theory	Continuous	Maximization of the objective function based on marginal analysis

Source: Adapted from (Williamson, 2000).

some of them have been reproduced in the country's economic culture since the 16th century (Hryniewicz, 2004). The cultural analyses of Edward Banfield (1958), Samuel Huntington (1996), Lawrence Harrison and Samuel Huntington (2000), David Putnam (1993, 2000), Francis Fukuyama (1995) and Manuel Castells (1998), to mention only a few, proved the long-lasting nature of the value patterns relating, among other things, to social capital, which had an impact on the diversified economic efficiency of various actions undertaken at the level of local communities and entire societies.

In this context, Harrison's apt assessment should be quoted, that "for most economists, cultural issues are inconvenient because they present definitional problems, are difficult to quantify, and function within a very broad psychological, institutional, political and geographical context" (Harrison and Huntington, 2000, p. 28) We are aware of the importance of cultural factors, but they are beyond the scope of this book and therefore we will be able to refer to them only in a very limited extent. As a side insight, it is worth adding in this context that the "patchwork" nature of capitalism in some countries of Central and Eastern Europe may be seen as a proof for the lack of "cultural adequacy" between new institutions on the one hand and values, attitudes and social aspirations on the other (Szomburg, 1994).

While defining the concept of institutional change it is also essential to distinguish the very process of change from the results it brings about. Table 1.2 highlights the most salient aspects of this distinction.

The content of Table 1.2 corresponds to a considerable extent with our own distinction between input and output institutional variables applied in the empirical part of the present study. Whereas the former describe determinants of the institutional matrix in various countries, the latter focus on outcomes (or economic performance) of different institutional setups in these countries (for details, see Chapters 3 through 9). These results are mainly influenced by institutional and structural factors, coherence and complementarity of institutions, but we do not lose sight of sociological and cultural factors related to internalized values (Nowak, 1979; Hausner, 2017).

In the scholarly literature on the sources and drivers of institutional change, two broadly opposing views may be traced. According to the first view, institutions change as a derivative of a spontaneous, unintentional and evolutionary

Table 1.2 Types of institutional change: processes and outcomes

		Result of change	
		Continuity	*Discontinuity*
Process of change	Incremental	Reproduction by adaptation	Gradual transformation
	Abrupt	Survival and return	Breakdown and replacement

Source: Streeck and Thelen (2009).

process, out of individual interactions (Hayek, 1967). On the other hand, institutional change has been interpreted as the outcome of the power of special (vested) interests and the effect of political compromise. This view has been representative in particular for the public choice theory (Buchanan and Tullock, 1962; Schmid, 1987; Gwartney and Wagner, 1988) and for the collective action paradigm (Olson, 1965). More recently it has also been articulated in the comparative capitalism literature (e.g. Aoki, 1994, 2001; Amable, 2003). In the latter current, institutional change has been perceived as a result of socio-political clashes (1) grounded in a complex distribution of power among different economic entities and (2) deeply rooted in path-dependent political legacies (Pierson, 2000; Jackson and Deeg, 2012).

A closer glance at the two perspectives on major determinants of institutional change reveals, however, that they are not necessarily rivals and may complement each other. This may be true particularly for two levels of institutional change in Williamson's analytical framework. At the highest level of analysis (level 1), which entails embeddedness, informal institutions are likely to be subject to only slow, gradual changes, which implies that the "evolutionary" view is more adequate in explaining the process of change. On the other hand, in the case of formal rules of the game which make up the institutional environment of an economy (level 2), this is the "political" interpretation that gives a better insight into the nature of changes concerned.

Bearing in mind the objectives and design of our research and the methodological approach adopted, in the subsequent parts of this book we will aim to reconcile the "evolutionary" and "political" interpretations of the way institutions change. It has to be emphasized in this context that the most crucial presumption of the analysis that follows is the *path-dependent nature* of institutional change, which is of special relevance for former socialist countries being the focal point of this book. As shown in many empirical studies on transition economies (e.g. Rapacki and Linz, 1992; Mokrzycki, 1997; Próchniak et al., 2016), one particular element of the path-dependence analytical framework, the command-economy legacy, has played a crucial role in these countries as a determinant of systemic transformation in particular and institutional development in general.

In addition to this institutional legacy, it is also worth pointing to a cultural heritage that combined to contribute to the diversity of results on the "output side" or performance of former socialist countries, despite the similarity of their institutional systems, both in the socialist era and in the initial period of systemic transformation, at the time of implementation of institutions copied from Western market economies without adjusting them to local conditions (Crowley and Ost, 2001). It is necessary therefore to take into account the phenomenon which we will call "varieties of socialism", clearly perceptible when comparing Poland, Hungary, the Czech Republic and Slovakia. This was particularly true of institutions related to the labor market, but also to industrial relations and economic mentality (Gardawski, 2003, 2009b).

In most general terms, the concept of *path dependence* refers to a property of contingent, non-reversible dynamical processes, including a wide array of biological and social processes that can properly be described as "evolutionary" (David, 2000). The path-dependence theory's core argument is that organizations and individuals, being players within the institutional setup, channel their behavior and activities along already established paths (Trouvé et al., 2010). These paths encompass institutions with their values and standards, which have been instilled by previous choices made in the past and as such create obstacles to institutional developments. Consequently, the main argument of this theory builds on the premise that once a path is chosen it is difficult to change it, because the underlying processes become instilled, institutionalized and are reinforced over time. It is also strenuous to reverse institutional choices because a failure of adhering to the rules established by preceding choices leads to ostracism and costs in terms of investment or coordination. Accordingly, prevailing institutions are modified rather than replaced, which in turn creates institutional inertia (Trouvé et al., 2010).

According to the path-dependence proposition, today's institutions have evolved to their present forms from recognizably similar structures, which had emerged in a particular historical moment with the end to meet a certain, then deemed important, societal need (David, 1994, p. 205). David (1994) illustrates the path-dependence approach, referring to Aristotle's distinction between genealogic explanations and teleological explanations. The former associate the current institutions with an initial context or initial conditions, and then make an interpolation of the sequence of events, in which the past exerts a considerable impact on the shape of the present. The latter interpret the current state of institutional development as a derivative of the implied functions today's institutions are supposed to perform in the future. Teleological explanations are characteristic of neoclassical economics (Colander, 2000), whereas genealogic interpretations are typical of institutional and evolutionary economics as well as economic sociology (Hodgson, 1988, 1993).[6] Obviously, this is the genealogic interpretation of the path-dependence proposition which will be internalized in our approach throughout the remaining parts of this book.

Institutional complementarity

Another key concept which is pivotal to our analysis of comparative capitalism in Central and Eastern Europe is *institutional complementarity*. This concept has been deeply rooted in social sciences (Lachmann, 1979) and has found applications across a wide range of institutional spheres, stretching from firm governance and industrial relations to varieties of capitalism and political reforms.

Institutional complementarity generally refers to situations that entail interdependence among institutions. This notion has been frequently used to explain the degree of institutional diversity that can be observed across and within different types of capitalism as well as its consequences for economic performance.

The canonical model of institutional complementarity was put forward by Aoki (2001) and relies on the theory of super-modular games developed by Milgrom and Roberts (1990). In his earlier studies, Aoki (1994) analyzed the role of institutional complementarities in contingent governance models of teams.

About the same time as the work by Aoki, in their seminal contribution to the field Peter Hall and David Soskice (2001) designed a broad theoretical framework to study institutional complementarities that characterize different political economies or varieties of capitalism. Having a specific focus on institutions of the political economy, the two authors developed an actor-centered approach for understanding the institutional similarities and differences among developed Western economies. According to Hall and Soskice's definition:

> Two institutions can be said to be complementary if the presence (or efficiency) of one increases the returns from (or efficiency of) the other. Conversely, two institutions can be said to be "substitutable" if the absence or inefficiency of one increases the returns to using the other. [. . .] This point about institutional complementarities has special relevance for the study of comparative capitalism. It suggests that nations with a particular type of coordination in one sphere of the economy should tend to develop complementary practices in other spheres as well.
>
> (2001, pp. 17–18)[7]

A very similar definition can be found in another trailblazing study of comparative capitalism published in 2003 by Bruno Amable. In his wording, institutions are believed to be complementary when the presence of one institution increases the efficiency of another. More precisely, institutional complementarities are present when the existence of or the particular form taken by an institution in one area reinforces the presence, functioning, or efficiency of another institution in another area (Amable, 2003).

As can be inferred from the foregoing definitions, the concept of institutional complementarity is inextricably connected (explicitly or implicitly) to the notions of effectiveness and efficiency of institutions. Both definitions imply, as a built-in, tacit assumption, a positive relationship between complementarity and efficiency (effectiveness), that is, more institutional complementarity is believed to result in higher efficiency. It seems advisable therefore to supplement the definition of institutional complementarity with at least very general definitions of these two notions. Thus, for the purpose of the present study we will understand the *effectiveness of an institution* as the degree of achieving the goals set for this institution. In turn, the *efficiency of an institution* may be conceived as the level of outcomes or performance resulting from the existence of this institution compared to the level of relevant costs and measured in terms of output/input ratio or the value of output (or other performance indicators) per unit of cost involved. This angle may be further extended from the level of a single institution to include the sets of institutions or the entire institutional area (see Chapters 3 through 9).

In addition to institutional variety, the concept of institutional complementarity has also motivated studies on institutional change, which aimed to explain why institutions are resistant to change and why introducing new institutions into a system often leads to unintended or suboptimal results. In this line of research, institutional complementarity has often been interpreted as a conservative factor ensuring stability of the institutional equilibrium. In the presence of institutional complementarity, institutional reforms require the simultaneous variation of different institutional domains, which in turn demands high coordination among the actors involved.

The generalizations formulated within the framework of economic sociology supplement the research perspective outlined above. Using the network analysis, and the analysis of interests and internalized economic values, economic sociology explains the persistence of incoherent institutional arrangements and institutional architectures with low levels of complementarity.

Comparative institutional advantage

As a result of diverse institutional endowments and divergent forms of institutional complementarities, particular countries or their clusters may also differ in their decisions on resource allocation and specialize in the production and exports of different types of products. In other words, they may exhibit different patterns of international competitiveness. This finding gave birth to a new concept in comparative capitalism dubbed "comparative institutional advantage", which aims to explain the ways institutions determine the types of countries' revealed comparative advantage. As a matter of example, Hall and Soskice (2001) argue that this is the prevailing method of coordinating economic agents' actions that provides the key to understand why the liberal market economies (LME) specialize in radical innovations while their CME (coordinated market economies) counterparts channel most of their resources to produce incremental innovations.

Model of capitalism

Taking account of the foregoing definitions of the core concepts pertaining to our research profile, and much in line with a view well-embedded in the literature (see e.g. Hall and Soskice, 2001; Amable, 2003; Sapir, 2006; Lane and Myant, 2007; Myant and Drahokoupil, 2011), for the purpose of the present book the "ideal-typical" model or variety of capitalism (in the Weberian sense, see the next section) may be defined as a system of complementary institutions, with a predominant role of private ownership and private markets as the main mechanism for resource allocation. The preceding definition will serve as a *theoretical* reference frame for our research. However, as the comparative study on the emerging post-communist capitalism in Central and Eastern Europe undertaken in this book is empirical by nature, we will predominantly interpret the results in terms of the Weberian "average types" of a statistical-empirical genre (Weber, 2002). This implies, among other things, that the real-life institutional orders evolving in CEE countries (and elsewhere in the European Union) may in many instances exhibit symptoms of institutional ambiguity or clear deficits of institutional complementarities, thus being quite distant from the "ideal-typical" definition. As a derivative, for the purpose of our empirical study we will later understand a model (variety) of capitalism as a cluster of countries sharing a similar set of institutions and displaying a clear-cut resemblance across the set of institutional measures selected for this study as a basis for comparative analyses.

1.2 Theoretical background

Seen in a historical perspective, the intellectual inspirations of the contemporary studies of comparative capitalism may be traced in the traditions of German historical school in economics and political science, and in particular in the works of Max Weber and Werner Sombart. They can be also found in the research of their American followers in the late 19th and early 20th centuries, such as Thornstein Veblen and John R. Commons, recognized today as the founding fathers of "old" institutional economics (Crouch, 2009; Chmielewski, 2011; Jasiecki, 2013; Staniek, 2017).

In the following subsections we will first outline the contribution of Max Weber to the development of comparative capitalism and next provide an overview of the contemporary antecedents of the two main reference points for our book: the Varieties of Capitalism (Hall and Soskice, 2001) and Diversity of Capitalism (Amable, 2003) conceptual and methodological frameworks.

Early pioneers – Max Weber and his inspirations

When formulating the basis of new economic sociology, Jens Beckert pointed out that Mark Granovetter brought to the fore the achievements of Karl Polanyi and his concept of "embeddedness", but he passed over Weber, Durkheim, Simmel or Marx (Beckert, 2007). It should be added, however, that Granovetter, while building his methodology in opposition to the "over- and under-socialized conceptions of sociology and economics" (Granovetter, 1985), was not far from the Weberian approach to social action. From the point of view of our research, the works of Max Weber are of particular relevance, since they allow to reconcile the leading NIE paradigm with the auxiliary paradigm of NES.

We will start with the Weberian category of rationality. It distinguishes two types of rational action: a goal-oriented rational action (*zweckrational*) and a value-oriented rational action (*wertrational*). Jerzy Szacki correctly grasped the differences between the two actions. The former is the kind of activity in which the maximum awareness of both the goals and the means is achieved, whereas in the latter the goal itself is left out the sphere of systematic reflection. In addition, Weber made a distinction between a traditional action and affective action:

> traditional activity is performed in accordance with established habits, but with a seed at least consciousness that makes this conformity something intentional and desirable. Emotional act is based on the overwhelming feeling of behaving in a certain way, regardless of the resulting effects, but it is not easy to relieve the tension without any involvement of consciousness.
>
> (Szacki, 1981, p. 528)

The category of rationality has been subject to a variety of criticism, ranging from the concept of bounded rationality of Herbert Simon (1955) to the contemporary controversies highlighted in the works of behavioral economists such as Kahneman and Tverski (for a critical review, see Tittenbrun, 2012, pp. 293–300). From our point of view the most important are, on the one hand, the differences between the action, the goal of which is subject to "maximum awareness" and the action that does not meet this condition and, on the other hand, between the routine, traditional and other actions.

Weber argued that a goal-oriented rational action, also referred to as instrumental action, adequately explains the behavior of actors shaped in Western capitalism, while it is not typical of actors coming from other cultural backgrounds characterized mostly by tradition and value-oriented action (China, India). This thesis has been challenged since the second half of the 20th century, in particular in view of the achievements of experimental psychology which cast some doubts over the validity of Weber's claim. The results of the pertinent research proved the historical and cross-cultural universality of goal-oriented rational actions. While accepting the results of the latest research in the field of social sciences, we try however to avoid one-dimensional or single-factor explanations. We believe that the interpretation of the mental legacy of state socialism and the disposition to appropriate behaviors requires a broader, multi-factoral perspective taking into special account the actions orientated by tradition and routine as well as by cognitive schemes, values and aspirations, often latent (Kotarbiński, 1955; Nowak, 1989; Kowalik, 2000; Hryniewicz, 2004, 2007; Gardawski, 2009a).

The preceding issue is related to Weber's typology of social action seen from the angle of three scientific disciplines: economic theory, sociology and economic sociology.

> Economic theory, in (Weber's) view, analyzes situations in which the actor is driven mainly by material interest and aims at utility but not takes the behavior of other actors into account (economic action). Sociology looks at action that is driven by ideal as well as material interest and that is also oriented to the behavior of others (social action). Economic sociology focuses on economic social action – that is, action that is driven mainly by material interests, is oriented to utility, and takes other actors into account. Social action and economic social action can also by driven by habit (or tradition) and emotions, typically in combination with interests.
>
> (Swedberg, 2000, p. 24)

This Weberian division provides the basis for a distinction between NIE and NES. The former is located between economic theory and economic sociology. Using the methodology of economics, it incorporates into the model those behavioral and institutional factors that are regular and could be subject to formalization. This allows the formulation of scientific laws and forecasting, for building nomothetic science (Becker's theory, Akerlof's PSA [psychology–sociology–anthropology] economics, etc.). In turn, economic social action – the subject of NES research – lays emphasis on the structural, cultural, political and cognitive embeddedness of social action that requires both kinds of analysis: nomothetic and idiographic. It casts NIE as a foundation of the pertinent analysis whereas NES enables deepening the interpretation involved, going beyond the behavioral and institutional regularities and often focusing on unique social situations. In a nutshell, the study of the remains of socialism as a determinant of institutions and social mentality requires using the tools of behavioral economics, public choice theory and Olson's collective action theory but also necessitates a humanistic sociological imagination and the tools sensitive to the cultural heritage and a value-driven action (Weberian "*Verstehen* sociology" – understanding perspective in sociology).

Another issue gathered from Weber which is relevant for our research is the broad contextual recognition of economic phenomena. Weber distinguished the economic phenomena in the strict sense from the economically relevant phenomena and economically conditioned phenomena. The former are phenomena that have economic significance (e.g. the market, banks, stock exchange). The latter have no economic significance as such, but in certain situations they may have a sizeable impact on economic phenomena – here Weber pointed, inter alia, to religion. Finally, the economically conditioned phenomena are those that do not belong to the first two categories but are influenced by economic phenomena. The third category may include all phenomena from the sphere of culture (Weber, 2004, p. 162).

These classes of phenomena have been studied or may be subject to scholarly examination through the lens of economic theory including the perspective shaped on the basis of the theory of rational action, but also by sociology, economic sociology, economic anthropology and related disciplines. Economic sociology considerably extends the field of research in comparison with the economic angle. As a result, according to Stanisław Kozyr-Kowalski, the perspective adopted by Weber is a good reference framework for analyzing the influence of the Protestant religion on the spirit of capitalism, as it avoids the tendency to single-factor interpretations:

> Weber does not claim [. . .] that the "spirit of capitalism" is solely a product of the Reformation: Ascetic denominations of Protestantism are indeed significant, but only as one of many factors that contributed to the emergence of the spirit of capitalism. Weber in "*Die Protestantische Ethik*" only wants to determine if and to what extent religious influences have contributed to [. . .] the expansion of this spirit in the world and what specific cultural aspects of capitalism depend on them.
>
> (Kozyr-Kowalski, 1967, pp. 216–217)

Weber showed that the complex of historical factors closed the path of capitalist development and Western-type rationalism to the societies of China and India. Despite the multiplicity of conditions that each of these factors is subject to, they can preserve identity and independent influence on historical processes. Hence, we can assume that, according to Weber, Protestantism in Europe, Confucianism and Taoism in China, or Hinduism and Buddhism in India, though important, were only factors conducive to the development of capitalism or preservation of traditional forms of economy and social life. By themselves, without entering into complex relationships with other factors, including economic ones, they cannot be considered as causative factors (Bendix, 1962/1975, pp. 67–68; Kozyr-Kowalski, 1967, p. 436). Weber, even though he generally valued Marx's oeuvre, rejected his historiosophy and theory, which presupposed a relatively uniform structure of social processes with the supreme position of the productive forces (the exception being the "Asiatic mode of production"). Weber believed that the genesis of modern capitalism, like other civilizations, cannot be determined a priori without an in-depth empirical research on the role played by individual factors.

Weber's inspiration facilitates the analysis of the state socialist "ethos" and its long-term effect on economic mentality and economic efficiency even nowadays. The study of the institutional order and culture of the CEE countries proves that the social mentality there has been shaped in a specific way by the prevailing ideology. Stefan Nowak dubbed this process with respect to Poland the "educational success of real socialism" (1979, 1989). The socialization in the state-socialist ideological and social practice had given rise to the formation of specific egalitarian attitudes ("moderate egalitarianism", according to Nowak), to a low level of social trust and social capital, the expectation of a free satisfaction of basic social needs by government (by "them"), the specific Poland's form of Banfield's "amoral familism" (Nowak defined it as "society as a federation of primary groups with very weak institutional ties" and "relativism of moral norms"), the disappearance of praxeological values, social acceptance for breaking or/and bypassing legal norms in the sphere of formal institutions (Skąpska, 2002, 2007) and an exceptionally large scope of resourcefulness in the private domain. To describe these processes, Adam Podgórecki coined the term "dirty community" (1990). At the same time, support for the market and competition must be emphasized, as confirmed by sociologists since 1980. They defined this phenomenon as a "myth of competition" (Kolarska-Bobinska and Rychard, 1982). Immediately after 1989, advocates of the so-called transitology believed that a change in economic, social and political conditions alone would bring about a relatively rapid change in the value systems, but this did not happen. The ethos developed in the conditions of socialism turned out to be resistant to change and has proved susceptible to reproduction. It should be pointed out that the general acceptance for the market and competition continued after 1989, although Poles used to commonly criticize the Polish capitalism. The analysis of those ambivalent and incoherent attitudes necessitates the tools of a contemporary version of *Verstehen* sociology.

The last issue to which we want to draw attention deals with the methodological aspect of comparative political economy and the possibility of linking it with Weber's "ideal types". The ideal type category allowed Weber to take a position in the *Methodenstreit* between the German historical school and marginalism. It should be emphasized that the procedure of building the "ideal type" served Weber mainly (though not exclusively) as a means to reconstruct the phenomena for which he assumed rationality. A contemporary researcher of Weber's output, Dirk Käsler wrote:

> The main task of the ideal type [. . .] is [. . .] the hypothetical assignment of the chaotic diversity of individual phenomena to "the ideal", i.e. to the imagined course of things. Weber's ideal types are "ideal" in two respects: first, they are always a product of purely logical thought perfection, they engage in the process of their creation and reflection to the imagined extremum; secondly, they also refer to "ideas", i.e. they are "mental images", and thought projects. [. . .] Weber repeatedly and repeatedly rejected the possibility of finding in his types the ideal "sense" of history, its "essence". He also repeatedly warned against the hypostasis of ideal types as the real driving forces of history.
>
> (Käsler, 2010, pp. 241–242)

Kozyr-Kowalski described such an ideal type as a "heuristic fiction", which has a modest role of ordering and describing a selected empirical material but cannot serve as a causative explanation (Kozyr-Kowalski, 1967, p. 476). Without entering into a highly sophisticated debate, we will only add that the main contemporary taxonomies of capitalism, especially the key typologies of Amable (2003), Hall and Soskice (2001) or Nölke and Vliegenthart (2009), have the character of ideal typologies in the Weberian sense. However, not all taxonomies of capitalism have such a nature; some of them correspond to another type which distinguishes Weber's methodology, namely the "average type". In the key section of "Economy and Society", which is crucial for his methodology, he described the relations between these types as follows:

> sociology must create pure ("ideal") types of creations [. . .] characterized by consistency of the best possible adequacy from the point of view of meaning, but therefore, in this absolutely perfect, pure form, occurring in reality as rarely as any physical reaction calculated with the assumption of absolute vacuum. It is only by referring to a pure ("ideal") type of sociological casuistry. It goes without saying that sociology also sometimes uses average types, from the empirical-statistical genre that do not require specific methodical explanations.
>
> (Weber, 2002, p. 16)

The above problem is of particular relevance to us, as the empirical analyses carried out in the subsequent chapters of this book consisted in comparing the structure of real-life institutions existing in individual Central and Eastern European states, with the countries of Western Europe representing various clusters or empirical variants of capitalism rather than with the ideal types like LME and CME. Nevertheless, some of the conclusions we formulate in the book are expressed in the language of "ideal types" and have been inspired by Weber's contribution to social sciences.

Contemporary antecedents

The present state of comparative capitalism studies, in particular the "varieties of capitalism" and "diversity of capitalism" frameworks, can be seen as a result of an evolutionary process. More specifically, it is the last stage in this process – being a derivative of an effort to go beyond three perspectives on institutional variation – that has dominated in the scholarly discussion on comparative political economies after the Second World War and in particular since the mid-1960s. All these perspectives – which we will call (1) state-centered, (2) trade union–centered and (3) firm-centered, respectively – followed a temporal sequence, as each of them was a response to the economic problems of its time (Hall and Soskice, 2001).

The first of these approaches provided a modernization (state-centered) perspective to comparative capitalism. Being devised in the aftermath of the war, it conceived the key challenge facing Western developed economies as the task of modernizing industries that suffered from war atrocities or/and were still dominated by pre-war practices.

The trailblazing work that laid the ground for the ensuing debates within this current was Andrew Shonfield's study on the diversity of industrial modernization strategies pursued in a number of Western European countries as well as in the United States and Japan (Shonfield, 1964). In his approach he put a special stress on the role of various institutions surrounding the economy – different branches of the state, banks and stock exchanges – as factors of success or failure in modernization efforts (Crouch, 2009). In his view, the main drivers of the post-war "economic miracles" in France and Germany should be seen in an increased government intervention in the free-market economy, intellectually grounded in economic theory of John Maynard Keynes (Jasiecki, 2013).[8] Based on his findings, and motivated by his concern with national politico-economic systems, Shonfield categorized the sample countries covered by his study as the *national varieties of capitalism.*

In the next two decades, the advocates of the modernization approach highlighted the role of institutional structures as a crucial driver of economic growth, with special emphasis on those institutions that would give the state leverage over the private sector, such as planning systems and public say over the flow of funds in the financial system (Cohen, 1977; Estrin and Holmes, 1983). Seen from this angle, countries were often classified, based on the structure of their state, into "strong" and "weak" states (e.g. Katzenstein, 1978).

In the aftermath of the first oil shock in 1973, with the burst of inflation as the main economic challenge in the Western Hemisphere and the failure of the Keynesian paradigm to explain the new reality, the second (trade union–centered) approach to comparative capitalism was born based on the concept of *neo-corporatism* (e.g. Schmitter and Lehmbruch, 1979). The neo-corporatist perspective was generally associated with the state's capacity to negotiate stable settlements with employers and trade unions that involved wages, working conditions and social and economic policy (Hall and Soskice, 2001). Intellectually it was rooted in the Olsonian logic of collective action, which implies that more encompassing unions can better internalize the economic effects of their wage settlements (Olson, 1965; Calmfors and Driffill, 1988). The adherents to the neo-corporatist perspective used to classify different capitalist economies largely based on the criterion of the organization of their trade union movement. In the light of this criterion, a nation's capacity for neo-corporatism and its institutional comparative advantage were believed to be a function of the centralization or concentration of the trade union movement and the ability of the state to ensure durable "political exchanges" (Przeworski and Wallerstein, 1982; Hall and Soskice, 2001).

During the 1980s and 1990s, the third (firm-centered) perspective on comparative capitalism, dubbed the *social systems of production* approach, gained popularity (Hall and Soskice, 2001; Jasiecki, 2013). The research conducted under this heading comprised a wide body of studies ranging from sectoral governance through national innovation systems to flexible production regimes. Many of these studies were influenced by the French *régulationiste* school (Boyer and Saillard, 1995) and stressed the movement of firms away from mass production toward new production patterns that depend on collective institutions at the regional, sectoral or national level (Schmitter and Streeck, 1985; Hollingsworth et al., 1994).[9] Among the most distinctive features of this line of research was its focus on the behavior of firms. Simultaneously, the "social systems of production" approach entailed a more comprehensive understanding (and a wider range) of institutions being analyzed, with an important component of the sociological perspective. As a result, one of the most interesting findings of this line of research on comparative capitalism was a more in-depth conception of the ways institutions generate trust and enhance learning within economic communities (Hall and Soskice, 2001).

As a wrap-up of this part of the discussion, it can be said that despite seeming differences between the foregoing three perspectives on comparative political economies in Western developed countries, all these approaches shared two properties. The first common thread was the starting research premise that the diversity of capitalism is a matter of co-existence or continuing multiplicity of forms rather than their evolutionary development or superseding. The second similarity boiled down to the resulting typologies of the co-existing *national* varieties of capitalism.

The first endeavors to go beyond the three perspectives on institutional variation of capitalism just outlined have been made since 1990. They brought the study of comparative political economy to a higher level of aggregation or generalization. The most distinctive feature of these endeavors was the presumption that – despite institutional differences – capitalist countries may be grouped into similar clusters and that the resulting typologies may exceed national boundaries. Seen from this angle, three such studies are particularly worth mentioning here, authored by Michel Albert (1991), Gøsta Esping-Andersen (1990) and Vivian Schmidt (2002), respectively. They can be seen as immediate predecessors of the pioneering contributions by Hall and Soskice (2001) and Amable (2003).

The first author who made a contribution to a pluralistic analysis of the diversity of capitalism and moved it above the national level was Michel Albert. In his study (1991), he offered a dichotomist taxonomy of two polar types of capitalism, labeled the Anglo-Saxon and Rhenish (Rhineland) models. The former embodies a free-market capitalism and is represented in the Anglophone countries. The latter takes its name from certain institutional characteristics shared by the riparian countries of the Rhine, such as Germany, the Netherlands, Switzerland and (to a lesser degree) France (Crouch, 2009). The set of classification criteria employed by Albert comprised the incidence of poverty, the scale of immigration, social security, wage differentiation, savings-to-income ratio, the scope of business regulation, the pattern of corporate governance and the role of firms as providers of education and vocational training (Jasiecki, 2013).

In contrast, both Esping-Andersen (1990) and Schmidt (2002) have gone beyond the dichotomy proposed by Albert (and similarly, by Hall and Soskice ten years later) and further extended the menu of possible ideal types of Western market economies to encompass three models of capitalism or capitalist welfare state.

Based on classification criteria relating to the outcomes of political struggle, or dominant political traditions, Esping-Andersen discriminated between three different types of welfare state co-existing in Western developed countries: (1) free-market or liberal capitalism, embodied again in the Anglophone cluster of countries; (2) the conservative continental European model (best exemplified by Germany); and (3) the social-democratic model, geographically associated with Scandinavia (Crouch, 2009).

In turn, Schmidt (2002) classified the sample countries into three distinct models of European capitalism: (1) the "market" or liberal model (approximating Hall and Soskice's LME ideal type), with a state offering greater autonomy to economic actors (the UK); (2) the "managed" model (roughly similar to the CME variety of capitalism), with an "enabling" state supporting associational governance and cooperation among private actors (Germany); and (3) the "state" model, with an interventionist state regulating private activities (France). Worth stressing is one particular trait of Schmidt's approach, which is hardly typical of the remaining studies discussed in this section. In her analysis, the author emphasized the importance of institutional change and its timing – she tried to understand how countries embodying each of the three models of capitalism respond to the challenges of globalization and Europeanization. A central hypothesis of her study is that these challenges have not been conducive to a simple institutional convergence. Governments of the countries concerned have responded in many different ways, giving rise to new forms of capitalist diversity (Crouch, 2009).

1.3 Concluding remarks

The discussion carried out in this chapter may be summarized under the following main headings.

1 The study of comparative capitalism constitutes an important thread in a broad and heterogeneous research stream in contemporary social sciences. The key idea underlying the "comparative capitalism" approach is the co-existence of

various models of capitalism or diverse sets of institutional arrangements in particular countries or their clusters.

2 The research on comparative capitalism has been deeply embedded in the new institutional economics (NIE) paradigm in particular and the new institutionalism (NI) in general, with their fundamental methodological premise that "institutions matter" as a key explanatory variable of socio-economic development and human behavior in a society. While the NIE paradigm constitutes the core reference framework of our research we also refer to the new economic sociology (NES) paradigm, which plays an auxiliary role in our study.

3 The key concepts inherent in the new institutional economics which are instrumental for comparative capitalism studies include the notions of institutions, institutional change, institutional complementarity and comparative institutional advantage. Simultaneously, the core concepts for the new economic sociology include networks, interests and embeddedness.

4 In a historical perspective, the intellectual inspirations of the contemporary studies of comparative capitalism may be traced in the traditions of German historical school, and in particular in the works of Max Weber, as well as in the research of their American followers or "old institutionalists" (Veblen, Mitchell and Commons). Seen from the angle of our own study, this is the Weberian contribution to social sciences that preserves its relevance as the most useful research reference framework.

5 Chronologically, three different perspectives on comparative capitalism after the Second World War can be distinguished, as a function of changing economic challenges and policy priorities: (1) modernization (state-centered) perspective; (2) neo-corporatist (trade union–centered) perspective; and (3) social systems of production (firm-centered) approach.

6 The research on comparative political economies in the Western developed world has also followed over time a noteworthy evolution in terms of the resulting typologies of capitalist diversity: (1) national varieties of capitalism, (2) dichotomist taxonomies and (3) more comprehensive classifications encompassing three or more models of capitalism.

7 Historically, the scholarly debate on comparative capitalism has gone through two distinct stages: (1) diversity seen as a matter of evolutionary development or superseding (e.g. Weber, Gramsci, Boyer and Saillard) and (2) diversity conceived as a matter of co-existence or continuing multiplicity of forms (most of post-war studies).

Notes

1 The term was first used by Jenő Szűcs (1983) as a key to understand the history of feudalism and capitalism in Central Europe in the 19th century and the first half of 20th century. See Chapter 10 for a more comprehensive discussion of this theme.

2 The very term was coined by Oliver Williamson (Williamson, 1975).

3 This refers in particular to two out of three main building blocks of new institutional economics (i.e. the economics of contracts and economics of institutions). Historically,

NIE did not start as a concerted scholarly initiative. According to Brousseau and Glachant (2008), the birth of NIE was a derivative of several waves of applied and analytical endeavors, driven by specific issues. These led to the development of three bodies of literature which were initially loosely connected to each other: (1) *economics of the firm and organizations* that started with the seminal article by Coase (1937) and developed in the 1950s; (2) *economics of contracts* initiated in the 1970s (with major development in the 1980s and 1990s); and (3) *economics of institutions*, born in the 1990s and inspired by the need to manage the challenges of economic development and systemic transformation, in a sheer opposition to the dominant neoliberal view and its economic manifesto – the Washington consensus. For an interesting discussion of this opposition in the context of transition economies, see Roland (2000).

4 As implied by recent advances in experimental psychology and behavioral economics, a limited mental capacity may stem, inter alia, from the co-existence of two different systems of thinking in human brains: fast and slow. The short-term dominance of fast thinking may often give rise to irrational decisions (Kahneman, 2012). A similar line of argument may be found in the recent book by Yuwal Noah Harari, who points to a dichotomist nature of human consciousness which seemingly consists of two distinct selves – the experiencing self and narrative self within us, with a strong bias toward the latter as a determinant of individual's actions and decision-making (Harari, 2017, pp. 342–343).

5 In a way, this outcome in NES may be compared with some corresponding threads in mainstream economics. For example, while the conception of Pareto optimality implies a single optimum in terms of efficiency, it is simultaneously consistent with multiple optima or many possible patterns of welfare distribution in terms of equity. With a certain simplification, some similarity may be also found in the proposition of new Keynesian economics, which implies the possibility of multiple long-run equilibria on the labor market entailing, inter alia, a prominent role of hysteresis.

6 For an interesting discussion, see also Karbowski (2017).

7 If this is the case and institutions from different areas (e.g. the labor market and education system or financial intermediation and the product market) are complementary, we can talk about an *institutional isomorphism* (see, e.g., Jasiecki, 2013) or a positive synergy stemming from the fact that different parts of the institutional architecture in a country are coherent.

8 In the case of Germany, an equally important source of intellectual inspiration should be seen in the idea of a "social market economy" instilled in German ordoliberalism, and in particular in the works of Walter Eucken.

9 The French school of regulation in turn, and by the same token the followers of this approach, were influenced by Antonio Gramsci's distinction between the classic free-market stage and the Fordist stage of capitalism, which he believed would succeed the former.

References

Albert, M. (1991). *Capitalisme contre capitalisme*. Paris: Seuil.

Amable, B. (2003). *The diversity of modern capitalism*. Oxford: Oxford University Press.

Aoki, M. (1994). The contingent governance of teams: Analysis of institutional complementarity. *International Economic Review*, 35, pp. 657–676.

Aoki, M. (2001). *Towards a comparative institutional analysis*, Cambridge, MA: MIT Press.

Aoki, M. (2007). Endogenizing institutions and institutional changes. *Journal of Institutional Economics*, 3(1), pp. 1–31.

Arrow, K. J. (1987). Reflections on the essays. In: G. Feiwel, ed., *Arrow and the foundations of the theory of economic policy*. New York: New York University Press, pp. 727–734.

Banfield, E., with the assistance of Banfield, L. F. (1958). *The moral basis of a backward society*. Glencoe, IL: The Free Press.

Beckert, J. (2007). The great transformation of embeddedness: Karl Polanyi and the new economic sociology, *MPIfG discussion paper* 07/1, Max Planck Institute for the Study of Societies, Cologne, Jan.

Beckert, J. and Streeck, W. (2008). Economic sociology and political economy: A programmatic perspective, *MPIfG working paper* 08/4, Max Planck Institute for the Study of Societies, Cologne.

Bendix, R. (1962/1975). *Max Weber. An intellectual portrait*. New York: Doubleday and Co. Inc. (Polish edition [1975], 'Max Weber. Portret uczonego'. Warszawa: PWN).

Boyer, R. and Saillard, Y., eds. (1995). *Théorie de la régulation: L'état des savoirs*. Paris: La Découverte.

Brousseau, E. and Glachant, J-M. (2008). *New institutional economics. A guidebook*. Cambridge: Cambridge University Press.

Buchanan, J.M. and Tullock, G. (1962). *The calculus of consent*. Ann Arbor: University of Michigan Press.

Calmfors, L. and Driffill, J. (1988). Bargaining structure, corporatism and macroeconomic performance. *Economic Policy*, 6, pp. 13–61.

Castells, M. (1998). *End of millennium. The information age: Economy, society and culture*, Vol. 3. Oxford: Blackwell.

Chmielewski, P. (2011). *Homo agens. Instytucjonalizm w naukach społecznych* [*Homo Agens. institutionalism in social science*]. Warszawa: Poltext.

Coase, R. (1937). The nature of the firm. *Economica*, 4(16), pp. 386–405. Blackwell Publishing.

Cohen, S. (1977). *Modern capitalist planning*. Berkeley and Los Angeles: University of California Press.

Colander, D. (2000). The death of neoclassical economics. *Journal of the History of Economic Thought*, 22, pp. 127–143.

Crouch, C. (2009). Typology of capitalism. In: B. Hancké, ed., *Debating varieties of capitalism*. Oxford: Oxford University Press.

Crowley, S. and Ost, D., eds. (2001). *Workers after workers' states: Labor and politics in postcommunist Eastern Europe*. Lanham: Rowman and Littlefield.

David, P. (1994). Why are institutions the 'Carriers of History?': Path dependence and the evolution of conventions, organizations and institutions. *Structural Change and Economic Dynamics*, 5, pp. 205–220.

David, P. (2000). Path dependence, its critics and the quest for 'historical economics'. In: P. Garrouste and S. Ioannides, eds., *Evolution and path dependence in economic ideas: past and present*. Cheltenham: Edward Elgar.

Esping-Andersen, G. (1990). *The three worlds of welfare capitalism*. Princeton: Princeton University Press.

Estrin, S. and Holmes, P. (1983). *French planning in theory and practice*. London: Allen & Unwin.

Etzioni, A. (1988). *The moral dimension. Toward a new economics*. New York: The Free Press.

Fukuyama, F. (1995). *Trust. The social virtues and the creation of prosperity*. London: Penguin Books.

Gardawski, J. (2003). *Konfliktowy pluralizm polskich związków zawodowych* [*Conflicting pluralism of Polish trade unions*]. Warszawa: wyd. Fundacja im. Friedricha Eberta.

Gardawski, J. (2009a). Pracujący Polacy wobec wyzwań ekonomicznych [Working Poles in the face of economic challenges]. In: J. Gardawski et al., eds., *Polacy pracujący a kryzys fordyzmu* [*Working Poles and the crisis of Fordism*]. Warszawa: Scholar.

Gardawski, J. (2009b). *Związki zawodowe na rozdrożu* [*Trade unions at the crossroads*]. Warszawa: Instytut Spraw Publicznych.

Granovetter, M. (1985). Economic action as social structure: The problem of embeddedness. *American Journal of Sociology*, 91.

Guillén, M., Collins, R., England, P. and Meyer, M. (2005). The revival of economic sociology. In: M. Guillén, R. Collins, P. England and M. Meyer, eds., *The new economic sociology developments in an emerging field*. New York: Russell Sage Foundation.

Gwartney, J. and Wagner, R., eds. (1988). *Public choice and constitutional economics*. Greenwich: JAI Press.

Hall, P. and Soskice, D. (2001). *Varieties of capitalism. The institutional foundations of comparative advantage*. Oxford: Oxford University Press.

Hanson, P. (2007). The tasks ahead in comparative economic studies: What should we be comparing? *Japanese Journal of Comparative Economics*, 44(1), Jan, pp. 1–14.

Harari, Y.N. (2017). *Homo deus. A brief history of tomorrow*. London: Vintage (Penguin Random House, UK).

Harrison, L.E. and Huntington, S.P. (2000). *Culture matters. How values shape human progress*. New York: Basic Books.

Hausner, J. (2017). Value economics vs. economic value. In: B. Biega et. al., eds., *Open eyes book two*. Kraków: Fundacja Gospodarki i Administracji Publicznej.

Hayek, F.A. (1967). Notes on the evolution of system of rules of conduct. In: *Studies in philosophy, politics and economics*. Chicago: Chicago University Press.

Hodgson, G. (1988). *Economics and institutions: A Manifesto for a modern institutional economics*, Cambridge, MA: Polity Press.

Hodgson, G. (1993). *Economics and evolution: Bringing life back into economics*, Ann Arbor: University of Michigan Press.

Hollingsworth, J.R., Schmitter, P.C. and Streeck, W. (eds.) (1994). *Governing capitalist economies: Performance and control of economic sectors*. New York: Oxford University Press.

Hryniewicz, J. (2004). *Polityczny i kulturowy kontekst rozwoju gospodarczego* [The Political and Cultural Context of Economic Development]. Warszawa: Wydawnictwo Naukowe Scholar.

Hryniewicz, J. (2007). *Stosunki pracy w polskich organizacjach* [Labor Relations in Polish Organizations]. Warszawa: Wydawnictwo Naukowe Scholar.

Huntington, S.P. (1996). *The clash of civilizations and the remaking of world order*. New York: Simon & Schuster.

Jackson, G. and Deeg, R. (2012). The long-term trajectories of institutional change in European capitalism. *Journal of European Public Policy*, 19, pp. 1109–1125.

Jasiecki, K. (2013). *Kapitalizm po polsku. Między modernizacją a peryferiami Unii Europejskiej* [*Capitalism Polish style. between modernization and European Union Periphery*]. Warszawa: Instytut Filozofii i Socjologii Polskiej Akademii Nauk.

Johnston, A. and Regan, A. (2018). Is the European Union capable of integrating diverse models of capitalism? *New Political Economy*, 23, pp. 145–159.

Kahneman, D. (2012). *Pułapki myślenia. O myśleniu szybkim i wolnym*. Poznań: Media Rodzina; [English edition: *Thinking, fast and slow*. New York: Farrar, Straus and Giroux, 2011].

Kahneman, D., Knetsch, J. L. and Thaler, L. (1986). Fairness as a constraint on profit seeking: entitlements in the market. *American Economic Review*, 76(4).

Kahneman, D., Slovic, P. and Tversky, A., eds. (1982). *Judgement under uncertainty: Heuristics and biases*. New York: Cambridge University Press.

Karbowski, A. (2017). *Analiza otoczenia instytucjonalnego systemu tworzenia wiedzy w krajach EŚW ze szczególnym uwzględnieniem "path dependence" [An analysis of the institutional environment of the knowledge creation system in CEE countries with special regard to 'path dependence']*, manuscript. Warsaw: SGH Warsaw School of Economics.

Käsler, D. (2010). *Weber. Życie i dzieło* [*Weber. Life and work*]. Warszawa: Oficyna Naukowa.

Katzenstein, P., ed. (1978). *Between power and plenty*. Madison, WI: University of Wisconsin Press.

Kolarska-Bobinska, L. and Rychard, A. (1982). Ład polityczny i ład ekonomiczny' [Political and economic order]. In: W. Adamski i inni, ed., *Polacy 91. Postrzeganie kryzysu i konfliktu*. Warszawa: PAN, Instytut Filozofii i Socjologii.

Kotarbiński, T. (1955). *Traktat o dobrej robocie* [The treatise on the good work]. Warszawa: PWN.

Kowalik, T. (2000). *Współczesne systemy ekonomiczne. Powstawanie, ewolucja, kryzys* [Contemporary economic systems: Emergence, evolution, crisis]. Warszawa: Akademia im. Leona Koźmińskiego.

Kozyr-Kowalski, S. (1967). Max Weber a Karol Marks [Max Weber vs. Karl Marx]. Warszawa: Książka i Wiedza.

Lachmann, L. M. (1979). *The legacy of Max Weber*. London: Heinemann.

Lakatos, I. (1978). *The methodology of scientific research programmes*. Cambridge: Cambridge University Press.

Lane, D. and Myant, M., eds. (2007). *Varieties of capitalism in post-communist countries*. Basingstoke: Palgrave Macmillan.

March, J. G. and Olsen, J. P. (1989). *Rediscovering institutions: The organizational basis of politics*. New York: The Free Press.

Ménard, C. and Shirley, M. M., eds. (2005). *Handbook of new institutional economics*, Dordrecht: Springer.

Milgrom, P. and Roberts, J. (1990). Rationalizability, learning and equilibrium in games with strategic complementarities. *Econometrica*, 58(6), pp. 1255–1277.

Mokrzycki, E. (1997). Od protokapitalizmu do prosocjalizmu: makrostrukturalny wymiar zmian ustroju [From protocapitalism to prosocialism: Macrostructural dimension of systemic change]. In: H. Domański, ed., *Elementy nowego ładu*. Warszawa: Instytut Filozofii i Socjologii PAN.

Myant, M. and Drahokoupil, J. (2011). *Transition economies: Political economy in Russia, Eastern Europe and Central Asia*. Hoboken, NJ: John Wiley & Sons.

North, D. (1991). *Institutions, institutional change and economic performance*. New York: Cambridge University Press.

North, D. (2004). *Understanding the process of economic change*. Princeton, NJ: Princeton University Press.

North, D. (2005). Institutions and the performance of economies over time. In: C. Ménard and M. M. Shirley, eds., *Handbook of new institutional economics*. Dordrecht: Springer.

Nowak, S. (1979). Systemy wartości społeczeństwa polskiego (Value Systems of the Polish Society]. *Studia Socjologiczne*, 4(75), pp. 155–173.

Nowak, S. (1989). The attitudes, values and aspirations of Polish society. In: W. W. Adamski and E. Wnuk-Lipiński, eds., *Sisyphus sociological studies*, Vol. V. Warsaw: PWN.

Nölke, A. and Vliegenthart, A. (2009). Enlarging the Varieties of Capitalism: The Emergence of Dependent Market Economies in East Central Europe. *World Politics*, 61(4).

Olson, M. (1965). *The logic of collective action*. Cambridge, MA: Harvard University Press.

Pierson, P. (2000). Increasing Returns, Path Dependence, and the Study of Politics. *American Political Science Review*, 94(2), pp. 252–267.

Podgórecki, A. (1990). Kontrola społeczna trzeciego stopnia [Third-degree social control]. In: A. Kojder et al., eds., *Elementy Socjologii Prawa* [*Selected Issues in the Sociology of Law*], Vol. 3. Warszawa: Wydawnictwo Uniwersytetu Warszawskiego.

Próchniak, M., Rapacki, R., Gardawski, J., Czerniak, A., Horbaczewska, B., Karbowski, A., Maszczyk, P. and Towalski, R. (2016). The emerging models of capitalism in CEE11 countries – a tentative comparison with Western Europe. *Warsaw Forum of Economic Sociology*, 7(2, 14), Autumn, pp. 7–70.

Przeworski, A. and Wallerstein, I. (1982). The structure of class conflict in democratic capitalist societies. *American Political Science Review*, 75, pp. 215–238.

Putnam, D. (1993). *Making democracy work: Civic traditions in modern Italy*. Princeton: Princeton University Press.

Putnam, D. (2000). *Bowling alone: The collapse and revival of American community*. New York: Simon & Schuster.

Rapacki, R. and Linz, S. J. (1992). Privatization in transition economies: Case study of Poland. *Econometrics and Economic Theory Papers*, No. 9011. East Lansing, MI: Department of Economics, Michigan State University.

Roland, G. (2000). *Transition and economics. Politics, markets and firms*. Cambridge, MA and London. England: The MIT Press.

Sapir, A. (2006). Globalization and the reform of European social models. *Journal of Common Market Studies*, 44(2).

Schmid, A.A. (1987). *Property, power, & public choice. An inquiry into law and economics*. New York: Praeger.

Schmidt, V. (2002). *The futures of European capitalism*. Oxford: Oxford University Press.

Schmitter, P. and Lehmbruch, G. (1979). *Trends toward corporatist intermediation*. London: SAGE.

Schmitter, P. and Streeck, W. (1985). *Private interest government*. London: SAGE.

Shonfield, A. (1964). *Modern capitalism*. Oxford: Oxford University Press.

Simon, H. A. (1955). A behavioral model of rational choice. *The Quarterly Journal of Economics*, 69(1), pp. 99–118.

Skąpska, G. (2002). Kultura prawna w procesie tworzenia wolnej gospodarki' [Legal culture in the process of building a free-market economy]. In: G. Skąpska, ed., *Buddenbrokowie czy piraci? Polscy przedsiębiorcy okresu głębokich przemian*. Kraków: Universitas.

Skąpska, G. (2007). Prawo w społeczeństwie w obliczu kryzysu [Law in the Society in the Time of Crisis]. *Studia Socjologiczne*, 2(185), pp. 7–31.

Smelser, N. J. and Swedberg, R. (2005). Introducing economic sociology. In: N. J. Smelser and R. Swedberg, eds., *The Handbook of economic sociology*. Princeton: Princeton University Press.

Staniek, Z. (2017). *Ekonomia instytucjonalna. Dlaczego instytucje są ważne* [*Institutional economics. Why do institutions matter*]. Warszawa: Diffin.

Streeck, W. and Thelen, K. (2009). Institutional change in advanced political economies. In: B. Hancké, ed., *Debating varieties of capitalism*. Oxford: Oxford University Press.

Swedberg, R. (2000). *Max Weber and the idea of economic sociology*. Princeton: Princeton University Press.

Swedberg, R. and Granovetter, M. (1992). Introduction. In: M. Granovetter and R. Swedberg, eds., *The sociology of economic life*, Boulder, San Francisco. Oxford: Westview Press.

Szacki, J. (1981). Historia myśli socjologicznej. Część druga [*History of sociological thought. Part Two*]. Warszawa: PWN.

Szomburg, J. (1994). Trzy wizje ustroju [*Three visions of the political system]. Przegląd Polityczny,* 25.

Szücs, J. (1983). The three historical regions of Europe: An outline. *Acta Historica Academiae Scientiarum Hungaricae*, 29(2–4), pp. 131–184.

Talmud, I. (2013). Economic sociology. *Sociopedia.isa.*

Tittenbrun, J. (2012). *Gospodarka w społeczeństwie. Zarys socjologii gospodarki i socjologii ekonomicznej w ujęciu strukturalizmu socjoekonomicznego* [Economy and society. An outline of sociology of economy and economic sociology in a socioeconomic structuralism approach]. Poznań: Zysk i S-ka.

Trouvé, H., Couturier, Y., Etheridge, F., Saint-Jean, O. and Somme, D. (2010). The path dependency theory: Analytical framework to study institutional integration. The case of France. *International Journal of Integrated Care*, 10.

Tversky, A. and Kahneman, D. (1981). The framing of decisions and the psychology of choice. *Science*, 211, pp. 453–458.

Weber, M. (2002). *Gospodarka i społeczeństwo. Zarys socjologii rozumiejącej* [Economy and society. An outline of understanding sociology]. Warszawa: Wydawnictwo Naukowe PWN (Biblioteka Socjologiczna).

Weber, M. (2004). „Obiektywność" poznania społeczno-naukowego i społeczno-politycznego. In: M. Weber and M. Holona, eds., *Racjonalność, władza, oczarowanie*, Poznań: Wydawnictwo Poznańskie. Original edition: 'Die "Objektivität' sozialwissenschaftlicher und sozialpolitischer Erkenntnis. In: *Archiv für Sozialwissenschaft und Sozialpolitik* (1904).

Williamson, O.E. (1975). *Markets and hierarchies. Analysis and antitrust implications.* New York: Free Press.

Williamson, O.E. (2000). The new institutional economics: Taking stock, looking ahead. *Journal of Economic Literature*, 38, pp. 595–613.

Zukin, S. and DiMaggio, P. (1990). Introduction. In: S. Zukin and P. DiMaggio, eds., *Structures of capital*. New York: Cambridge University Press.

2 Emerging models of post-communist capitalism in Central and Eastern Europe

Survey of the literature[1]

Ryszard Rapacki, Adam Czerniak, Juliusz Gardawski, Bożena Horbaczewska, Adam Karbowski, Piotr Maszczyk and Mariusz Próchniak

Introduction

In the present chapter we pursue two main goals. First, we conduct a survey of the most representative theoretical and empirical research in the mushrooming literature on the emerging varieties or models of post-communist capitalism in Central and Eastern Europe (CEE). We critically review both standard conceptual frameworks and their applications (e.g. Hall and Soskice, 2001; Amable, 2003; Hanson, 2006; Knell and Srholec, 2007; and Mykhnenko, 2005) their derivatives (Nölke and Vliegenthart, 2009; Babos, 2010; Farkas, 2011; and Ahlborn, Ahrens and Schweickert, 2016) and non-standard approaches (such as those by King and Szelenyi, 2005; Myant and Drahokoupil, 2011; and Bohle and Greskovits, 2012). Second, while summarizing the main findings which stem from the survey of the literature on comparative capitalism in the post-communist world we highlight the major peculiarities of the institutional architecture in CEE countries and its evolution which make a direct application to this category of countries of both standard and (to a lesser degree) non-standard theoretical frameworks problematic (Rapacki et al., 2019).

The chapter has been structured as follows. Section 2.1 outlines the major standard conceptual frameworks and their applications in the ongoing scholarly debate on the diversity of post-communist capitalism emerging in Central and Eastern Europe. Section 2.2 discusses the most representative non-standard theoretical approaches and typologies of the emerging capitalism in transition countries, with special reference to the CEE11 group, the new EU members from that region. Section 2.3 summarizes the major findings of the comparative research on post-communist capitalism surveyed in the chapter.

2.1 Standard conceptual frameworks and their applications

The role of institutions in economic analysis has been often neglected for multiple reasons, including the difficulties with incorporating institutional factors

DOI: 10.4324/9780429056901-3

into formal economic models. However, with the outbreak of the global economic crisis in 2008, problems with quantitative accounting of major differences in the design, operation and outcomes of institutions existing in various countries diminished in importance. Instead, a new approach has become increasingly popular; it aims at explaining the diversity of institutional setups in different countries and, based on their empirical analysis, at classifying the co-existing varieties or models of capitalism. In accordance with the definition adopted earlier in Chapter 1, and in line with a widespread view in the literature (see e.g. Hall and Soskice, 2001; Amable, 2003; Sapir, 2006; Lane and Myant, 2007; Myant and Drahokoupil, 2011), in the text that follows we will understand the model (variety) of capitalism as a system of complementary institutions (Rapacki et al., 2019).

In assessing the possible effect of institutions and institutional changes on economic performance in the context of their complementarity, it is necessary to note that the "institutional comparative advantage" may be seen as a key driver of countries' international competitiveness. Specific institutional arrangements can either enhance or constrain the efficiency and effectiveness of an economic system selected via political decisions or shaped in an evolutionary manner.

As a matter of illustration, inflexible labor markets are likely to adversely affect the competitiveness of economies that derive their comparative advantage from cheap labor (e.g. Portugal, Greece and Spain), but it will not have a negative impact on countries whose primary source of competitive advantage is the high quality of manufactured products (e.g. Germany and Sweden). Similarly, whereas a system of corporate governance based on universal banks, coupled with high participation of employees at various levels of management and reconciling the interests of all stakeholders involved, works well in economies geared toward gradual and continuous improvements of products and processes (e.g. Austria and Germany), it inhibits the potential for groundbreaking innovations. For the latter scenario to materialize, it is far more desirable to use capital markets instead as a main vehicle fueling the corporate governance system, accompanied by mechanisms aimed at financing investment ideas/projects at early stages of their life cycle (such as business angels and venture capital) and promising high average rates of return to investors (as in the United States).

The "institutional comparative advantage" factor is particularly important in countries at lower levels of economic development, in which the patterns of international specialization have been constantly changing. While in the US or German economies, it is safe to assume that their production profiles have been subject to only minor changes for the last few decades, in CEE countries the foundations of their international competitiveness have experienced dramatic shifts since 1990. It seems therefore that a key challenge these countries face boils down to skillful institution matching in response to a changing external and internal environment, with a view to maintain their comparative advantage. Institutions that boost growth based on imitation and the inflow of foreign direct investment (FDI) will perform poorly at a stage of development when the focus shifts from the production of components within the supply chains of multinational corporations to the manufacture of final products with high value added and based on cutting-edge technologies. In fact, a lack of an adequate and timely institutional change will hinder necessary changes in the mix of factors fueling fast and sustained economic growth.

Originally, the very idea of "comparative capitalism" or studying the co-existing varieties of capitalism in the contemporary world was confined to the Western Hemisphere. As a derivative, the methodological and conceptual frameworks developed toward this end were designed for developed market economies. This was in particular the case of two major contributions to the field made at the beginning of the past decade – the studies of Peter Hall and David Soskice (2001) and Bruno Amable (2003), referred to as the Varieties of Capitalism (VoC) and the Diversity of Capitalism (DoC) approaches, respectively. Notwithstanding their primary focus and objectives, the VoC and DoC propositions have triggered a new line of research geared toward a direct application of the original frameworks involved to former socialist countries undergoing systemic transformation from a centrally planned toward a market-driven economy, with an end to explain the emerging post-communist models of capitalism there. Simultaneously, based on the original VoC and DoC concepts and typologies, some attempts have also been made to take account of institutional peculiarities or specific "rules of the game" (North, 1990) inherent in the post-communist transition and to extend the existing standard classifications with derivative categories that would accommodate transition countries too, as the emerging types of post-communist capitalism. These trends have become particularly pronounced since the Eastern enlargement of the European Union in 2004 and 2007 encompassing ten CEE new member states (followed by Croatia in 2013). The next two sections give an account of these endeavors.

Varieties of Capitalism approach

The key idea underlying the Varieties of Capitalism (VoC) approach (Hall and Soskice, 2001) is that different capitalist countries can survive and thrive with somewhat different sets of social arrangements or institutions aimed at coordinating production decisions.

In their study, Hall and Soskice used two basic classification criteria for Western developed market economies that best characterize their institutional setups. The first, general criterion was the *prevailing mode of coordinating* actions of economic agents and the second entailed the innovative capability of an economy – its *ability to create* either *radical or incremental innovations*. While the former criterion highlights the "input" side of the institutional infrastructure (legislation, regulatory framework, etc.) of an economy, the latter illustrates its "output" side or selected dimensions/results of its performance.

The two authors have also singled out five spheres where firms must develop successful relationships to resolve coordination problems crucial to their core competencies.

1 *Industrial relations*: the problem enterprises face is how to coordinate bargaining over wages and working conditions with their labor force, trade unions and other employers;

2 *Vocational training and education*: firms face the problem of securing a workforce with suitable skills, while workers must decide how much to invest in what skills;
3 *Corporate governance*: to which firms turn for access to finance and where investors seek assurances of returns on their investments;
4 *Inter-firm relations*: the relationships a company forms with other firms and notably its suppliers or clients, with a view to securing a stable demand for its products, appropriate supplies of inputs, and access to technology;
5 *Relations with employees*: to ensure that they have requisite competencies and cooperate well with others to advance the objectives of the firm: labor market institutions.

As a result of applying the above taxonomic criteria, two varieties of capitalism have been distinguished (Hall and Soskice, 2001): *liberal market economy* (LME) and *coordinated market economy* (CME).

In liberal market economies (US, UK, Ireland, Australia, New Zealand), firms coordinate their activities primarily via hierarchies and competitive market arrangements. Market relationships are characterized by the arm's-length exchange of goods or services in a context of competition and formal contracting. In response to price signals generated by such markets, the actors adjust their willingness to supply and demand goods or services, often on the basis of marginal analysis stressed by neoclassical economics. In many respects, market institutions provide a highly effective means for coordinating the endeavors of economic actors.

A coordinated market economy (best represented by Germany, Austria, France, Belgium, and to a certain degree also by Greece, Italy, Portugal, Spain and the Scandinavian countries) operates with a great deal of strategic cooperation, both between firms, between banks and firms, and between unions and firms. Investment finance depends more heavily on banks; wage bargaining may be coordinated at the national level; employees have greater job security, personal and income taxes are likely to be more progressive, and income inequality, other things equal, is relatively low.

Table 2.1 provides a comparative picture, based on a more detailed breakdown of classification criteria and the most characteristic traits of the two varieties of capitalism concerned.

Hall and Soskice's contribution gave rise to a number of interesting applications and empirical extensions of their original approach, aimed at including transition countries to the VoC framework too. The most representative studies for this line of research are those conducted by Knell and Srholec (2005, 2007), Hanson (2006, 2007), Babos (2010), and Ahlborn, Ahrens and Schweickert (2016).

Taking Hall and Soskice's typology as a starting point, Mark Knell and Martin Srholec (2005, 2007) embarked on a tentative assessment of the institutional architecture in post-communist economies against the patterns established for Western industrialized countries. Drawing on three key components of their analysis (institutional arrangements in the field of social cohesion, labor market regulation and business regulation), they distinguished various "mixed" types of

Table 2.1 Varieties of capitalism – a comparative picture

Criterion/feature	*LME*	*CME*
Coordination mechanism	Competitive market arrangements	Non-market relations
Equilibrium	Demand/supply and hierarchy	Strategic interaction among firms and other actors
Inter-firm relations	Competitive	Collaborative
Mode of production	Direct product competition	Differentiated, niche production
Legal system	Complete and formal contracting	Incomplete and informal contracting
Institutions' functions	Competitiveness; freer movement of inputs	Monitoring; sanctioning of defectors
Employment	Full-time; general skills; short-term; fluid	Shorter hours; specific skills; long-term; immobile
Wage bargaining	Firm level	Industry level
Training and education	Formal education from high schools and colleges	Apprenticeship imparting industry-specific skills
Unionization rate	Low	High
Income distribution	Unequal (high Gini)	Equal (low Gini)
Innovation	Radical	Incremental
Comparative advantage	High-tech industries and services	Manufacturing
Policies	Deregulation, anti-trust, tax breaks	Encourages information sharing and collaboration of firms

Source: Authors' own elaboration.

capitalism in the transition world that – to a greater or lesser extent – resemble one of the "ideal types" singled out by Hall and Soskice in their classification (i.e. LME or CME). Their findings show that social cohesion in a former socialist country is tightly linked to its level of economic development. Based on these criteria, the majority of post-communist countries fall into a group featuring low gross domestic product (GDP) and relatively liberal forms of social coordination (see also Lane and Myant, 2007). The picture is not as consistent when it comes to the labor market regulation component. In the group of post-communist countries, Knell and Srholec (2007) distinguished highly regulated (e.g. Ukraine) and relatively liberal (e.g. Russia) national labor markets. A similar, mixed picture can be drawn for the business regulation axis, the third major component of the analysis. On one end of the spectrum, then, we have countries like Russia or Lithuania that are relatively "liberal", and on the other end, there are economies like the Czech Republic or Poland that seem more "coordinated" in terms of business regulation. Summing up the three sub-indices for each field, the two authors arrived at the aggregate coordination index indicating the prevailing mode of coordination in each country. Not surprisingly, the results show again quite an ambiguous picture: the range of indices involved is very wide (between −9.6 for Russia and +8.9 for Belarus); simultaneously, out of 27 transition economies in the sample, nearly half (13) exhibit features of a coordinated market economy while the others (14) can be classified as LME. Based on their results, Knell and Srholec (2007) claimed that there was no one single, specific model of the emerging post-communist capitalism, and the footprint of state socialism remained a major determinant of the nature and characteristics of institutional architecture prevailing in these countries on their road from central planning to a fully-fledged market-driven economy.[2]

The foregoing results prompt an important, early reservation (their more comprehensive list will be developed in Chapter 3). Namely, all such endeavors as the one by Knell and Srholec, aimed at directly applying standard conceptual frameworks – developed for Western industrialized economies – in the transition world, encounter a serious methodological impediment. This is due to a substantial gap between formal measures of the institutional environment in transition economies and informal institutions which may give rise to surprising or dubious results if we rely on the former rather than on the latter (e.g. a relatively liberal labor market in Russia compared to a highly regulated one in Ukraine in the Knell and Srholec study).

Applying, with some extensions (e.g. indicators showing the ease of doing business, the quality of governance and the incidence of perceived corruption), a similar framework to that of Knell and Srholec, Phil Hanson (2006, 2007) focused on the role of the European Union as a factor of institutional change in the new CEE member countries. He argued that the EU accession has not pushed the CEE states toward a welfarist, continental European pattern of institutional arrangements (in terms of social cohesion, labor market regulation and business regulation). The major reason is that accession requirements and the *acquis communautaire* leave a vast room for institutional variation within an acceding state's economic and social institutions. According to Hanson (2006), the trend toward greater institutional heterogeneity has become even more pronounced with the EU Eastern enlargement (i.e. accession of the new CEE members).

The VoC framework has also been applied in the study by Pavol Babos (2010), who embarked on an empirical exercise to identify the type of capitalism emerging in eight CEE countries that joined the EU in 2004. Based on the character and strength of coordination mechanisms among the economic actors concerned, he constructed a composite coordination index.

Babos conceived coordination from the angle of its outcomes (or outputs) resulting from particular types of institutional arrangements. He believed that it is the coordination of institutions that may enhance the country's international comparative advantage and lead to an improved economic performance. With a view to measure the strength and the prevailing mode of coordination, he identified 18 variables (e.g. stock market capitalization, trade union density and social protection expenditures). The coordination index has been computed not only for individual CEE countries but also for their clusters, such as the Baltics and the Visegrad Group. The results of his study indicate that Slovenia was the closest to a coordinated market economy, while the Baltic countries were more akin to the LME benchmark (which is consistent with earlier empirical studies). The most striking finding in his analysis was the status of Poland, which can be categorized as a liberal market economy with the prevailing mode of coordination even more market-based than in the case of Latvia. For Lithuania, the score suggested more liberal coordination than for Estonia (in contrast to the pattern established in the literature). In turn, Hungary, Slovakia and the Czech Republic seemed to have their capitalisms not yet institutionally embedded.

The most recent research undertaken along similar lines is the study by Ahlborn, Ahrens and Schweickert (2016), who applied the modified and extended VoC approach to analyze the sample countries' allocation into various clusters depending on the prevailing type of capitalism and to assess the time stability of clusters. Their study encompasses 25 EU countries (the current EU members excluding Luxembourg, Malta and Cyprus) as well as Norway, Switzerland, the United States, Canada, Australia, New Zealand, Japan and Turkey (33 countries altogether). The authors are particularly interested in the behavior of the CEE countries: they try to answer the question whether these countries embody their own type of capitalism or whether they converge toward a specific Western European model. Ahlborn, Ahrens and Schweickert focus on three aspects of the analysis that have been neglected or completely ignored in earlier studies on the subject, including the original VoC approach: (1) the government activity, (2) economic performance (related to financial stability and income distribution) and (3) the transition process. For the first aspect, they adopt three variables measuring government activity: (1) size of government (including general government consumption spending, transfers and subsidies, government enterprises and investment, and top marginal tax rate); (2) transfers and subsidies; and (3) regulation (based on credit market regulations, labor market regulations and business regulations). All these three variables are taken from the Economic Freedom of the World database. Three other indicators measuring the economic performance represent welfare state objectives: (1) the (Gini) index, (2) innovation (based on the World Bank Knowledge Assessment Methodology) and (3) fiscal debt. The transition process is accounted for by looking at cluster history and principal component analysis for different sub-periods. This may be seen as an advancement in the comparative capitalism studies in the transition world, as it adds a more dynamic perspective to the analysis and enables capturing the pertinent changes.

The research methodology is composed of two methods: cluster analysis and principal component analysis (PCA). Under the cluster analysis, the authors build dendrograms, where individual countries are grouped based on their similarities in terms of the examined indicators. Under PCA, the number of variables is reduced from six to two or three principal components (three main principal components explain 81% of the data variation). The analysis covers the 1995–2009 period, which has been divided into four observations covering the years 1995, 2000–2003, 2004–2006, and 2007–2009, respectively (the last three observations are sub-period averages over three-year time spans).

The analysis carried out by Ahlborn, Ahrens and Schweickert (2016) indicates that among the CEE countries two different varieties of capitalism could be identified, sharing features of the ideal types of either liberal market economies or coordinated market economies. The former cluster includes Bulgaria, Estonia, Latvia, Lithuania, Romania and Slovakia, while the latter hosts Croatia, the Czech

Republic, Hungary, Poland and Slovenia (plus Spain from the Mediterranean region). The CEE countries have not developed their own (hybrid) model of post-communist capitalism, unlike the Mediterranean states that (according to the three authors) form a distinct variety of capitalism dubbed *mixed market economies* (MME).

When comparing various sub-periods covered by the study, it turns out that between 1995 and 2009, the CME cluster of the CEE countries (CEEC CME) has caught up with the CME variety of capitalism, while the LME cluster of the CEE countries (CEEC LME) has converged toward the liberal type of capitalism.

As can be seen from the foregoing concise overview of the selected most representative applications of the original conceptual and methodological framework devised by Hall and Soskice (2001), the picture of the emerging post-communist capitalism in transition countries (with special regard to Central and Eastern Europe) is far from being unequivocal or coherent. Depending on the methodology and assumptions adopted in different empirical studies on the subject, the same individual transition economies or their clusters (e.g. the Baltic countries) may substantially differ in their institutional characteristics and be allocated either to the LME or CME type (i.e. to the opposite varieties of capitalism).

These ambiguities gave birth to yet another offspring of the Varieties of Capitalism approach. Taking the standard conceptual VoC framework as a starting point, Andreas Nölke and Arjan Vliegenthart (2009) suggested to extend the original classification and to add a third category, dubbed a *dependent market economy* (DME).[3] The term was coined specifically for selected CEE countries (namely the Visegrad Group) with a view to better capture their peculiar institutional features while at the same time implying some crucial similarities to their Western LME or CME prototypes. At the same time, however, Nölke and Vliegenthart's proposition is rooted in the stream of reflection on dependent economies and draws heavily from the Latin American "dependence school" tradition (e.g. Cardoso and Faletto, 1979). According to the two scholars, the Visegrad economies or DMEs are coordinated largely by hierarchical intra-firm relationships within transnational corporations. In their view, these economies exhibit a comparative advantage in the assembly and production of relatively complex and durable consumer goods. The comparative advantage in question is based on (1) institutional complementarities between skilled, but relatively cheap labor, (2) the transfer of technological innovations within transnational enterprises and (3) the provision of capital through FDI. The authors also claim that in CEE economies, decisions regarding knowledge production are not dominated by concerns regarding the long-term innovation potential of national economies but rather by their current profitability. Moreover, the organization of the innovation system within CEE economies differs considerably from those within LMEs (where innovations are transferred through market mechanisms) and CMEs (where innovations are spread by means of industrial cooperation). In the case of CEE economies, most research and development (R&D) activity is conducted outside the region and then imported into the production process through transnational networks that bind together different places of production. Modern technologies are transferred to CEE economies under the strict control of transnational corporations. For Nölke and Vliegenthart (2009) and Högselius (2003), innovation in CEE countries is predominantly imitative rather than creative. Technological activities in firms are skewed toward downstream non-analytical and non-R&D activities like testing or standards. In CEE economies, public vocational training takes place largely outside of corporations. For example, in Hungary a rapid shift of training provision from employers (business firms) to vocational schools occurred during the Hungarian transformation from socialism to capitalism (Noelke and Horn, 2014). The substitution of employer-provided training with school-provided training has resulted in higher unemployment and lower job quality, particularly upon leaving school.

Summarizing the hitherto scholarly discussion on the emerging varieties of capitalism in Central and Eastern Europe, Bluhm (2010) shows that it has been marked by two different theoretical strands. On the one hand, attempts have been underway to directly apply the VoC framework; on the other hand, the dependency and world-system theory (Hopkins and Wallerstein, 1982) has undergone a renaissance, taking a critical stance vis-à-vis the VoC approach. The author argues that the strengths and weaknesses of both strands may be seen as complementary.

Diversity of Capitalism approach

The most significant contribution to the ongoing scholarly debate on the diversity of capitalism was made by Bruno Amable (2003). In his insightful and trailblazing book, he rejected the functionalist view adopted by Hayek (1967), who claimed that institutions develop and function due to efficiency reasons. Amable raised two important questions. First, what mechanisms ensure the efficiency of emerging institutions? Second, and more importantly, how should institutional efficiency be defined and from which perspective should institutions be efficient? According to this author, the development of specific institutions represents the "political compromise" between various groups having their own contradictory interests. Thus, each institutional reform violates the existing set of interests and requires a strong social support needed for its implementation. Hence, Amable's models of capitalism reflect "specific social compromises in terms of institutions"; as a result, "institutional change is basically the area of interest of political economy" (Amable, 2003, pp. 9–10).

The core element in Amable's approach is the concept of institutional complementarities, examined earlier by Aoki (1994). He defines complementarity as a relationship between institutions where the presence of one institution increases the efficiency of another. For example, the labor market can be organized as a laissez-faire market or may be subject to strong government regulation. If a fluid labor market co-exists with financial markets which allow for a rapid accumulation of inputs and a fast creation of new jobs, such a labor market will work more efficiently compared to a scenario where firms are financed mainly by the banking sector. Amable concludes that the models of capitalism should be analyzed not only as a set of separate institutions but also in a broader perspective, including the relationships among institutions, with special emphasis on their complementarity (Amable, 2003, p. 6).

The conceptual framework developed by Amable differs in several crucial respects from the earlier study of Hall and Soskice (2001). First, he singled out five major institutional areas or key elements of the overall institutional architecture of a country:

- Product market competition;
- Wage-labor nexus and labor market institutions;
- Financial intermediation sector and corporate governance;
- Social protection sector;
- Education and knowledge sector.

In the next step, for each of the five areas concerned he selected a set of indicators that best describe the most salient features of their institutional setups. Similar to Hall and Soskice, Amable applied both "input" and "output" measures of the institutional architectures involved.[4] His selection of the dataset, however, was not fully consistent, as in some institutional areas (e.g. the social protection system) only the input side was represented, while in other areas both sides – though in different proportions – were involved. The following stage entailed the empirical test of five sets of indicators aimed at detecting the strongest and most statistically significant regularities, including institutional complementarities both within each area and between all of them. To this end, two basic statistical methods were applied: the principal component analysis and the cluster analysis. As a result of selecting the most important indicators (components) and clustering, Amable identified five models of capitalism co-existing in the Western Hemisphere:

- Anglo-Saxon model (UK, US, Australia, New Zealand, Ireland);
- Social-democratic model (also dubbed the Nordic or Scandinavian model: Sweden, Norway, Denmark, Finland);
- Continental European model (France, Germany, the Netherlands, Austria);
- South European (Mediterranean) model (Greece, Italy, Spain, Portugal);
- Asian model (Japan, South Korea).

Similar to the Hall and Soskice's case, the proposition put forward by Amable inspired other scholars to apply and extend the original DoC framework with a view to incorporate former socialist countries. Two such attempts are particularly worth discussing here.

The first study on post-communist capitalism emerging in CEE, based on the DoC methodology, was conducted by Vlad Mykhnenko (2005). On the one hand, compared to other such studies, including those by Hanson (2006, 2007) and Knell and Srholec (2007), the scope of his paper is narrower as it covers only two CEE countries, Poland and Ukraine. On the other hand, however, it is more comprehensive as it scrutinizes all five Amablean institutional areas in the two countries concerned.

The most important results of this study seem to support the claim that post-communist countries have not evolved into any of the four pure models of capitalism described by Amable. The findings established by Mykhnenko imply that while in some respects either of the two countries examined appears to resemble one particular model of capitalism, in some other respects they tend to converge to quite a different variant. And more specifically, whereas in Poland the mix of institutional characteristics in most areas (four out of five) points to a similarity of the emerging variant of capitalism to the Mediterranean model, the dominant features of the fifth area (the social protection system) are more akin to the Continental European model. Likewise in Ukraine, while the nascent capitalism appears to resemble in most respects the Continental European model, the most salient properties of its social protection sector seem to exhibit much more similarity to the liberal Anglo-Saxon model of capitalism (Mykhnenko, 2005).

Another conclusion to be drawn from Mykhnenko's research is that – at least in case of Poland and Ukraine – as a consequence of systemic transformation and then EU membership (Poland), the convergence process toward the institutional patterns prevailing in Western Europe has taken place. However, the two countries have apparently been heading for quite distinct benchmarks exhibiting significant differences in their emerging models of capitalism. Equally interesting is the downward trend in institutional complementarities in both countries ("institutional ambiguity" in Mykhnenko's terminology), which tends to adversely affect the efficiency of all institutions involved.[5]

The most plausible explanation of the possible reasons underlying the "institutional ambiguity" in Poland and Ukraine, and pars pro toto in the whole group of CEE economies, may be synthesized under two headings. First, this is the uncompleted process of building the "post-communist capitalism" in transition economies that makes their institutional infrastructure still a "work in progress" (Rapacki, 2012). Second, at least a part of the institutional environment analyzed by Amable has been formatted under a strong impact of exogenous factors or external entities, such as foreign investors, multinational corporations or international organizations (EU, IMF, EBRD or the World Bank). Still another part (first of all the social protection sector) has been determined mostly by endogenous drivers such as politics, history, values represented by the majority of the society or just the amount of money available in this area (path dependence). As a consequence, some parts of the institutional matrices predominating in CEE countries are not consistent with other parts, as is usually the case in developed countries representing various models of Western capitalism.

The second research that capitalizes on the DoC approach with a view to extend its reach and to delve into the intricacies of the emerging post-communist capitalism was conducted by Beata Farkas (2011, 2013). Farkas addressed the question of how the institutions in the new CEE members of the European Union (CEE11) match the institutional order of the old EU countries, and whether they resemble any of the four models of European capitalism singled out by Amable (2003) or rather form a distinct one.

Following Amable's conceptual structure that encompasses five institutional areas and using data from OECD, Eurostat, the European Central Bank, the World Bank, Fraser Institute and UNCTAD, Farkas made an attempt at a modified DoC typology incorporating the CEE countries. To this end, she applied the cluster analysis and multidimensional scaling based on measurable data (whenever available) and three-year average values.

The empirical analysis carried out by Farkas implies that the CEE countries evolved into their own, new model of post-communist capitalism. This author, in contrast to the prevailing consensus in the literature, claims that the institutional disparities between these countries and the old EU member states representing Amable's four models of European capitalism are more remarkable than the differences between post-communist economies alone. Only one CEE country, Slovenia, seems to approach the Continental European model.

According to Farkas, there are three main reasons that may explain a new institutional development path of the CEE11 economies: all post-communist countries suffered from (1) the lack of capital and (2) featured a weak civic society; and parallel to that (3) the EU institutions exerted a strong impact on their economies (Farkas, 2011). The lack of capital made foreign investment necessary. A substantial part of FDI went to the financial sector, and in particular to the banking industry, which was conducive to the development of bank-based financial systems (Farkas, 2013). There was no domestic, internationally competitive business-led R&D system. The levels of social protection and welfare distribution in those countries were closely correlated with the strength of civil society or traditions of social institutions (Farkas, 2013).

Hence, as may be inferred from Farkas's argument, the CEE11 countries are subject to path dependence. As a derivative, they have developed their own pattern of institutional architecture, being a response to their historical legacy and consistent with the initial conditions of systemic transformation. In her view, there is no reason to believe that the emerging model of post-communist capitalism in these countries is just a temporary situation, which will one day converge into any of the Western European varieties or models of capitalism (Farkas, 2011).

2.2 Non-standard approaches

With the benefit of hindsight, it may be claimed that the discussion on the emerging post-communist capitalism, triggered by the trailblazing studies of Hall and Soskice (2001) and Amable (2003), also gave rise (with a certain time-lag) to still another line of research on the subject taking a different methodological and conceptual perspective or, at times, being even rooted in a different research tradition.

The key premise for the proponents of a new, non-standard approach was that – due to the peculiar nature of systemic transformation – a straightforward application of the standard analytical framework embedded in the VoC and DoC paradigms is impossible (or at least very difficult) for transition economies. Hence a different set of assumptions and conceptual framework should be designed with the resulting tentative classification, which would take account of the specific features that make these economies a distinct case, compared to the advanced Western European countries. One of the most comprehensive examples of such tentative taxonomies, comprising the whole group of 27 transition economies, is the proposition put forward by Martin Myant and Jan Drahokoupil (2011).

They start from the presumption that although "institutions matter", they are neither the only nor the most important determinant of the emerging model of capitalism in transition economies. Even more, for these scholars, institutions are a precondition for the emerging model of post-communist capitalism rather than its determinant.

The first step in Myant and Drahokoupil's approach in devising a new framework which would better correspond to the conditions of transition economies consists in distinguishing various forms of their integration with the international economy. The main criteria used for drawing up such a typology include in particular the patterns prevalent in the balance and structure of their current accounts and the commodity composition of their exports (Myant and Drahokoupil, 2011). As a derivative, they singled out six forms of international integration of post-socialist countries:

- Export-oriented FDI in complex sectors;
- Export-oriented complex sectors without FDI;
- Simple manufacturing subcontracting to multinational companies (MNCs);
- Commodity exports;
- Dependence on remittances and aid;
- Dependence on financialized growth.

The above typology has been supplemented by other criteria that are best fitted to the unique conditions of post-communist countries and also include internal factors. They were used by Myant and Drahokoupil to distinguish the varieties of post-communist capitalism emerging in transition countries. The full list of these classification criteria includes:

- The mode of international integration;
- The nature of property rights;
- The role of the state;
- The nature of business-government relations.

Based on the foregoing criteria, the two authors distinguished five distinct models/varieties of capitalism in former socialist countries (Myant and Drahokoupil, 2011):

1 *FDI-based (second rank) market economies*, present most notably in Central and Eastern Europe. The most salient characteristics of this model are democratic political systems, integration with the European Union and export structures increasingly built around highly processed manufactured goods produced by foreign-owned MNCs.

2 *Peripheral market economies*, to be found mostly in southeastern Europe and the Baltic states (Romania, Bulgaria, Estonia, Latvia, Lithuania). These countries rely on less sophisticated and thus less stable manufactured exports while at the same time displaying many features of a financialized growth pattern including a significant dependence on remittances. They have democratic political systems and ensure basic legal and institutional conditions for business. They also exhibit a low level of welfare provision and large income disparities.
3 *Oligarchic (clientelistic) capitalism*, represented predominantly by the former Soviet republics and in particular by Russia, Ukraine and Kazakhstan in Central Asia. This model shares the relatively authoritarian political systems and high incidence of rent seeking due to close links between politics and the business world. Social and employment protection are generally underdeveloped, similar to the regulatory framework for new business expansion.
4 *Order states*, where the scope of market and institutional reforms is the most limited (e.g. Belarus and some Central Asian republics, such as Uzbekistan and Turkmenistan). The most salient features of this model are authoritarian political systems, the dominant role of the state in economic decision-making, state support for commodity or manufactured exports as a channel for international integration, a poor institutional environment for private business and a high level of welfare provision.
5 *Remittance- and aid-based economies*, a category ascribed to a number of low-income countries in the Commonwealth of Independent States (CIS) and Eastern Europe (Albania, Kyrgyz Republic, Bosnia and Herzegovina). This model is compatible with a very low level of institutional development and highly depends on labor market conditions in other countries; hence it implies no internal institutional preconditions for international integration of a country concerned.

As can be seen, the taxonomy put forward by Myant and Drahokoupil is definitely distinct from those designed for advanced market economies. The authors have focused on differences between post-socialist countries and the incumbent EU members. Taking into account the whole analyzed group, it seems obvious that these disparities are important. However, in case of a much narrower group of FDI-based (second rank) market economies and peripheral market economies (with special regard to CEE11 countries that joined the EU), these differences are not so important, even more so if the Mediterranean model of capitalism is taken as a benchmark. For this group, Myant and Drahokoupil's classification seems insufficient to capture all peculiarities that differentiate, for example, Poland from the Czech Republic or Hungary.

Another interesting and inspiring attempt at capturing the most relevant features of the nascent post-communist capitalism in Central and Eastern Europe and to come up with a more tailored-made typology, outstanding from the standard VoC/DoC approach, was made by Dorothee Bohle and Bela Greskovits. They argued (2007) that the VoC framework is ill-suited to study the emergence of institutions, their international embeddedness and the semi-peripheral character of Central and Eastern European capitalisms.

Bohle and Greskovits (2012) relied on theoretical inspirations (Karl Polanyi) and research traditions quite distinct from the VoC and DoC approaches to describe political economies or types of capitalism emerging in CEE countries. Extending Polanyi's original triadic scheme of politics, protection and market (Polanyi, 1957), they proposed a hexagonal or diamond-shaped scheme that consists of the following categories: government, corporatism, welfare state, macroeconomic coordination, market efficiency and democracy. Based on these dimensions, they discriminated between four different regimes or types of post-communist capitalism:

1 *Pure neoliberal* type (Estonia, Latvia and Lithuania), whose most salient features combine market radicalism with weak compensation of transaction costs and quite limited influence of citizens and their groups on politics.
2 *Embedded neoliberal* type (Visegrad group: Czech Republic, Hungary, Poland, Slovakia and additionally Croatia), whose most typical characteristics include a continuous search for a compromise between market transformation and social cohesion, in particular in more inclusive yet not always effective systems of democratic governance.
3 *Neocorporatist* type, hosted in Slovenia, which has chosen a radical market-building strategy coupled with compensation schemes for all those who were made worse off as a consequence of systemic transformation. This type of capitalism embodies many features of a democratic regime where multi-level relationships between business, employees and the state are being negotiated with a view to forge a workable compromise.
4 *Non-regime* countries (southern Europe).

Yet another important contribution to the ongoing debate on the nature of the emerging capitalism in the transition world was made by Laurence King and Ivan Szelenyi (2005). Unlike Myant and Drahokoupil or Bohle and Geskovits, King and Szelenyi adopted a more dynamic perspective in their analysis, focusing on the paths former socialist countries followed on their road from plan to market or the way capitalism has been formed. Based on this criterion, they singled out three distinct categories or varieties of post-communist capitalism:

1 *Capitalism from below*, also dubbed *hybrid capitalism* (China, Vietnam), has evolved in rural communities in Asia as a systemic blend encompassing small private local firms co-existing with large state-owned enterprises in the dominant command-economy environment. In this model, the nascent capitalist class has had a "grass-root" record and emerged in the private, market-oriented sector not subject to the rules of central planning. The hybrid nature of this variety of capitalism stems from the unique combination of a non-capitalist state sector with private entrepreneurship.

2 *Capitalism from above*, also called *patrimonial capitalism* (e.g. Russia, Ukraine), has been a derivative of "top-down" revolutions initiated by new-old state elites, that is former communist party leaders or functionaries now in power who attempted to transform socialist economies applying the neo-liberal prescriptions for market reforms. Under this scenario, the new class of capitalists has been formed mainly from former *nomenklatura* members and their cronies, including the birth of a very special new social stratum of "oligarchs" (Åslund, 2002; Jasiecki, 2013).

3 *Capitalism from without (from abroad)*, also denoted *liberal capitalism* (Czech Republic, Hungary, Poland, and to a lesser degree Slovakia and the Baltic states) has emerged, similar to "capitalism from above", as a result of a "top-down" implementation of the neoliberal strategy of systemic transformation. In contrast to the former, however, the key role in the birth and evolution of "capitalism from without" has been performed by foreign investors and the cooperation of domestic firms with MNCs. As a consequence, the countries embodying this variety of capitalism developed quite advanced market institutions in a relatively short time, well integrated with the global economy.

It is worth indicating in this context that – despite essential differences in the very approach and classification criteria – the last category in King and Szelenyi's typology ("capitalism from without" representative for CEE countries) appears to exhibit clear similarities to the notion of "dependent market economy", a variety of capitalism introduced by Nölke and Vliegenthart (2009).[6]

As a wrap-up of the foregoing discussion, the following section gives an account of the most important findings in our survey of the scholarly debate on the nature of the emerging post-communist capitalism.

2.3 Main findings

As a starting remark, it may appear quite striking that – while departing from the command economy system – the former socialist countries entered the road from plan to market without a clear *explicit* vision of the end point or the target model of capitalism they were aiming to build. Following a distinction made by Heiduk and Rapacki (2009), and similarly by Myant and Drahokoupil (2011), and Rapacki (2016) it can be inferred that the overwhelming majority of these countries have undergone the process of "systemic transformation" (i.e. a process of change without a clear end point) rather than "transition" or a movement toward a defined target. Despite undeniable progress in pushing through structural reforms and building the institutional infrastructure of the market in these countries, it sounds like a plausible hypothesis that the results achieved so far on the road from plan to market are very diverse in individual transition countries and quite different from the patterns established in advanced market economies (Myant and Drahokoupil, 2011).

This conclusion appears to correspond well with the major findings stemming from our survey of the pertinent research on the emerging capitalism in former socialist countries, with special emphasis on the CEE economies, carried out in this chapter. The findings in question may be summarized as follows.

First, it should come as no surprise that after nearly 30 years of systemic transformation there emerged no one common post-communist type of capitalism, even in the relatively homogenous group of CEE11 countries. This conclusion seems consistent with the findings of all but one study (Farkas, 2011) on post-communist comparative capitalism in the transition world, irrespective of the analytical framework being applied (i.e. the standard vs. non-standard approach).[7]

Second, the trajectory of institutional development followed by former socialist countries, including the CEE11 economies, in their quest for capitalism after 1990 has entailed both the convergence and divergence trends. Institutional divergence has taken place in particular within the whole group of transition economies, although in some respects it has also occurred toward their Western capitalist prototypes.

Third, in terms of outcomes, the emerging post-communist capitalism seems to share a number of interesting properties. In the first place these include the *institutional ambiguity* which boils down to missing or incomplete complementarities within various institutional areas and between those areas (along the lines of Amable's approach). Simultaneously, the evolving capitalism in the transition world displays strong symptoms of a *hybrid nature* or heterogeneity of its institutional architecture (a blend of different models or varieties of capitalism co-existing in the same country). This pattern seems to hold even in the case of a relatively institutionally developed group of CEE11 states.[8]

Fourth, in the ongoing scholarly debate on comparative capitalism in the post-communist world, a good deal of research effort has also been devoted to establishing possible reasons that would explain the three findings outlined above. In the debate concerned, three categories of such factors are believed to play the most vital role:

- Diverging pathways of pre-1990 development, including especially different models of socialism hosted until 1989 in individual countries or their groups (e.g. Soviet-style centralization, Yugoslav labor-management, Hungarian market socialism or Polish mixed model with predominantly private agriculture and a relatively wide margin of openness to the West);
- The significance of path dependence or endogenous factors as a key explanatory variable underlying the pervasive institutional dissimilarities among post-socialist countries on their road to a market-driven capitalist system; of special interest here (though less so over time) are the initial conditions of systemic transformation and the persistence and inertia of the command-economy legacy (especially in axiological, mental and behavioral terms; see, e.g., Rapacki and Linz, 1992);
- Exogenous factors, including the external anchor (the prospects of and then accession to the European Union in case of CEE11 countries); this category

encompasses such variables as the place of a country on Europe's periphery, its position vis-à-vis the global networks of multinational companies and exposure to pressures from international organizations (the Washington consensus).

As a concluding remark and a sort of tentative generalization, it may be argued that – at the level of the main pillars of the institutional architecture – the political economies of the CEE countries entail the co-existence of "tradeable" and "non-tradeable" institutional areas.[9] The concept of "dependent market economies" put forward by Nölke and Vliegenthart (2009) suggests that DMEs (mostly the Visegrad countries) are coordinated largely by hierarchical relationships within transnational corporations; as a result, decisions on knowledge production are not dominated by concerns regarding the long-term innovation potential of the host CEE countries but rather by their current profitability. A similar pattern can be tracked in some other areas, such as product market competition, labor market and industrial relations, and financial intermediation. In contrast, the social protection system, as it was of little interest to MNCs, was designed in a fully autonomous way in each CEE11 country. Clearly, it would be a mistake to neglect other factors that might have affected the design of this institutional area, including the inclination to copy well-functioning institutions from countries perceived by political and social elites in Central and Eastern Europe as "institutional benchmarks". Even under such a scenario, however, the decisions on both the scope of emulation and the country selected as a benchmark used to be simultaneously influenced by internal, mostly political constraints, which could not be ignored by any government.

Notes

1 This chapter capitalizes on a more extensive version of the text prepared as an article by the same team of authors and forthcoming in *Europe-Asia Studies* in 2019.

2 Much the same conclusion was reached by Cernat (2006), who applied the term "cocktail capitalism" to define the nature of a post-communist political economy as a blend of the command-economy (socialist) legacy and new building blocks of a capitalist institutional architecture.

3 Quite similar lines of thinking can be traced in King's proposition, who conceptualized the CEE countries as "liberal dependent (post-communist) capitalism (*with proto-CME and LME elements*)" because of the liberal nature of the state there and the dependent nature of their economies (King, 2007). See also King and Szelenyi (2005) and section 2.2 of this chapter.

4 Whereas input variables represent key features/components of a pertinent institutional architecture, the output measures show the outcomes of institutional determination or performance in a given institutional area. For more details, see Chapter 3.

5 Interestingly enough, it has to be noted that Mykhnenko made also another contribution to the ongoing debate, based on the VoC approach. In his other study he argued that both the Polish and Ukrainian versions of emerging capitalism may be interpreted as "mixed- or 'weakly' coordinated market economies" (Mykhnenko, 2007).

6 See note 3.

7 The heterogeneity of post-communist capitalism is most clearly visible when a comparison with the established models of Western European capitalism is made, and in particular when the institutional architecture of CEE11 economies is scrutinized using the standard analytical framework designed by Hall and Soskice or Amable for developed market economies. Most comparative studies on the diversity of post-communist capitalism adopt the tacit assumption that CEE11 countries have followed and are likely to follow in the future the convergence path toward one of the models identified in the early 21st century.
8 The "hybrid nature" of post-communist capitalism can be also seen as a symptom of confirmation bias, being a side effect of the research method applied. When something is different than any chosen benchmark or includes elements of more than one benchmark, the term "hybrid" comes to mind naturally.
9 Reinterpreting the conceptual framework developed by Balassa (1964) and Samuelson (1964), the institutional areas concerned can be divided into two categories: "tradeables", which emerged and then evolved under at least a partial influence of non-domestic factors; and "non-tradeables", which in principle were free of such influence.

References

Ahlborn, M., Ahrens, J. and Schweickert, R. (2016). Large-scale transition of economic systems: Do CEECs converge towards Western prototypes? *Discussion paper 280*, Center for European Governance and Economic Development Research, Göttingen.

Amable, B. (2003). *The diversity of modern capitalism*. Oxford: Oxford University Press.

Aoki, M. (1994). The contingent governance of teams: Analysis of institutional complementarity. *International Economic Review*, 35(3), pp. 657–676.

Åslund, A. (2002). *Building capitalism. The transformation of the former Soviet bloc*. Cambridge: Cambridge University Press.

Babos, P. (2010). Varieties of capitalism in Central and Eastern Europe: Measuring the coordination index of a national economy. *SEER Journal for Labour and Social Affairs in Eastern Europe*, 4, pp. 439–458.

Balassa, B. (1964). The purchasing power parity doctrine: A reappraisal. *The Journal of Political Economy*, 72(6), pp. 584–596.

Bluhm, K. (2010). Theories of capitalism put to the test: Introduction to a debate on Central and Eastern Europe. *Historical Social Research/Historische Sozialforschung*, 35(2).

Bohle, D. and Greskovits, B. (2007). The state, internationalization, and capitalist diversity in Eastern Europe. *Competition and Change*, 11(2), pp. 89–115.

Bohle, D. and Greskovits, B. (2012). *Capitalist diversity on Europe's periphery*, Ithaca and London: Cornell University Press.

Cardoso, F.H. and Faletto, E. (1979). *Dependency and development in Latin America*. Berkeley: University of California Press.

Cernat, L. (2006). Domestic institutions and economic performance: 'Cocktail Capitalism'. In: *Europeanization, varieties of capitalism and economic performance in Central and Eastern Europe. Studies in economic transition*. London: Palgrave Macmillan.

Farkas, B. (2011). The Central and Eastern European model of capitalism. *Post-Communist Economies*, 23(1), pp. 15–34.

Farkas, B. (2013). Changing development prospects for the Central and Eastern European EU member states'. *Paper presented at the 2nd annual SPERI conference*, Sheffield, 1–3 July, University of Sheffield, Working Paper 48172 (MPRA).

Hall, P. and Soskice, D. (2001). *Varieties of capitalism. The institutional foundations of comparative advantage*. Oxford: Oxford University Press.

Hanson, P. (2006). *The European Union's influence on the development of capitalism in Central Europe*. London: Mimeo.

Hanson, P. (2007). The tasks ahead in comparative economic studies: What should we be comparing? *Japanese Journal of Comparative Economics*, 44(1).

Hayek, F.A. (1967). Notes on the evolution of system of rules of conduct. In: *Studies in philosophy, politics and economics*. Chicago: Chicago University Press.

Heiduk, G. and Rapacki, R. (2009). The road from plan to market: Comparing Poland and China. In: R. Frank and S. Burghart, eds., *Driving forces of socialist transformation: North Korea and the experience of Europe and East Asia*. Vienna: Praesens Verlag.

Högselius, P. (2003). Can East European countries innovate? *Paper presented at the Danish research unit for industrial dynamics winter conference*, Aalborg, 16–18 Jan.

Hopkins, T.K. and Wallerstein, I.M. (1982). *World-systems analysis: Theory and methodology*. Beverly Hills: Sage.

Jasiecki, K. (2013). *Kapitalizm po polsku. Między modernizacją a peryferiami Unii Europejskiej* [*Capitalism Polish style. Between modernization and European Union periphery*]. Warszawa: Instytut Filozofii i Socjologii Polskiej Akademii Nauk.

King, L.P. (2007). Central European capitalism in comparative perspective. In: B. Hancké, M. Rhodes and M. Thatcher, eds., *Beyond varieties of capitalism. Conflict, contradictions, and complementarities in the European economy*. Oxford: Oxford University Press.

King, L.P. and Szelenyi, I. (2005). Post-communist economic systems. In: N.J. Smelser and R. Swedberg, eds., *The handbook of economic sociology*. Princeton: Princeton University Press.

Knell, M. and Srholec, M. (2005). Emerging varieties of capitalism in Central and Eastern Europe. *Paper presented at the conference on varieties of capitalism*, University of Paisley, Paisley, 23–24 Sept.

Knell, M. and Srholec, M. (2007). Diverging pathways in Central and Eastern Europe. In: D. Lane and M. Myant, eds., *Varieties of capitalism in post-communist countries*. Basingstoke: Palgrave Macmillan.

Lane, D. and Myant, M., eds. (2007). *Varieties of capitalism in post-communist countries*. Basingstoke: Palgrave Macmillan.

Myant, M. and Drahokoupil, J. (2011). *Transition economies: Political economy in Russia. Eastern Europe and Central Asia*. Hoboken, NJ: John Wiley & Sons.

Mykhnenko, V. (2005). What type of capitalism in Eastern Europe? Institutional structures, revealed comparative advantage, and performance of Poland and Ukraine. Discussion paper 6, Centre for Public Policy and Regions, University of Glasgow, Glasgow.

Mykhnenko, V. (2007). Strengths and weaknesses of 'weak' coordination: Economic institutions, revealed comparative advantages, and socio-economic performance of mixed market economies in Poland and Ukraine. In: B. Hancké, M. Rhodes and M. Thatcher, eds., *Beyond varieties of capitalism. Conflict, contradictions, and complementarities in the European economy*. Oxford: Oxford University Press.

North, D. (1990). *Institutions, institutional change and economic performance*. New York: Cambridge University Press.

Noelke, C. and Horn, D. (2014). Social transformation and the transition from vocational education to work in Hungary: A differences-in-differences approach. *European Sociological Review*, 30(4), first published online 28 Mar. doi:10.1093/esr/jcu048.

Nölke, A. and Vliegenthart, A. (2009). Enlarging the varieties of capitalism: The emergence of dependent market economies in East Central Europe. *World Politics*, 61(4).

Polanyi, K. (1957). *The great transformation: The political and economic origins of our time*. Boston: Beacon Press.

Rapacki, R. (2012). Emerging varieties of capitalism in transition countries of East Central Europe and Central Asia. In: R. Rapacki and P. Maszczyk, eds., *Varieties of capitalism in transition countries*. Warsaw: Warsaw School of Economics.

Rapacki, R. (2016). The institutional underpinnings of the prospective euro adoption in Poland. In: Y. Koyama, ed., *The Eurozone enlargement: Prospect of new EU member states for euro adoption*. New York: Nova Science Publishers.

Rapacki, R., Gardawski, J., Czerniak, A., Horbaczewska, B., Karbowski, A., Maszczyk, P. and Próchniak, M. (2019). Emerging varieties of post-communist capitalism in Central and Eastern Europe: Where do we stand? *Europe-Asia studies*, forthcoming.

Rapacki, R. and Linz, S.J. (1992). Privatization in transition economies: Case study of Poland. *Econometrics and economic theory papers*, 9011. Department of Economics, Michigan State University, East Lansing, MI.

Samuelson, P. (1964). Theoretical notes on trade problems. *Review of Economics and Statistics*, 46, pp. 145–154.

Sapir, A. (2006). Globalization and the reform of European social models. *Journal of Common Market Studies*, 44(2).

3 Methodological framework

Adam Czerniak and Piotr Maszczyk

Introduction

This chapter discusses the major methodological challenges faced in comparative studies on the emerging post-communist capitalism in CEE countries. They are a derivative of the peculiar nature of the institutional endowment of these countries, being an outcome of systemic transformation and the command-economy legacy, and in broader terms, their path dependence. In this chapter we describe the methodological framework and the approach applied throughout the remaining chapters of the book. Against this background we also provide justification for our choice of the research method used in the empirical part of the study, and in particular the subspace clustering machine-learning technique. Simultaneously we specify the data employed.

3.1 Peculiarities of post-communist capitalism and the applicability of standard methodological approaches

As was already mentioned in the preceding chapters, the very idea of "comparative capitalism" studies was originally confined only to the co-existing varieties/models of capitalism in the Western Hemisphere. As a derivative, the methodological and conceptual frameworks developed toward this end were designed for advanced market economies alone. This was in particular the case of two major contributions to the field made by Hall and Soskice (2001), and Amable (2003), referred to as the Varieties of Capitalism (VoC) and the Diversity of Capitalism (DoC) approaches, respectively. Notwithstanding their primary focus and objectives, the VoC and DoC propositions have triggered a new line of research aimed at a direct application of the original frameworks involved to the former socialist countries undergoing systemic transformation, with an intent to explain the emerging post-communist models of capitalism there. Simultaneously, based on the original VoC and DoC concepts and typologies, some attempts have also been made to take account of institutional peculiarities inherent in the post-communist transition, and to extend the existing standard classifications with derivative categories that would accommodate transition countries too, as the emerging types of post-communist capitalism. These trends have become particularly pronounced

DOI: 10.4324/9780429056901-4

since the Eastern enlargement of the European Union from 2004 onward (Rapacki et al., 2019). The survey of the most representative theoretical and empirical research on the emerging varieties or models of post-communist capitalism in Central and Eastern Europe was conducted in Chapter 2.

The VoC and DoC methodological frameworks enable highlighting the institutional differences between countries (clearly not in the whole institutional environment, as it is very complex, but only in those institutional domains that are included in identification of the models of capitalism under a methodology in question). The way institutions matter as the explanatory variable of economic performance is also an interesting research question by itself, but answering it calls for much more in-depth analyses which are beyond the scope of this book.

Based on the survey of the pertinent research on comparative capitalism in the post-communist world carried out in Chapter 2, we arrived at the conclusion that transition economies display a number of peculiar features that make a direct application of the standard methodological and conceptual framework embedded in the "varieties (diversity) of capitalism" paradigm problematic or at least difficult. As a follow-up and extension of the findings articulated in Chapter 2, in this chapter we delve into the main methodological difficulties faced in comparative studies on the emerging post-communist capitalism being a derivative of a peculiar nature of the institutional endowment in former socialist countries. In particular, the following problems deserve special attention (Rapacki et al., 2019).

The first difficulty, especially if one tries to make use of Hall and Soskice's (2001) analytical framework, lies in the choice of an appropriate dependent variable while explaining the comparative economic performance of transition countries as a function of their "comparative institutional advantage". Under the standard VoC approach, the independent variable is the ability of a country to reach a leading position in the world in a particular branch of economic activity on the basis of radical innovation. As of today, no transition economy has gained such a position, which may suggest that we need a more appropriate dependent variable for this group of countries (Myant and Drahokoupil, 2011).[1]

The second difficulty is linked with the choice of the right independent variable. Unlike in advanced Western capitalist countries, where formal institutions or rules of the game (North, 1990) tend to guide the behavior of economic agents, transition economies have been experiencing quite a sizeable gap between formal and informal institutions with a strong bias toward the latter. As a derivative, the proxy for independent variable or "comparative institutional advantage" in former socialist countries should be defined differently compared to Western countries with established and reliable institutional environments.

The third problem is that institutions are not the only determinant of post-communist evolution in transition economies; they are a necessary but not always sufficient condition. Other important factors, including the inherited economic structures (in particular, the scope for new business expansion and the nature of welfare systems; see Myant and Drahokoupil, 2011) and the command-economy legacy play a vital role as co-determinants of their development trajectories.

The fourth difficulty in applying the VoC/DoC frameworks to transition economies is that they are built on the assumption of long-term continuity and stability of existing institutions. In contrast to developed market economies, the process of systemic transformation entails a high degree of discontinuity and volatility. It is hard to predict, therefore, which institutional characteristics existing in former socialist countries are permanent and are likely to have lasting consequences, and which are only of a temporary nature. Similarly, as it was pointed out earlier in the text, this is the question of the "hybrid" nature of post-communist models/varieties of capitalism raised in the literature. Given the fast track of institutional evolution in former socialist countries, it is often very difficult to foretell whether an institutional arrangement is to be "hybrid" in the long run or whether it is just in the middle of the transformation process and will soon become less ambiguous than it used to be.

In view of the peculiarities of systemic transformation as an historically unprecedented process and the difficulties with a direct application of the standard VoC/DoC frameworks to transition economies, outlined above, it seems advisable to adjust this framework with the end to better capture the specific conditions prevailing in former socialist countries. The remaining part of this chapter introduces and substantiates such a modified analytical framework that enables a more precise description of the institutional architecture involved. At the same time, the adjusted framework allows a more refined clustering of the sample countries and enables the resultant tentative classification of the models of post-communist capitalism emerging in Central and Eastern Europe (CEE11) against a broader backdrop of the incumbent EU member states excluding Luxembourg (EU14).

As a starting point in our approach, we adopt in essence the analytical framework devised by Amable (2003) but with substantial modifications, amendments and extensions. In our view, compared to its alternatives such as the VoC conception, described in more detail in the preceding chapter, the DoC scholarly agenda is the most versatile and comprehensive research vehicle for the purpose of studying comparative capitalism, as it allows to capture all key interconnected institutional areas and emphasizes the importance of institutional complementarities as key drivers of the institutional comparative advantage of a country.[2]

Before depicting the main lines of our adjusted approach, two methodological remarks or caveats of a more general nature seem appropriate. First, we bear in mind the objections that have been often propounded against quantitative analytical methods in the research field of institutional economics (see, e.g., Rutherford, 2001; Lissowska, 2008; Farkas, 2011), while at the same time realizing that any dataset of institutional measures is only an imperfect approximation of the existing institutional environment of an economy. Nevertheless, we take the position that quantitative analysis as a method of comparative research on the diversity of institutional arrangements in a broad sample of countries is purposeful and appropriate as it allows to group similar institutional regimes, to measure the scope of institutional variance between groups and to trace the evolution path of each model of capitalism. This is particularly important when the overriding objective of such research is to classify largely heterogeneous countries, like the EU member states, into institutionally approximate clusters rather than to describe in detail the existing institutions and modes of coordination in particular countries or areas, as in the case method being frequently used in institutional analysis (North, 1990; Williamson, 2000).

Second, an important methodological caveat should be formulated, namely the feasibility of comparing studies on the co-existing models/varieties of capitalism carried out at various levels of generalization and idealization. The approach proposed by Amable (similar to that by Hall and Soskice in this respect) has the status of an ideal typology in the sense of Max Weber. In turn, many other studies on comparative capitalism are largely empirical in nature and they lack coherence in imaging the institutions involved. Seen from this perspective, none of the real-life models of capitalism is coherent. There is a good deal of research indicating the incidence of non-market coordination in countries embodying the LME variety of capitalism (US, UK and other examples of liberal models); simultaneously there are many studies pointing to liberal solutions present in countries representing the CME model, such as the Scandinavian economies (Regini, 2000; Koźmiński, 2016). Uwe Becker (2009) in his concept of "Open Varieties of Capitalism" refers to the idea of diversity of capitalism put forward by Karl Polanyi (1957) and recognizes that every real-life institutional architecture is a hybrid. Hence the research challenge is to measure the extent of inconsistency, or rather the distance from the ideal type.

Starting from the foregoing insights, we made two significant modifications to Amable's original research methodology. First, the approach employed in this study, similar to the Amablean inspiration, takes a predominantly macroeconomic perspective as it builds on a premise that a wide range of variables (aka institutional measures) describing a specific institutional area can be applied to approximate the nature of a model of capitalism and to analyze how it operates in broader macroeconomic terms. However, as an essential amendment, we combined the macroeconomic analytical perspective with selected components of the microeconomic foundations derived from the works of Hall and Soskice (2001); apart from a country clustering exercise we also scrutinized in detail the coordination mechanisms prevalent in each cluster and assessed their complementarity with both formal and informal institutions. For the purpose of the present study, we define the *coordination mechanism* as the way in which society enforces cooperation in favor of common interests. In this context, we pay special attention to the difference between market-based mechanisms, which are characteristic of liberal market economies, and non-market mechanisms, which are typical of coordinated market economies. We decided to supplement the macroeconomic focus of our analysis with a microeconomic element to better grasp the uniqueness of capitalism in Central and Eastern European countries, where the state still plays an important role in the organization of social and economic relations, at least in some institutional areas. This extension gives rise to positive synergies as it allows to add a qualitative dimension while interpreting the quantitative results of our empirical study.

Second, we discarded the tacit assumption made by Amable that the number of possible institutional arrangements (or models/varieties of capitalism) in the

European Union is finite and predetermined by the typology crafted 15 years earlier for a distinct group of countries. Hence, at the start of our research we do not presuppose any particular number of the co-existing models of capitalism either in the entire EU or in the CEE11 group. Similarly, we do not assume an a priori continuity of the four models of Western European capitalism singled out by Amable in 2003.

In addition to the aforementioned major methodological novelties compared to the original Amablean approach, the following amendments have been also made in the research agenda and research method applied:

1 Unlike in Amable's original exercise, which boiled down to a snapshot or a static picture of different models of capitalism prevailing in the Western developed world during the 1990s and 2000s, under the adjusted research scheme the major focus was placed on the dynamics of institutional architecture in CEE11 countries, which enabled capturing the evolution of the emerging capitalism in these countries. Such an extension of the pertinent method is essential for the study of post-communist capitalism in Central and Eastern Europe, as it is still in a state of flux – systemic transformation that started in the early 1990s and accelerated again on the eve of the EU accession remains unfinished. Such a dynamic perspective, though not as comprehensive compared to our proposal, has been adopted in a few studies on comparative capitalism in post-communist countries discussed in Chapter 2, including the works by King and Szelenyi (2005) and Ahlborn, Ahrens and Schweickert (2016).

2 An important extension to the Amablean method is the inclusion of the housing market as the sixth institutional area in the set of basic research categories. The global financial and economic crisis from 2008 on has vividly shown that there exists a very strong link between general economic conditions and the state of the housing market, as well as between the housing market condition and its institutional surroundings. It may be argued, therefore, that organization of the residential market should be explicitly included in the adjusted research agenda as the sixth institutional area for discriminating between different types of capitalism in CEE11 countries. In this regard, we draw mainly on the concept of varieties of residential capitalism developed by Schwartz and Seabrooke (2009); see Chapter 9 for a more in-depth discussion of this theme. As a result, our study covers six institutional areas:

   - Product market competition;
   - Labor market and industrial relations;
   - Financial intermediation;
   - Social protection;
   - Knowledge system;
   - Housing market.

3 A very essential issue to be accounted for in the adjusted approach is the complementarity between "deep" or "broad" (i.e. informal) institutions (e.g. the

perceived role of family and of an individual in the society, the desirable level of income disparities or the scope of state intervention in the economy) and formal institutions. The concept of institutional complementarities allows also a better understanding of why institutional reforms are so difficult to implement and are subject to path dependence. In the case of strong complementarities among institutions, reforms are only feasible once all the interrelated areas of institutional setup are changed simultaneously. A clear distinction between formal and informal institutions ought also to be made, as the latter play a much more important role in post-communist societies compared to established Western market economies.

It has to be emphasized at this point, however, that all the foregoing amendments and extensions are contingent upon an in-depth understanding of the nature of capitalism and its forms. The resulting definition of capitalism will help in going beyond just provisional and often postulative labels of various capitalistic forms.

4 In the empirical part of the research agenda, we employ more complex and advanced quantitative methods compared to the original DoC approach. They include a more sophisticated technique that identifies the common traits and differences between the CEE11 economies and Western European models of capitalism and can be used for the analysis of a larger, and hence more comprehensive, set of indicators, encompassing both the "input" and "output" sides of the institutional architecture in the CEE11 countries. This so-called subspace clustering machine-learning method is described in the next section.

3.2 Research method

The first point on our research agenda was to identify as many different institutional dimensions as possible in each of the six analyzed areas. We tried to pinpoint both formal (e.g. legal surrounding, public spending policy, existence and modus operandi of public institutions) and informal institutions (e.g. market praxis, economic actors' preferences, government's soft power enactment) and to isolate cultural values in which they are embedded (e.g. thrift, desire of economic freedom and social protection, gender equality). Moreover, we also attempted to identify the praxis in which mechanisms of coordination reveal themselves (e.g. collective agreements). Basing on such premises, we gathered the best available measures of these institutions for 25 EU countries for two points in time – the first existing observation after the EU enlargement (usually 2005, hereinafter the "2005 dataset") and the last available observation at the time we have started our research (usually 2014, hereinafter the "2014 dataset"). With a view to better assessing institutional differences between countries and minimizing the risk of mismeasurement, we searched for as many available indicators as possible, dividing them into two groups: (1) input measures of institutions that assess the regulatory, social and policy framework of each area and are best suited to measure formal and informal institutions; and (2) output yardsticks of institutions (e.g. the market structure or economic performance and actual decisions of economic actors) that are designed to capture the latent aspects of the institutional surrounding from values to coordination mechanisms. The importance of discriminating between these two types of measures of a social system has already been widely discussed in sociological literature (Almond and Verba, 1989).

For the purpose of this research we have used various data sources, from official data warehouses like Eurostat, the OECD, the World Bank and the ECB, through data gathered for our previous research papers, to our own calculations based on microdata (like the World Value Survey) or information on economic policies of different EU countries (e.g. the TenLaw project). Altogether we have gathered over 150 variables out of which about two dozen were dropped or merged in the process of cluster identification.[3] This results in approximately 25 indicators (aka institutional dimensions) per one institutional area being scrutinized.

Such a big number of indicators requires a sophisticated tool for cluster identification. The standard, principal component approach cannot be used because it is prone to the so-called curse of dimensionality (i.e. in a space with many dimensions, all the points are very far from each other). This means that the identification of clusters is impossible and needs to be preceded by the elimination of irrelevant dimensions – those measures of institutions that are randomly distributed among 25 EU countries and do not reveal any commonalities in the models of capitalism. Such kind of a problem can be solved by applying a subspace clustering machine-learning method.[4]

There exist already a large variety of subspace clustering algorithms (Parsons, Haque and Liu, 2004) that can be divided into two main groups: bottom-up and top-down search algorithms. In the bottom-up approach, an algorithm first creates a histogram for each dimension and selects those bins with densities above a given threshold. The algorithm proceeds until there are no more dense units. Adjacent dense units constitute a cluster. This is not always easy, as one cluster may be mistakenly reported as two smaller clusters, and other clusters may overlap. As a result, this group of subspace clustering algorithms is not suitable for institutional analysis, since one country cannot fall into two distinct institutional clusters at the same time.

The second group of algorithms is much more appropriate to be used for discriminating between different models of capitalism. The algorithms of this sort start by finding an initial approximation of the existing clusters in the full space with equally weighted dimensions. Then the dimensions are weighted according to the number of potential clusters they host. The weights are used in the next iteration to regenerate clusters. Top-down algorithms create clusters that are partitions of the dataset, meaning each instance is assigned to only one cluster. The drawback of this method is that it is highly sensitive to parameter tuning. One needs to set the number of clusters and subspace dimensions prior to the clustering procedure. However, while maintaining vigilance, one can use this method to properly assess both the number and dimensionality of final clusters.

After having tested a series of alternative algorithms, we found the "arbitrarily oriented projected cluster generation" (ORCLUS) proposed by Aggarwal and Yu

(2000)[5] to be the most suitable subspace clustering method for our purposes. In the output of this algorithm, one can find not only a cluster classification but also a subspace consisting of a predefined number of dimensions that is created from a vector of weights of all the initial dimensions. In the majority of other subspace clustering algorithms, the dimensions of the subspace are chosen from the set of the full space, which increases the risk of wrongly choosing the right amount of dimensionality and, hence, omitting important measures of institutions due to an arbitrary choice of parameters. Besides, the algorithm provides as an output the cluster sparsity coefficient which can be used to evaluate the correctness of the arbitrarily set subspace dimension.

The ORCLUS top-down algorithm looks for non-axis parallel subspaces; this routine arose from the observation that many datasets contain inter-attribute correlations. This is a very important remark, as a dataset of institutional measures intrinsically exhibits such properties and, hence, the ORCLUS algorithm is best suited to analyze models of capitalism. It is divided into three steps: clusters assignment, subspace weights determination and merger of clusters. During the assignment phase, the algorithm assigns observations to the nearest cluster center. The distance between two observations (in our case, countries) is defined in a subspace, that is, a set of orthonormal vectors in some space consisting of a predefined number of dimensions. Subspace weights determination redefines the subspace associated with each cluster by calculating the covariance matrix for a cluster and selecting the orthonormal eigenvectors with the smallest eigenvalues. Clusters that are near each other and have similar directions of eigenvalues are merged during the merger phase.

In the ORCLUS algorithm, the final number of clusters (k), the initial number of clusters (k_0), the cluster number reduction per iteration (a), the repetition of iterations with the same number of clusters (*loop*) and the size of the subspace dimensionality (l) must be specified. For the sake of simplicity, we assumed the l parameter to be equal to 1. This assumption holds for each analyzed institutional area, as the obtained cluster sparsity coefficients did not indicate that setting a higher dimensionality would be of benefit to the accuracy of the results. Additionally, we set the parameters a and *loop* to be equal 0.5 and 1, respectively.[6]

The choice of the final number of clusters (k) was more complicated, as we used our own procedure to assess the number of institutional clusters in 25 EU countries for the 2014 dataset. We always began with setting k equal to 2, and then we increased the number of clusters stepwise by 1 until the algorithm broke down and was not able to provide additional, sufficiently coherent clusters of countries. As a control procedure we checked each additional two- or three-country cluster that the algorithm identified for its spuriousness. If countries in a small cluster that appeared in any iteration were not pinpointed as exhibiting similar institutions in the literature prior to our research, we decided to drop that cluster.[7] We always set the initial number of clusters to follow a simple mathematical rule: $k_0 = k + 1$.

The previously described procedure of identifying models of capitalism for the 2014 dataset has three outputs: a vector assigning countries to clusters in each institutional area (see maps[8] depicted in Chapters 4 through 9), a vector of weights that constitutes each cluster subspace in which countries assigned to a given cluster are gathered around or at the cluster center, and the previously described cluster sparsity coefficient. The output vector of weights is most useful for the purpose of institutional analysis, as it allows to perform three types of actions: (1) identify which measures constitute a given cluster (i.e. which institutions are similar in a given cluster of countries and which are irrelevant for models of capitalism identification); (2) define the subspace in which one can measure the institutional distance of each country from a given cluster center; and (3) measure changes in the institutional distances (aka institutional divergence and convergence) between countries and identified cluster centers.

In order to identify the most important institutions that determine a given cluster in each institutional area, we transformed the vector of weights for the 2014 dataset through multiplying it by the transposed vector of standard deviations for each variable in the whole group of 25 EU member states in the 2014 dataset and dividing it by the standard deviation (i.e. dispersion measure) of data points for all countries in the one-dimensional subspace that this vector creates. As a consequence, we obtained a vector of standardized (within and between subspaces) values that allow to arrange institutional measures in their order of importance for cluster distinction (see Tables A4.5 through A9.5 in the appendices to Chapters 4 through 9). We performed these computations separately for each cluster in every institutional area.

With a view to comparing the institutional distance between a given country and different models of capitalism along institutional areas, we constructed a standardized measure of distance for the 2014 dataset. To this end, we computed the absolute distance between a country's data point and the cluster center and divided it by the standard deviation of data points for all countries in the one-dimensional subspace in which this cluster exists. The results are shown in Tables A4.4 through A9.4 in the appendices to Chapters 4 through 9.

Finally, to analyze the process of institutional convergence or divergence of CEE countries toward (from) various clusters identified in the course of our empirical exercise, we used the vector of weights for each cluster in each area to assign a data point for every EU CEE member state in the subspace it constitutes, using the values of institutional measures from the 2005 dataset. Afterwards we calculated the difference between the absolute distance of a given country's data point (for the 2014 dataset) from the cluster center and the absolute distance of that country's data point (for the 2005 dataset) from the cluster center, multiplied it by −1 and divided by the standard deviation of data points for all countries in the one-dimensional subspace in which that cluster center exists. As a result, for each CEE11 economy we obtained a standardized measure which takes a positive value whenever that country converged in the examined period to a given cluster (i.e. its institutional characteristics became more similar to those exhibited by countries that made up that cluster in 2014), and takes a negative value whenever that country experienced a divergence from a given model of capitalism in the institutional area concerned. The results of this part of our empirical exercise can be found in Tables 4.3 through 9.3 in Chapters 4 through 9.

In addition, the applied subspace clustering method enabled us to also perform a qualitative analysis of the complementarity of institutions in CEE11 countries, both within and between six institutional areas involved. To assess whether formal and informal institutions are complements and whether they are coherent with values and the predominant mechanism of coordination in each area, we examined the importance of different input and output measures of institutions for cluster distinction. Based on the existing literature on the subject and our own expertise, we have judged whether the identified salient features of various models of capitalism are complementary (i.e. whether they satisfy needs of socio-economic actors and do not generate inner frictions, social tensions or systemic inefficiencies). Of special relevance to us was an assessment of whether input and output measures coherently indicate the same model of capitalism or, rather, they reveal fault lines resulting from the transplantation of Western European formal institutions to CEE countries (as reflected by input measures) with non-complementary informal institutions or values inherited from the communist period or a more remote past (as indicated by output measures). Furthermore, with a view to assessing the complementarity of institutions across different areas, we analyzed whether CEE11 countries are assigned to similar clusters in each of the six examined institutional areas. In this way we also tested the validity of the implicit assumption made by Amable (2003), that countries fall in the same cluster in all institutional dimensions of analysis.

The next six chapters describe in detail and interpret the results of our empirical study based on quantitative and qualitative institutional analysis. They discuss in particular the institutional measures used and the cluster classification of all 25 EU member states in 2014 together with a description of their prevalent characteristics, and they examine with scrutiny the evolution of the models of capitalism in CEE11 countries between 2005 and 2014 – the recent history, the current state and the vector of possible institutional development.

Notes

1 In this regard Amable "bypassed" the problem, assuming that all five models of capitalism he singled out do not essentially differ in terms of efficiency and did not include economic performance to his classification criteria. One of the possible solutions of this problem, which seems more appropriate for transition countries, would be to replace the dependent variable expressed in absolute terms (levels) with an indicator showing the pace of changes or progress in economic performance. For CEE11 countries, this could be for example the measure of a real income convergence process vis-à-vis the EU15 average (gross domestic product per capita in purchasing power parity terms).

2 Additionally, it may be also argued that today – notwithstanding the fact that the DoC framework was originally designed exclusively for Western market economies – some 15 years after its first application (based on the data from the 1990s), the question of its applicability to the most economically and institutionally advanced post-socialist countries from the CEE region looks different. In the last 20 years a significant real income and institutional convergence toward Western Europe has occurred in CEE11 countries, especially since their EU accession. This trend has been corroborated, inter

alia, in three recent empirical studies by Ahlborn, Ahrens and Schweickert (2016), Matkowski, Próchniak and Rapacki (2016) and Rapacki (2016).

3 The final number of institutional measures that were used in the subspace clustering was 132. The detailed lists of indicators used and their sources are provided in Chapters 4 through 9 (Tables 4.1 to 9.1, respectively).

4 Hereby we would like to express our gratitude to Martyna Kobus, PhD, who suggested the application of this method to our analytical problem.

5 We have used the algorithm implemented in the "orclus" package for the open source R project software environment for statistical computing and graphics.

6 The sensitivity analysis conducted did not yield any substantially different results for other values of *a* and *loop*. We tested *a* equal to 0.3, 0.7 and 0.9, and *loop* equal to 1, 2 and 3.

7 Such a situation happened only once for the product market competition analysis, where two spurious clusters were identified: one consisting of Portugal, Bulgaria and the Czech Republic and the other comprising Ireland, Croatia and Poland.

8 Maps were generated with the use of the "maps", "mapdata", "ggplot2", "maptools" and "ggthemes" packages for the open source R project software environment for statistical computing and graphics.

References

Aggarwal, C.C. and Yu, P.S. (2000). *Finding generalized projected clusters in high dimensional spaces.* In: Proceedings of the 2000 ACM SIGMOD International Conference on Management of Data, SIGMOD '00, Vol. 29, pp. 70–81.

Ahlborn, M., Ahrens, J. and Schweickert, R. (2016). *Large-scale transition of economic systems: Do CEECs converge towards Western prototypes? Discussion Paper 280*, Center for European Governance and Economic Development Research, Göttingen.

Almond, G.A. and Verba, S. (1989). *The civic culture: Political attitudes in five democracies.* Princeton: Princeton University Press.

Amable, B. (2003). *The diversity of modern capitalism.* Oxford: Oxford University Press.

Becker, U. (2009). *Open varieties of capitalism: Continuity, change and performances.* Houndmills: Palgrave Macmillan.

Farkas, B. (2011). The Central and Eastern European model of capitalism. *Post-Communist Economies*, 23(1).

Hall, P. and Soskice, D. (2001). *Varieties of capitalism. The institutional foundations of comparative advantage.* Oxford: Oxford University Press.

King, L.P. and Szelenyi, I. (2005). Post-communist economic systems. In: N.J. Smelser and R. Swedberg, eds., *The handbook of economic sociology.* Princeton: Princeton University Press.

Koźmiński, A. (2016). *Wyobraźnia ekonomiczna* [*Economic imagination*]. Warszawa: Poltext.

Lissowska, M. (2008). *Institutions for market economy. The case of Poland.* Warsaw: C.H. Beck.

Matkowski, Z., Próchniak, M. and Rapacki, R. (2016). Real income convergence between Central Eastern and Western Europe: Past, Present, and Prospects. *Ekonomista*, 6, pp. 853–892.

Myant, M. and Drahokoupil, J. (2011). *Transition economies: Political economy in Russia, Eastern Europe and Central Asia.* Hoboken, NJ: John Wiley & Sons.

North, D. (1990). *Institutions, institutional change and economic performance.* New York: Cambridge University Press.

Parsons, L., Haque, E. and Liu, H. (2004). Subspace clustering for high dimensional data: A review. *ACM SIGKDD Explorations Newsletter – Special Issue on Learning from Imbalanced Datasets*, 6(1).

Polanyi, K. (1957). *The great transformation: The political and economic origins of our time*. Boston: Beacon Press.

Rapacki, R. (2016). The institutional underpinnings of the prospective euro adoption in Poland. In: Y. Koyama, ed., *The Eurozone enlargement: Prospect of new EU member states for euro adoption*. New York: Nova Science Publishers.

Rapacki, R., Gardawski, J., Czerniak, A., Horbaczewska, B., Karbowski, A., Maszczyk, P. and Próchniak, M. (2019). Emerging varieties of post-communist capitalism in Central and Eastern Europe: Where do we stand? *Europe-Asia Studies*, forthcoming.

Regini, M. (2000). Between deregulation and social pacts: The responses of European economies to globalization. *Politics & Society*, 28(1).

Rutherford, M. (2001). Institutional economics: Then and now. *Journal of Economic Perspectives*, 15(3), pp. 185–190.

Schwartz, H. M. and Seabrooke, L. (eds.) (2009). *The politics of housing booms and busts*. London: Palgrave Macmillan. doi: 10.1057/9780230280441.

Williamson, O. (2000). The new institutional economics: Taking stock, looking ahead. *Journal of Economic Literature*, 3(38), pp. 595–613.

Part II

Empirical results

4 Product market competition

Mariusz Próchniak

Introduction

Product market competition is the institutional area that influences the behavior of firms and the performance of the product markets. It can be analyzed from two interconnected perspectives. The first one involves the institutional architecture of the product market. It affects the ease of establishing and running enterprises, the costs of entry to the industry, the extent of product market regulations, the rate of corporate income taxes (and more broadly the fiscal burden of firms), the complexity of the administrative burden in running enterprises (e.g. the number of permits or procedures necessary to start up and run enterprises) and the size of state control over competition. The second perspective highlights the outcomes or performance of product market competition, that is the degree of competitiveness of the markets in different industries. This area can be measured by the concentration ratio, the Herfindahl-Hirschman index or the Boone indicator. These variables show the level of competition in individual industries and the market power of single firms. The cross-country analyses for the Central and Eastern European (CEE) countries carried out from the institutional perspective do not appear frequently in the economic literature. For example, Jackson and Deeg (2012) analyze institutional changes in product markets in six Western economies and in Hungary and Slovakia. Farkas (2011) examines the product market competition in ten CEE countries compared with Western European economies by assessing the relationship between market liberalization and international integration. She finds five clusters in the examined group of countries. All in all, the literature on the CEE economies is relatively scarce and there is still much room for new studies on the subject.

4.1 Measurement of institutions

Before one can categorize the models of capitalism in the product market competition area, it is necessary to define the scope of analysis, as this area is embedded in a broad set of institutions. Theoretical and empirical studies include a large array of indicators that measure product market competition. They may be grouped into three categories (Próchniak, 2018): (1) microeconomic variables at

DOI: 10.4324/9780429056901-6

the firm level (e.g. price markup on costs, Lerner index, profit margin, number of firms or competitors, Boone indicator); (2) microeconomic variables at the industry level (e.g. Herfindahl-Hirschman index [HHI], concentration ratio); and (3) macroeconomic variables (e.g. product market regulation indicators). The variety of product market competition yardsticks has been also discussed by Alexeev and Song (2013). These authors empirically test the relationship between corruption and product market competition for some 60 countries on the basis of six product market competition measures: (1) the number of competitors, (2) costs markup, (3) consumer reaction to a hypothetical price increase, (4) share in the domestic market, (5) share in the local market and (6) HHI. In more general terms, there is a good amount of studies in the field whose authors employ numerous product market competition gauges to examine various relationships between macroeconomic variables (for recent studies, see, e.g., Nicoletti and Scarpetta, 2003; de Rosa et al., 2006; McMorrow, Röger and Turrini, 2010; Bloch, 2012; Jean and Jiménez, 2011; Bertinelli, Cardi and Sen, 2013).

While measuring in this study institutions in which the product market competition is embedded, we follow Amable's (2003) approach, who focuses on "competition at the aggregate level, not at the disaggregate, industry level". Similar to the study by Amable, we do not analyze firm-level data (such as the Boone indicator) or industry-level data (such as concentration indices). We focus instead on macroeconomics indicators – primarily on "input" variables, that is institutional determinants of product market competition, but also on a few "output" measures, showing the performance of the product market.

In our study, we use 23 indicators of product market competition altogether. They originate from three sources: the Heritage Foundation, the World Economic Forum (Global Competitiveness Index [GCI]) and the World Bank (World Development Indicators [WDI]). The variables employed in this study are listed in Table 4.1. The economic coverage of our data is, nevertheless, akin to the dataset applied by Amable. The data taken from the Heritage Foundation and WDI databases represent primarily state control over competition – mainly the level of taxation and the ease of starting and running enterprises. The variables from the GCI database show not only the government involvement in product markets but also the quality of private institutions. The variables concerned represent mainly the institutional architecture of product market competition (i.e. determinants of competition). Global competitiveness index and its selected components (e.g. intensity of local competition) are "outputs" of competition (in the case of aggregated indicators, only partly).

For the sake of conciseness, we do not describe the exact method of calculating all the variables. These are given in the source references. As a matter of example, the variable called "Institutions" (gci_inst) includes seven areas: (1) property rights (including intellectual property protection); (2) ethics and corruption (diversion of public funds, public trust in politicians, irregular payments and bribes); (3) undue influence (represented by judicial independence and favoritism in decisions of government officials); (4) government efficiency (measured by wastefulness of government spending, burden of government regulation, efficiency of

Table 4.1 Data sources

Variable name	*Variable description*	*Data source*
hef_fiscal	Index of Economic Freedom component: Fiscal freedom	Heritage Foundation
hef_gov	Index of Economic Freedom component: Freedom from government spending	Heritage Foundation
hef_business	Index of Economic Freedom component: Business freedom	Heritage Foundation
gci_inst	GCI component: Institutions	GCI
gci_loccom	GCI component: Intensity of local competition	GCI
gci_mardom	GCI component: Extent of market dominance	GCI
gci_effec	GCI component: Effectiveness of anti-monopoly policy	GCI
gci_tax	GCI component: Total tax rate (% profits)	GCI
gci_domcom	GCI component: Domestic competition	GCI
gci_tradeb	GCI component: Prevalence of trade barriers	GCI
gci_forown	GCI component: Prevalence of foreign ownership	GCI
gci_busimp	GCI component: Business impact of rules on FDI	GCI
gci_forcom	GCI component: Foreign competition	GCI
gci_com	GCI component: Competition	GCI
gci_marsize	GCI component: Market size	GCI
gci_compind	Global competitiveness index	GCI
wdi_costbusi	Cost of business start-up procedures (% of GNI per capita)	WDI
wdi_newbus	New business density (new registrations per 1,000 people aged 15–64)	WDI
wdi_taxpaym	Tax payments (number)	WDI
wdi_timeenfor	Time required to enforce a contract (days)	WDI
wdi_timeregpro	Time required to register property (days)	WDI
wdi_timestartbu	Time required to start a business (days)	WDI
wdi_timepaytax	Time to prepare and pay taxes (hours)	WDI

GCI – Global Competitiveness Index Database by World Economic Forum; WDI – World Development Indicators Database by the World Bank.

Heritage Foundation variables range from 0 to 100, where higher value indicates greater scope of economic freedom. GCI indicators (except total tax rate) range from 1 to 7, where higher value indicates greater competition.

Source: Author's elaboration based on Heritage Foundation (2017), World Bank (2017) and World Economic Forum (2017).

legal framework in settling disputes, efficiency of legal framework in challenging regulations and transparency of government policymaking); (5) security (i.e. business costs of terrorism, business costs of crime and violence, organized crime, reliability of police services); (6) corporate ethics (measured by ethical behavior of firms); and (7) accountability (strength of auditing and reporting standards, efficacy of corporate boards, protection of minority shareholders' interests and strength of investor protection). As we can see, the variable "Institutions" measures both public and private institutions. The first five areas refer to public institutions, whereas the last two areas show the quality of private institutions.

We collected the values of all indicators involved for two years: the year close to the EU Eastern enlargement (2005, if possible) and the last available year (typically 2014). Due to various data sources and many missing observations, the exact years for which individual indicators were available may differ.

4.2 Models of capitalism in the EU member states – product market competition

While examining the data gathered on institutional measures with the ORCLUS subspace clustering algorithm, two distinct groups of countries that share a similar set of institutions were identified.

As a matter of fact, our study has shown that the institutional architectures in the area of product market competition in the incumbent EU member states (EU14) exhibit a substantial degree of resemblance. As a result, the subspace clustering method has not allowed to distinguish too many clusters. The EU14 countries (Western European members excluding Luxembourg) were found to fall into two clusters of uneven size.

The smaller cluster (denoted as cluster 1) comprises only two Mediterranean economies, Italy and Greece, and is labeled the *regulation-driven cluster*. The larger cluster (cluster 2) includes 12 countries: Austria, Belgium, Denmark, Finland, France, Germany, Ireland, Netherlands, Portugal, Spain, Sweden and the UK. For the purpose of this study it was labeled the *liberal cluster*. Map 4.1 provides a more detailed breakdown.

Such outcomes stem from the fact that the institutional matrices in Western European countries, as a rule, are relatively similar in the area of product market competition. Long-lasting EU membership made these countries subject to a process of institutional convergence as they had to adopt many regulations enhancing competition. It is worth mentioning in this context such factors as the unification of pertinent regulations by the European Commission, the important role of European courts (including the European Court of Arbitration) and benefits of the common market. The last factor is of special relevance as it results, among others, from the unification of tariffs and other trade barriers at the external borders of the EU, the introduction of standardized procedures of public tenders within the EU and the common competition policy aimed at confining the incidence of restrictive business practices and prohibiting cartels. For example, Article 102 of the Treaty on the Functioning of the European Union prohibits firms holding a dominant position on a market to abuse that position (e.g. by cutting down on the level of output or charging unfair prices). The "old" EU members had enough time to adjust their institutional environment to the requirements of acquis communautaire. The only exception may have taken place in the case of some Western European "latecomers" to the EU, that is the Mediterranean economies (e.g. Greece), which joined the EU in the 1980s. Indeed, our results are to some extent consistent with this conjecture.

The main differences between clusters 1 and 2 are mostly linked with variables that measure the time effort needed to carry out various economic activities. They

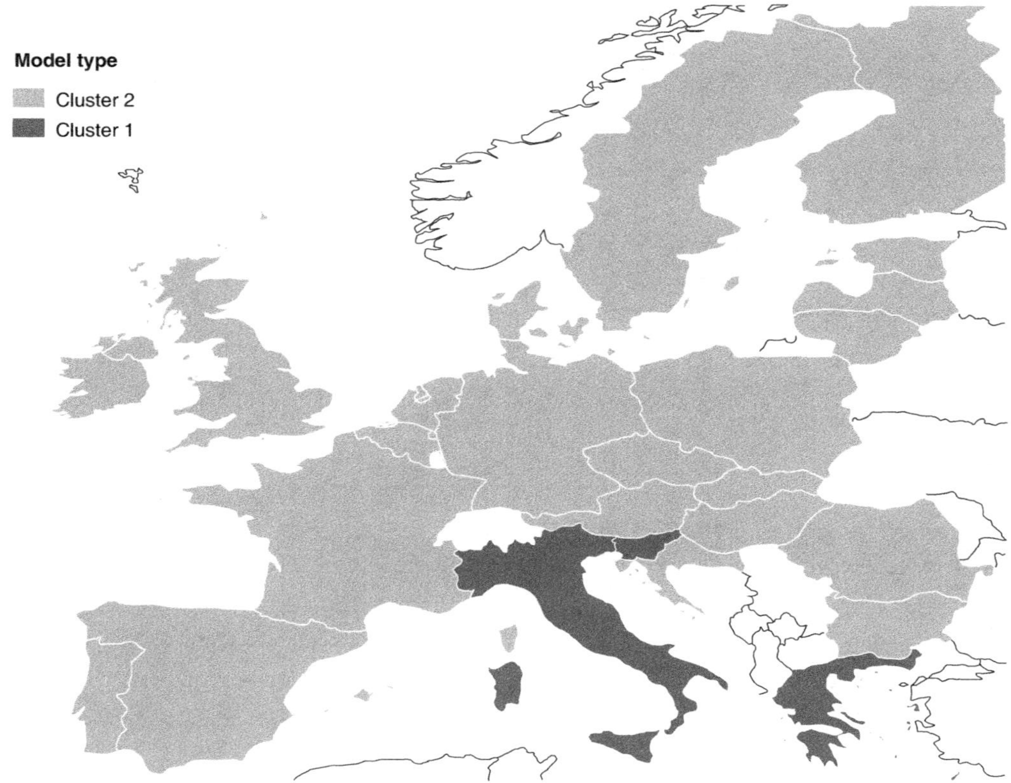

Map 4.1 Models of capitalism in the European Union: product market competition

Source: Author's elaboration.

stem from the fact that in the regulation-driven cluster the bureaucratic burden is higher, as firms must cope with a bigger number of administrative procedures during the registration process and at the subsequent stages of starting and running a business. In the liberal cluster (cluster 2), the degree of regulation is lower and the markets are more competitive. The most important variable that defines this cluster narrowed down to the group of Western European (EU14) economies is the time required to enforce a contract. Similarly, the most essential variable responsible for identifying the regulation-driven cluster (cluster 1) is the time to prepare and pay taxes. In cluster 2, the variable time required to start a business also ranks very high (4th). In cluster 1, the set of five most important variables includes two other "time" variables: time required to enforce a contract (3rd) and time required to register property (5th). One component of the Heritage Foundation index of economic freedom, namely freedom from government spending, is also a crucial variable in determining both clusters (the 3rd and 2nd ranks in the liberal and regulation-driven clusters, respectively).

The regulation-driven cluster features much less business-friendly regulations in the area of product market competition compared with the liberal cluster. For example, the average time required to enforce a contract in Italy and Greece amounts to 1,350 days, while in the remaining 12 Western European countries it is only 455 days. Similarly, preparing and paying taxes takes about 231 hours in the two Mediterranean states, while in the liberal cluster this takes approximately 145 hours. In Italy and Greece, time required to start a business amounts to 9.8 days, while in the remaining EU14 countries it stands at 8.1 days.

A more in-depth analysis of the coordination mechanism and the complementarity of institutions involved shows, however, that the institutional architecture in EU14 countries is not fully coherent. For instance, in some areas the countries making up cluster 2 exhibit more business-friendly regulations, whereas in some other areas the opposite is true. A good example is the assessment of three components of the index of economic freedom. In case of two such components (freedom from government spending and business freedom), the "liberal" countries perform better from the viewpoint of promoting product market competition. The mean value of the freedom from government spending variable (hef_gov) equals 23.7 for the 12 countries classified in the liberal cluster, whereas for two Mediterranean economies (Italy and Greece) the average stands at 11.1. The freedom from government spending indicator is calculated on the basis of only one variable (aggregated government spending) in such a way that a higher level of government spending means a lower score (the highest score of 100 would be assigned to a country with no public expenditures whatsoever). These outcomes indicate that in countries representing the regulation-driven cluster, the level of government expenditures is on average higher.

However, in the case of fiscal freedom (hef_fiscal), the results are different. The mean value for the 12 Western European countries equals 55.4, while the average for Greece and Italy amounts to 60.1. This variable includes three components (top marginal tax rate on individual and corporate income as well as total tax burden as a percentage of gross domestic product). The higher the level of taxation, the lower the pertinent score. The outcomes show that the two Mediterranean countries are characterized on average by lower taxes compared to the remaining Western European economies. This result can be explained partly by the fact that the latter group includes the Scandinavian countries in which taxes are relatively high.

The product market competition in two southern European or cluster 1 countries is less intense than in cluster 2 because the institutional environment there features a broader scope of regulations and larger incidence of administrative hindrances in this area. As a result, compared to cluster 2, it is more cumbersome in Greece and Italy to start and run a private business.

The CEE region does not constitute its own, distinct cluster. In the light of the results of subspace clustering, the CEE11 countries are dispersed among both clusters 1 and 2. The majority of these countries were identified as part of the liberal cluster. Only Slovenia was classified into the regulation-driven cluster.

As a consequence, at the level of the whole research sample most of the EU25 members – despite some country-specific dissimilarities in the institutional architectures of product market competition – were classified into one cluster (i.e. the liberal one). The liberal cluster comprises 22 countries altogether, including 12 EU14 and 10 CEE11 economies. In turn, three peripheric countries – two from Western Europe (Greece and Italy) and one from Central and Eastern Europe (Slovenia) – are classified in the regulation-driven cluster. As the dissimilarities concerned are not so clear and regular, the subspace clustering method does not allow to group the sample economies into more than just two clusters. The regulation-driven cluster contains very few countries, which are outliers compared with the majority of EU member states. This implies that the area of product market competition de facto hosts one main cluster of member countries in the enlarged EU pointing to a convergence trend and the resulting unification of institutional patterns in the European Union.

This outcome suggests that the overwhelming majority of CEE11 countries have implemented necessary reforms which have made their product markets performance comparable to that prevailing in the EU14 group. As a derivative, they do not lag behind their Western peers in this regard. They introduced a great many of institutional changes with a view to facilitate establishing and running private businesses, dismantling bureaucratic hurdles faced by private entrepreneurship, increasing the scope of economic freedom, reducing product markets regulations and so forth. This may be interpreted as one of the key reasons why the CEE countries have not formed their own cluster in this institutional area.

The variables employed in this part of our study measure, to a large extent, the level of economic freedom, ease of doing business, clear and simple legal and tax systems and other institutions that affect the product market competition of the sample countries. All these factors combined are indirectly linked with the level of economic development of a country (since they are supply-side economic growth determinants) and with the EU membership. During the process of EU accession, the CEE newcomers to the European Union were obliged to implement multiple reforms to make their product markets more competitive and to safeguard common standards in the single European market. As a result, the diffusion of Western European institutions into the CEE region took place. The main diffusion channels encompassed, inter alia, intensified international trade between new and old EU members and a massive inflow of foreign direct investment (FDI) into the CEE countries which facilitated the adoption of well-tested Western-type institutional arrangements and best practices. The fact of EU membership implies that many dimensions of product market competition (e.g. prohibition of favoring domestic companies or restrictions on the level of public aid) tend to be unified across the analyzed group due to the EU policies aimed at promoting competition. Moreover, the new CEE member states have been consistently improving their business environment well before their EU accession (i.e. since the beginning of the 1990s) or the outset of systemic transformation from socialism to capitalism.

Table 4.2 shows the average values of all the indicators used in our empirical exercise for the two clusters in the enlarged EU. Based on these data, we can describe the most salient features of the coordination mechanism driving product market competition. They clearly show that the liberal cluster is characterized by much better regulations seen as a vehicle of promoting product market competition. The three component variables of the index of economic freedom assume

Table 4.2 Cluster-average values for all variables (EU25 countries)

	Cluster 1 *Regulation-driven*	*Cluster 2* *Liberal*
hef_fiscal	59.6	67.7
hef_gov	7.4	36.0
hef_business	75.4	78.2
gci_inst	3.7	4.6
gci_loccom	5.1	5.4
gci_mardom	4.2	4.3
gci_effec	3.6	4.4
gci_tax	49.1	42.7
gci_domcom	4.4	4.8
gci_tradeb	4.5	4.6
gci_forown	3.7	5.2
gci_busimp	3.5	4.9
gci_forcom	4.5	5.3
gci_com	4.4	4.9
gci_marsize	4.4	4.5
gci_compind	4.3	4.8
wdi_costbusi	5.4	2.7
wdi_newbus	2.5	5.1
wdi_taxpaym	10.7	9.8
wdi_timeenfor	1286.7	486.3
wdi_timeregpro	28.5	23.8
wdi_timestartbu	9.0	10.3
wdi_timepaytax	235.7	186.9

Source: Author's elaboration.

higher values in this cluster compared to its regulation-driven counterpart. For the 22 EU economies classified in cluster 2, fiscal freedom equals 67.7 points on average, freedom from government spending amounts to 36.0 points, while business freedom stands at 78.2 points. The same indicators for the three countries making up the regulation-driven cluster (or cluster 1) amount to 59.6, 7.4, and 75.4 points, respectively. Much the same disparities between the two clusters involved are also visible in case of all indicators gathered from the GCI database (representing both competition "inputs" and, to a lesser degree, "outputs"). Except the variable gci_tax (total tax rate), the remaining indicators originating from the GCI database range from 1 to 7, where the score of 7 reflects the greatest scope of competition. The countries identified to be part of the liberal cluster are characterized on average by higher values of these variables meaning that product markets are more competitive than those in the regulation-driven cluster. In other words, these outcomes indicate that Italy, Greece and Slovenia perform atypically in terms of product market competition compared to most of the EU members. In this regard they may be conceived again as outliers vis-à-vis the 22 countries in the liberal cluster. Their product markets conditions are less favorable to competition due to, among others, their government policies. The culture and history might have also played a vital role. It is visible notably in Slovenia, characterized by a high significance of state-owned enterprises in many industries and sectors of the economy.

The differences between the liberal cluster and three countries found in cluster 1 are also clearly seen if indicators from the WDI database are considered. As regards input variables, in the regulation-driven cluster the cost of business start-up procedures equals 5.4% of gross national income (GNI) per capita and is double the level recorded in the liberal cluster (2.7% of GNI per capita); the number of tax payments is slightly higher (10.7 and 9.8, respectively); while time required to enforce a contract, register property and pay taxes is significantly higher in cluster 1 (1,286.7 days, 28.5 days, and 235.7 hours compared to 486.3 days, 23.8 days, and 186.9 hours in cluster 2).

When comparing ten CEE countries identified as part of the liberal cluster with Slovenia being in the regulation-driven cluster, we should admit that the institutional environment in the CEE10 sub-group as a rule is more favorable to competition, but the differences involved vary depending on individual indicators. For example, as far as fiscal freedom and freedom from government (hef_fiscal and hef_gov variables) are concerned, the CEE10 group scores on average 82.6 and 50.7 while the respective figures for Slovenia are much lower and amount to 58.6 and 0.0. The last value is interesting as it indicates that the level of government spending in Slovenia is extremely high. This outcome makes this country resemble Greece, which also shows a score of 0.0 in this area. No other country, even the Nordic states, recorded a comparable score of 0.0 for the level of public spending (although Finland, Denmark and France are close). On the other hand, under the heading of business freedom Slovenia outperforms the CEE10 (i.e. it exhibits a larger scope of freedom, which may be attributed to more business-friendly regulations than those in the CEE10 economies). Time required to enforce a contract is much longer in Slovenia compared with the CEE10 average (1,160 vs.

524 days), whereas time required to start a business is shorter (7.5 days in Slovenia and 13.0 days in the remaining CEE countries).

As regards the distances of individual countries in our sample from the other cluster, shown in Table A4.4 (see Appendix), the following findings are worth highlighting. Among the three economies representing the regulation-driven cluster, Slovenia is the most distant from the liberal cluster (3.85), followed by Greece (3.31) and Italy (0.95). This outcome indicates that Slovenia and Greece reveal a pretty high degree of similarity in terms of the institutional distance from the remaining 22 EU countries. This result can be partly explained by the fact that with respect to freedom from government spending (hef_gov indicator), Slovenia and Greece both achieve boundary values which are very distinct from the levels recorded in the remaining EU economies.

Looking at the distances of countries in the liberal cluster from its regulation-driven counterpart, it can be ascertained that this is Estonia that stands out in this respect (2.75). This is due to the fact that this country has excelled in enacting a good deal of business-friendly regulations and features a large scope of economic freedom and intense competition. For example, the aggregated global competitiveness indicator (gci_compind) for Estonia amounts to 4.74, which by far exceeds the values recorded in the remaining new CEE member states. As a derivative, Estonia was found to be situated far away from the regulation-driven cluster. The next farthest CEE countries in terms of their institutional gap toward that cluster include Romania (2.16), Lithuania (2.04), Croatia (1.78), Latvia (1.59) and Slovakia (1.54). For Hungary, Poland, Bulgaria and the Czech Republic, the distance from the regulation-driven cluster is much smaller. It may suggest a lower level of product market competition prevailing in the latter four CEE countries compared to other economies in the liberal cluster.

Table A4.5 (see Appendix) provides the ranking of most important variables for cluster identification in the whole group of EU25 countries. As regards the regulation-driven cluster, the following variables are ranked among the most important determinants of our classification: time required to register property (wdi_timeregpro), total tax rate as percent of profits (gci_tax) and time required to start a business (wdi_timestartbu). This indicates that these are variables representing inputs to product market competition, or the institutional determinants of this domain that take the top three ranks as cluster identifiers. In the regulation-driven economies, it is much harder to run private firms as product markets are more regulated. On the one hand, it is more cumbersome to start a new business: it takes more effort to go through all bureaucratic hindrances involved. On the other hand, once a new firm has been established, it must cope with much stronger fiscalism. In the regulation-driven economies, the total tax rate consumes on average a larger proportion of profits compared to the liberal economies.

The liberal cluster is primarily identified by a number of GCI indicators. These are related with foreign and local competition, the extent of market dominance, market size and effectiveness of anti-monopoly policy. In particular, the variable "Institutions" (gci_inst), which measures the quality of both public and private institutions, ranks second among the most important identifiers of this cluster.

In the next section, we will assess the course and directions of institutional changes in the area of product market competition in CEE11 countries between 2005 and 2014. This will allow to shed some new empirical light on time stability of the patterns established so far on the evolution of institutional architectures in this area since the largest EU enlargement onwards.

4.3 Evolving models of capitalism in CEE countries between 2005 and 2014

The general trend prevailing in the CEE11 countries in the institutional area involved in the 2005–2014 period can be summarized as a consistent tendency toward fewer regulations and more intense product market competition. Referring to our classification which singles out two clusters identified earlier in the chapter, it is equivalent to say that the CEE economies were on their convergence trajectory toward the liberal cluster.

In the case of new EU member states from Central and Eastern Europe, path dependence played a prominent role in the development of their product markets. The institutional environment of these markets in CEE11 countries has undergone gradual progress[1] encompassing most of the indicators used in our empirical exercise. However, in the case of a few institutional yardsticks, some symptoms of a backlash have also appeared.

In general, it may be argued that the institutional environment affecting product market competition improved in the CEE countries. This was brought about by the advancements in systemic transformation and the effects of the integration anchor. The institutional changes implemented by CEE11 countries during the 2005–2014 period complied with the EU standards and requirements aimed at promoting competition and adjusting the domestic law to common policies. For example, the caps on the level of public aid to state-owned enterprises were imposed. The enactment of this law entailed, inter alia, shutting down of the shipyard in Szczecin (Poland) as it was forced by the European Commission decision to return a public subsidy received from the Polish government. Another illustration of this tendency involves a rule that foreign firms cannot be discriminated in domestic markets. Implementation of this rule was conducive to boosting bilateral trade between countries. As a matter of example, PESA Bydgoszcz, the Polish manufacturer of rail rolling stock (including locomotives and trams), sells intensively its products to other European countries (e.g. to Germany and Italy) by winning tenders for rail rolling stock supplies. Solaris, the Polish producer of buses, sells its buses and trolleybuses to many European cities (e.g. Tallinn and Bratislava). Tax regulations were also unified in line with the EU requirements. For instance, the value-added tax (VAT) rates are relatively similar in the CEE countries. In 2018, the basic rate of the VAT ranged from 19% in Romania to 27% in Hungary, with eight CEE countries having a basic tax rate between 20% and 23%.

Institutional reforms concerned also individual industries and sectors of the economy. For example, deregulation of the railway industry took place (including a separation of ownership of the railway network from the carrier function, which led to enhanced competition in the railway services market). Similar reforms were undertaken in other industries or sectors which are natural monopolies. In the telecommunication and energy sectors, third-party access to infrastructure has been liberalized (at least partially) and the number of sellers increased. These reforms were implemented in all CEE11 countries, though the "outcomes" did not necessarily need to be the same (for instance, in Poland there are many more rail operators and the Polish railway market is more competitive than that of Slovenia).

The developments discussed above are confirmed by the data in Table A4.6 (see Appendix). The CEE countries improved their scores for input variables, including all three counts related to economic freedom variables (the most remarkable change took place in the case of fiscal freedom). A clear progress was also witnessed for all variables derived from the WDI database. Between 2005 and 2014 for CEE11 countries as a whole, the cost of business start-up procedures decreased from 10.0% to 3.4% of GNI per capita, the number of tax payments fell from 32.6 to 10.8 (i.e. by two-thirds), the time required to enforce a contract diminished from 587 days to 582 days while the time to register property exhibited a dramatic fall, from 178.6 days to 25.0 days. Time required to start a business shrank from 32.7 days to 12.5 days whereas time to prepare and pay taxes was reduced from 346 hours to 238 hours. There was also an upward trend in the case of output variables – new registrations per 1,000 people aged 15–64 rose from 3.6 in 2005 to 5.8 by 2014. Most variables from the GCI database also showed improvement in the institutional environment of the CEE countries; nevertheless, the aggregated GCI did not change during the 2005–2014 period.

The foregoing tendencies have been corroborated by the results of the subspace clustering exercise. Table 4.3 shows whether individual CEE countries were

Table 4.3 Change in absolute distance from 2014 clusters for each CEE11 country and each subspace dimension between 2005 and 2014 (standardized values)

	Cluster 1 Regulation-driven	*Cluster 2 Liberal*
Bulgaria	1.31	4.21
Croatia	1.57	5.80
Czech Republic	5.03	7.20
Estonia	−0.05	5.46
Hungary	−0.43	5.62
Latvia	−0.26	7.26
Lithuania	0.45	3.83
Poland	0.19	7.81
Romania	0.03	20.97
Slovakia	−1.14	8.80
Slovenia	0.13	1.30
Median change	***0.13***	***5.80***

Source: Author's elaboration.

converging toward or diverging from either cluster 1 or 2 between 2005 and 2014. A positive sign means that a CEE country became more similar to a given cluster. Data in Table 4.3 indicate that, on the one hand, all CEE11 economies were converging to the liberal cluster. The largest institutional convergence was recorded for Romania (20.97 standard deviations), followed by Slovakia (8.80), Poland (7.81), Latvia (7.26), the Czech Republic (7.20), Croatia (5.80), Hungary (5.62), Estonia (5.46), Bulgaria (4.21), Lithuania (3.83), and Slovenia (1.30). Slovenia represents the regulation-driven cluster and hence its performance vis-à-vis the liberal cluster was to be expected.

On the other hand, the prevailing pattern of institutional evolution of CEE countries toward the regulation-driven cluster proved different. The distance with respect to this cluster shrank significantly only in Czechia (5.03). For six CEE economies, the narrowing of the institutional gap toward cluster 1 was negligible (ranging from 0.03 in Romania to 1.57 in Croatia), whereas for four other new EU member states (Estonia, Hungary, Latvia and Slovakia) the distance even augmented, as illustrated by the respective negative values in Table 4.3.

To summarize, when looking at the median change, we can see that during the 2005–2014 period the CEE11 economies were subject to a clear-cut convergence trend toward the liberal cluster while the institutional gap to the regulation-driven cluster remained roughly constant. This implies that structural reforms undertaken by new EU member states during the first decade of their EU membership proved very similar and led to enhanced product market competition. The upgrading of the institutional architecture was focused, among other things, on boosting competition in the product markets, broadening the scope of economic freedom, facilitating start-ups of new businesses, and dismantling bureaucratic barriers to private entrepreneurship.

We may reasonably expect that these tendencies will continue in the near future. It even seems likely that in a few years only one cluster in the product market competition domain will remain as the process of institutional convergence among the EU member states will be unfolding. However, at this point in time, it is difficult to make more detailed forecasts of the future evolution of product market competition.

Note

1 When talking about progress, the default reference point is "best practice", that is, countries holding top places in relevant rankings (or the best performers among the EU countries in this respect).

References

Alexeev, M. and Song, Y. (2013). Corruption and product market competition: An empirical investigation. *Journal of Development Economics*, 103, pp. 154–166.

Amable, B. (2003). *The diversity of modern capitalism*. Oxford: Oxford University Press.

Bertinelli, L., Cardi, O. and Sen, P. (2013). Deregulation shock in product market and unemployment. *Journal of Economic Dynamics & Control*, 37, pp. 711–734.

Bloch, L. (2012). Product market regulation, trend inflation and inflation dynamics in the new Keynesian Phillips curve. *Economic Modelling*, 29, pp. 2058–2070.

de Rosa, D., Steiner, F., Nicoletti, G. and Conway, P. (2006). Regulation, competition and productivity convergence. *OECD Economics Department Working Papers*, 509, OECD Publishing, Paris.

Farkas, B. (2011). The Central and Eastern European model of capitalism. *Post-Communist Economies*, 23, pp. 15–34.

Heritage Foundation (2017). *Index of economic freedom database*. [online] Available at: www.heritage.org/index/ [Accessed 30 June 2017].

Jackson, G. and Deeg, R. (2012). The long-term trajectories of institutional change in European capitalism. *Journal of European Public Policy*, 19, pp. 1109–1125.

Jean, S. and Jiménez, M. (2011). The unemployment impact of immigration in OECD countries. *European Journal of Political Economy*, 27, pp. 241–256.

McMorrow, K., Röger, W. and Turrini, A. (2010). Determinants of TFP growth: A close look at industries driving the EU-US TFP gap. *Structural Change and Economic Dynamics*, 21, pp. 165–180.

Nicoletti, G. and Scarpetta, S. (2003). Regulation, productivity and growth: OECD evidence. *OECD Economics Department Working Papers*, 347, OECD Publishing, Paris.

Próchniak, M. (2018). The impact of product market competition on GDP per capita growth in the EU countries: Does the model of capitalism matter? *Post-Communist Economies*, 30, pp. 131–155.

World Bank (2017). *World development indicators database*. [online] Available at: http://databank.worldbank.org [Accessed 30 June 2017].

World Economic Forum (2017). *The global competitiveness report database*. [online] Available at: http://reports.weforum.org/ [Accessed 30 June 2017].

Appendix 4

Table A4.4 Distance from cluster in each subspace dimension (absolute, standardized values)

	Cluster 1 Regulation-driven	*Cluster 2 Liberal*
Slovenia	0	3.85
Greece	0	3.31
Italy	0	0.95
Czech Republic	0.37	0
Portugal	0.51	0
Bulgaria	0.51	0
Poland	0.74	0
Hungary	1.07	0
Germany	1.24	0
Slovakia	1.54	0
Latvia	1.59	0
Croatia	1.78	0
Belgium	1.79	0
Denmark	1.94	0
Spain	1.95	0
Lithuania	2.04	0
Netherlands	2.16	0
Romania	2.16	0
United Kingdom	2.29	0
Sweden	2.29	0
Austria	2.36	0
Ireland	2.38	0
France	2.41	0
Finland	2.49	0
Estonia	2.75	0

Source: Author's elaboration.

Table A4.5 Measures for cluster distinction in order of importance (EU25 countries)

Cluster 1 Regulation-driven	*Cluster 2 Liberal*
wdi_timeregpro	gci_forcom
gci_tax	gci_inst
wdi_timestartbu	gci_mardom
gci_forown	gci_loccom
gci_tradeb	gci_marsize
gci_compind	gci_busimp
gci_inst	gci_effec
wdi_taxpaym	wdi_newbus
hef_fiscal	hef_fiscal
hef_gov	wdi_timeenfor
gci_loccom	wdi_timeregpro
gci_forcom	wdi_timepaytax
gci_busimp	hef_gov
gci_effec	hef_business
gci_domcom	wdi_costbusi
gci_com	wdi_timestartbu
gci_mardom	gci_tax
gci_marsize	wdi_taxpaym
wdi_newbus	gci_compind
wdi_timeenfor	gci_forown
wdi_costbusi	gci_com
wdi_timepaytax	gci_tradeb
hef_business	gci_domcom

Source: Author's elaboration.

Table A4.6 Change in value of variables between 2005 and 2014 (average for CEE11 countries)

	2005	*2014*	*Change between 2005 and 2014*
hef_fiscal	72.8	80.4	7.6
hef_gov	44.2	46.1	1.8
hef_business	68.6	71.6	2.9
gci_inst	3.9	3.9	0.1
gci_loccom	5.0	5.2	0.3
gci_mardom	4.0	3.8	−0.2
gci_effec	4.1	3.9	−0.3
gci_tax	47.8	39.2	−8.5
gci_domcom	4.3	4.6	0.3
gci_tradeb	5.0	4.5	−0.5
gci_forown	5.2	4.8	−0.3
gci_busimp	5.0	4.5	−0.5
gci_forcom	4.6	5.2	0.5
gci_com	4.4	4.7	0.3
gci_marsize	4.1	3.9	−0.2

	2005	2014	Change between 2005 and 2014
gci_compind	4.4	4.4	0.0
wdi_costbusi	10.0	3.4	−6.6
wdi_newbus	3.6	5.8	2.1
wdi_taxpaym	32.6	10.8	−21.8
wdi_timeenfor	587.2	581.6	−5.5
wdi_timeregpro	178.6	25.0	−153.6
wdi_timestartbu	32.7	12.5	−20.2
wdi_timepaytax	346.4	238.1	−108.3

Calculations are based on the original dataset with exact values of the variables (without rounding). Hence, the data in the last column may not be exactly equal to the difference between the third and second column due to rounding.

Source: Author's elaboration.

5 Labor market and industrial relations

Juliusz Gardawski and Rafał Towalski

Introduction

Industrial relations are frequently described as a study of employment relations (Kaufmann, 2010), or as an analytical focus defined as governance of employment relations (Sisson, 2010). Employment relations are by definition a relationship between employees and an employer. They can be an individual or a collective. According to Eurofound (2018), "industrial relations deal with collective, rather than individual aspects of the employment relations".

The collective aspects of employment relations refer to the regulations of these relations through arrangements that go beyond the individual worker (Furåker, 2005). This collective mechanism is a bargaining between employers' and workers' representations, sometimes with government intervention.

Although industrial relations emerged as a separate research field within the social sciences well before the Second World War in North America (Kaufmann, 2010), it was the economic and social transformation that many countries underwent after the war, coupled with accelerated economic growth and social and political stabilization, that contributed to the development of industrial relations as a highly specialized discipline (Trigilia, 2002).

Industrial relations can be understood and interpreted in a wider political, economic or social context. At the same time, they are subject to different analytical perspectives: unitarist, pluralist, Marxist or systems perspective.

The concept of the industrial relations system was introduced by John Thomas Dunlop in his classic book, *Industrial Relations System*. He believed that a systematic approach can help to define actors of industrial relations, rules and contexts (Dunlop, 1958). He suggested that

> the multiple usage of the term only require that the reference to scope be made clear in each instance. The formulation has the merit of facilitating comparisons (and contrasts) within the country, . . ., and between industrial relations systems of countries taken as a whole.
>
> (Dunlop, 1958, p. 24)

Since that time, the concept of industrial relations system has undergone significant modifications, reflecting the vigorous debate on the definition of industrial relations.

DOI: 10.4324/9780429056901-7

Salamon (1998) argues that any definition must assume and emphasize a particular view of the nature and goals of industrial actors involved. One of the most influential research approaches to industrial relations is comparative analysis, although we have to keep in mind that there is no one and only "right approach" (Salamon, 1998, pp. 3–4). There are also significant differences in the comparative methods employed, being reflected in the set of indicators applied in particular studies.

Various definitions and conceptions of industrial relations do not exclude each other and emphasize different elements, the central ones of which can be identified as follows:

- Processes of control over work relations and regulations of employees' and employers' interest;
- Web of institutionalized relationships between actors, organizations and institutions;
- Collective relations;
- Different actors and arenas;
- Different levels of industrial relations and interplay between them;
- Legal and institutional framework;
- Cooperative and conflictual relationships;
- Diversity of the existing national models.

(Weiler, 2004; p. 13)

In one of the latest reports of the European Foundation for Living and Working Conditions (Eurofound, 2016) discussing the results of comparative analyses in the field of industrial relations, an interesting breakdown of variables was proposed to study the area of industrial relations from a comparative perspective. All variables can, according to the authors of the study, be attributed to one of the factors shaping the pattern of industrial relations. The first factor or category of variables is the quality of work, which was measured by means of such variables as workplace health and well-being, employment security and skills development (Eurofound, 2016). The second category involves competitiveness, measured by work efficiency and the employment rate. The third factor is "industrial democracy", measured in terms of the coverage of collective agreements, the level of unionization or the scope of employee participation practices, for example (Eurofound, 2016). The last category is social justice, approximated, inter alia, by the percentage of long-term unemployed people. It is easy to notice that the Eurofound study combines increasingly traditional yardsticks characterizing the systems of industrial relations with indicators reserved so far for the description of the labor market and treats them all as output variables.

Comparative research gives rise to typologies, often generalized in the form of varieties of capitalism. Lucie Davoine, Christine Erhel and Mathilde Guergoat-Larivière, in their study (Davoine, Erhel and Guergoat-Larivière, 2008) based on cluster analysis, presented the map of job quality in the European Union and then grouped the member states in several distinctive clusters. The results confirmed the heterogeneity of job quality across Europe. In 2005–2006, the EU member countries were classified by the three authors into five clusters. The

Northern cluster included Sweden, Denmark, Finland and the United Kingdom. It was characterized by high participation rates in education and training, high employment rates and high job satisfaction. The Continental cluster comprised Germany, France, Belgium, Luxembourg, Austria, the Netherlands, Ireland and Slovenia. The Southern cluster included Spain, Italy, Portugal, Greece and Malta, which were characterized by a high proportion of early school leavers, a high gender employment gap and poor levels of education and training. The authors also took into consideration the new member states, which were allocated into two more clusters: the first cluster contained Poland and Slovakia, while the second cluster comprised the remaining new EU members (Estonia, Latvia, Lithuania, Cyprus, the Czech Republic, Hungary, Bulgaria and Romania). The former cluster, with Poland and Slovakia, displayed high long-term unemployment rates and low employment rates. The latter cluster was characterized by very low levels of productivity but high rates of productivity growth, which is typical of countries in a catching-up process.

The study of job quality by Davoine, Erhel and Guergoat-Larivière (2008) highlighted the dissimilarities between the Northern countries and most of the EU new member states in terms of working conditions and socio-economic security. The Northern countries were characterized by high wages and good working conditions but also by high intensity at work. In contrast, the new EU members experienced low socio-economic security (low wages and long-term unemployment rate) and pretty bad working conditions. In turn, the Southern countries featured unsatisfactory social dialogue.

Another typology of industrial relations regimes may be found in a report of the European Trade Unions Institute (2012), where the 27 EU member states were grouped into five clusters: North European, Central-West European, South European (Mediterranean model), Liberal-West European (Anglo-Saxon) and Central-East European. The author of the report used the following classification criteria: trade union density, collective bargaining coverage, predominant level of collective bargaining, practices to extend collective agreements, statutory minimum wage, role of social partners in policymaking and the role of the state in collective bargaining. The North European cluster included Denmark, Finland and Sweden. The Central-West European cluster comprised Austria, Belgium, Germany, Luxembourg, the Netherlands and Slovenia. The remaining ten CEE countries were allocated to the Central-East European cluster. The United Kingdom, Ireland, Malta and Cyprus were classified into the Liberal-West European (Anglo-Saxon) cluster, whereas France, Greece, Italy, Portugal and Spain were assigned to the South European cluster (ETUI, 2012).

The foregoing brief survey of pertinent typologies and classifications implies both the dynamic nature of industrial relations and the key role of research perspectives and variables employed in industrial relations models. We will add to this pretty obvious conclusion one more insight, which is of utmost significance from the viewpoint of our further analysis (both in this chapter and in the whole book). It concerns a relatively low level of institutionalization of industrial relations in the CEE countries, which gives birth to a specific slippage of institutional arrangements inherent to "patchwork" capitalism. Institutional volatility is a common feature in present turbulent times, it also affects Western European political economies, but its intensity is particularly high in the CEE countries. An important clue to a better understanding of these processes has been provided by the research on cultural conditions of industrial relations and their variability. This issue was taken up by many scholars whose research allowed a deeper interpretation of the differences in the institutional structure of industrial relations between. for example, Poland and the Czech Republic, Slovenia and the rest of the CEE, Baltic countries, especially Estonia and Latvia, etc. (Crawley and Ost, 2001).

5.1 Measurement of labor market and industrial relations institutions

Given the results of empirical studies showing a dispersion in industrial relations and labor market systems discussed above, a dataset of 19 indicators was created encompassing both input and output variables. We assume that measures such as the coverage of collective agreements, predominant level of bargaining or trade union density rate, directly related to industrial relations, are input variables. In turn, output variables depict the quality of work and employment. We share a widely accepted view (Dunlop, 1958; Salamon, 1998; Eurofound, 2016) that the system of industrial relations encompassing employee and employer organizations, labor law, collective agreements and state bodies is an institutional input, which generates outcomes at both the macro- and microeconomic levels such as the employment rate, forms of employment or labor costs.

We may suppose that a particular industrial relations regime leads to a particular balance of power between "capital" and "labor". The institutional traits of industrial relations, like organizational capabilities of employers and employees, the form and scope of employment regulations and the industrial relations practices embedded in the political culture and social capital vary across the European Union, leading to different labor market outcomes in particular member countries.

We collected the values of all institutional measures involved for two years: the year close to the EU Eastern enlargement (2005) and the last available year (typically 2014). Due to various data sources and many missing observations, the exact years for which individual indicators were available may differ. A description of all these measures together with data sources are provided in Table 5.1.

5.2 Models of labor market and industrial relations in the European Union

The analysis of the data gathered on institutional measures describing the labor market and industrial relations area with the ORCLUS subspace clustering algorithm made it possible to identify four distinct groups of countries among the EU member states that share a similar set of institutional traits. Two of them comprise only EU14 countries, one is a mixture of old and new member states (the statist cluster) and one comprises only CEE11 countries and is described in the next section.

Table 5.1 Data sources

Variable name	*Variable description*	*Data source*
adjcov	Adjusted bargaining coverage rate: proportion of all wage earners with right to bargaining	ICTWSS
govint	Government intervention in wage bargaining	ICTWSS
level	The predominant level at which wage bargaining takes place	ICTWSS
ri	Routine involvement of unions and employers in government decisions on social and economic policy	ICTWSS
tc	Existence of a standard (institutionalized) tripartite council concerning social and economic policy (private sector)	ICTWSS
ud	Union density rate, net union membership as a proportion of wage earners in employment	ICTWSS
wc_rights	Rights of works councils	ICTWSS
ownaccwork	Own account workers (those workers who, working on their own account or with one or more partners, hold the type of job defined as a self-employed job, and have not engaged on a continuous basis any employees to work for them during the reference period)	International Labour Office (based on the International Classification by Status in Employment (ICSE). This indicator is part of the *ILO Estimates and Projections* series, analyzed in the ILO's World Employment and Social Outlook reports)[1]
labcost	Labor costs per hour in euros, whole economy (excluding agriculture and public administration), cover wage and non-wage costs less subsidies. They do not include vocational training costs or other expenditures such as recruitment costs, spending on working clothes, etc.	Eurostat. Labour costs in the EU. Hourly labor costs ranged from €3.8 to €40.3 across the EU member states in 2014. *Eurostat news releases*[2]
labprod	Nominal labor productivity per person employed (ESA 2010) – Index (EU28 = 100) [tec00116] Gross domestic product (GDP) is a measure for the economic activity. It is defined as the value of all goods and services produced less the value of any goods or services used in their creation. GDP per person employed is intended to give an overall impression of the productivity of national economies expressed	Eurostat[3]

	in relation to the European Union (EU28) average. If the index of a country is higher than 100, this country's level of GDP per person employed is higher than the EU average and vice versa. Basic figures are expressed in PPS (i.e. a common currency that eliminates the differences in price levels between countries allowing meaningful volume comparisons of GDP between countries). Please note that the term "persons employed" does not distinguish between full-time and part-time employment.[4]	
avewoho	Average number of usual weekly hours of work in main job, by sex, professional status, full-time/part-time and economic activity	Eurostat
precemp	Precarious employment by sex, age and NACE Rev. 2 activity (lfsa_qoe_4ax1r2)	Eurostat
neets	Young people neither in employment nor in education or training (NEET). It provides information on the transition from education to work and focuses on the number of young people who find themselves disengaged from both education and the labor market.	Eurostat
lowskill	Employment rate of low-skilled persons, age group 20–64	Eurostat
emprat	Employment rate by sex, age group 20–64 (t2020_10)	Eurostat
emplidur	Employees with a contract of limited duration (annual average) (tps00073)	Eurostat
lump	The long-term unemployment rate expresses the number of long-term unemployed aged 15–74 as a percentage of the active population of the same age. Long-term unemployed (12 months and more) comprise persons aged at least 15, who are not living in collective households, who will be without work during the next two weeks, who would be available to start work within the next two weeks and who are seeking work (have actively sought employment at some time during the previous four weeks or are not seeking a job because they have already found a job to start later). The total active population (labor force) is the total number of the employed and unemployed population. The duration of unemployment is defined as the duration of a search for a job or as the period since the last job was held (if this period is shorter than the duration of the search for a job). The indicator is based on the EU Labour Force Survey.[5]	Eurostat

(*Continued*)

Table 5.1 (Continued)

Variable name	*Variable description*	*Data source*
empprot[6]	The OECD indicators of employment protection are synthetic indicators of the strictness of regulation on dismissals and the use of temporary contracts. For each year, indicators refer to regulation in force on 1 January. For more information and full methodology,[7] employment protection index based on strictness of employment protection – individual dismissals (regular contracts). For Bulgaria and Romania, the data used in our study come from Tonin (2009): average value of the employment protection legislation index (weighted), dismissals from regular employment (weighted), procedural inconveniences (weighted), difficulty of dismissal (weighted). The value was estimated for 2004. For 2014 we applied the same value.	OECD, Tonin (2009)
anyrep	Positive answers to the question: "Does your organization have a trade union, works council or a similar committee representing employees?" European Working Conditions Survey 2015.[8]	Eurofound

1 http://www.ilo.org/ilostat/faces/oracle/webcenter/portalapp/pagehierarchy/Page3.jspx?MBI_ID=32&_afrLoop=1898393051472906&_afrWindowMode=0&_afrWindowId=7gf0yk1aq_1#!%40%40%3F_afrWindowId%3D7gf0yk1aq_1%26_afrLoop%3D1898393051472906%26MBI_ID%3D32%26_afrWindowMode%3D0%26_adf.ctrl-state%3D7gf0yk1aq_45 (access: 10 April 2018).

2 http://ec.europa.eu/eurostat/documents/2995521/6761066/3-30032015-AP-EN.pdf/7462a05e-7118-480e-a3f5-34e690c11545 (access: 10 April 2018).

3 http://ec.europa.eu/eurostat/tgm/web/table/description.jsp (access: 10 April 2018).

4 http://ec.europa.eu/eurostat/tgm/table.do?tab=table&init=1&language=en&pcode=tec00116&plugin=1 (access: 10 April 2018).

5 http://ec.europa.eu/eurostat/tgm/table.do?tab=table&init=1&language=en&pcode=tesem130&plugin=1 (access: 12 April 2018).

6 http://www.oecd.org/els/emp/oecdindicatorsofemploymentprotection.htm (access: 12 April 2018).

7 http://stats.oecd.org/Index.aspx?DataSetCode=EPL_R (access: 12 April 2018).

8 https://www.eurofound.europa.eu/data/european-working-conditions-survey (access: 12 April 2018).

Cluster 1, labeled the *Anglo-Saxon cluster*, encompasses only two countries: the United Kingdom (UK) and Ireland. These two countries share a variety of traits, formed on the basis of a common institutional and cultural heritage of the early 1970s and the liberal response to economic challenges that the government of Margaret Thatcher as well as its Irish counterpart at that time had to face. In comparison with other clusters, it is characterized by a decentralized bargaining system, where bargaining takes place at the company level. The most important measure that defines this cluster (see Table A5.5 in the Appendix) is the adjusted bargaining coverage rate, which takes much lower values in the UK and Ireland than in the rest of the EU14 group – 35% in comparison to 85.8% in the continental cluster (see Table 5.2). At the same time, the government intervention in wage bargaining is limited to providing conflict resolution mechanisms linked to the wage disputes settlement across the industry and is at the lowest level among all EU25 countries. The second most important characteristic of this cluster is a relatively small share of people employed for a definite period; only 23.3% of total employment works on such contracts – twice as low as in countries found in clusters 2 and 3. This is accompanied by the highest labor productivity in the whole sample, a high employment rate and the lowest employment protection among all identified clusters (see Table 5.2 for exact values of each measure). A high degree of labor utilization combined with deregulation of labor relations can be derived from extensive company-level human resources management practices. Similar conclusions can be found in the recent Eurofound report, whose authors

Table 5.2 Cluster-average values for all variables

	Cluster 1 Anglo-Saxon	*Cluster 2 Continental*	*Cluster 3 Statist*	*Cluster 4 Deregulated*
adjcov	35.0	85.8	49.3	22.8
govint	2.3	2.9	3.3	2.9
level	1.0	3.3	2.0	1.3
ri	0.5	1.3	1.0	0.7
tc	0.5	1.2	1.5	1.1
ud	29.7	38.3	19.6	12.8
wc_rights	1.0	2.3	1.3	1.1
ownaccwork	12.2	11.0	11.0	9.4
labcost	27.8	32.6	13.8	7.0
labprod	123.8	112.8	78.3	66.9
avewoho	36.2	35.8	40.3	39.6
precemp	3.8	7.2	13.9	31.2
neets	13.6	10.5	13.4	13.9
lowskill	52.4	53.8	45.7	45.8
emprat	71.6	71.3	64.6	68.6
emplidur	23.3	45.0	47.3	13.4
lump	4.5	4.1	8.3	5.1
empprot	1.3	2.4	2.6	2.2
anyrep	49.0	60.1	39.0	39.1

Source: Authors' elaboration.

emphasize the ongoing erosion of more collective forms of employee representation and substitution of these with "direct" and more individualized forms of worker involvement in the UK (Eurofound, 2016, p. 14).

Another important characteristic inherent to these countries is low involvement of unions and employers in the government's political decisions, which refers mostly to the United Kingdom rather than Ireland, where the National Economic and Social Council as a tripartite social dialogue institution remains a stable element of the industrial relations system. Moreover, the union density in these two countries is much lower than in continental EU14 member states, which is one of the main differences between cluster 1 and cluster 2.

Cluster 2, labeled the *continental model*, comprises almost all EU14 countries except United Kingdom, Ireland, Greece and Portugal (see Map 5.1).

The most salient characteristic of the continental model is a well-developed industrial democracy, compared to other clusters. This observation may be supported by a number of indicators from our dataset, including in particular the highest adjusted bargaining coverage rate, which is the most important measure defining this cluster (see Table A5.5 in the Appendix) and stays in these countries at 85.8% on average – twice as much as in all other EU25 member states (see Table 5.2). Other indicators implying a well-developed industrial democracy include the highest level of unionization among all identified clusters (38.3% compared to almost 20% in cluster 3 and around 13% in cluster 4) and various forms of strongly embedded employee representations, such as works councils. These conclusions may sound surprising, given the significant differences in the level of unionization between individual countries in cluster 2 (the best example is a clear-cut gap in this respect between France and Denmark). We believe, however, that these discrepancies have been more than offset by the prevalence of other forms of representation (60% in cluster 2 and less than 40% in clusters 3 and 4), which have outweighed those clear differences.

The second most important feature of the continental labor market model is its "solidaristic" face. It is characterized by the highest proportion of employed people with the lowest qualifications (53.8%) among EU25 states and a small share of precarious workers among employees (7.2%); only the Anglo-Saxon countries exhibit a smaller precariat. On top of that, countries embodying the continental model exhibit a relatively low share of long-term unemployed people among all those who do not have a job (4.1% compared to 4.5% in cluster 1, 5.1% in cluster 4, and 8.3% in cluster 3), as well as a small percentage of young people who do not study or work (NEETs) – around 10% in cluster 2, 13.6% in cluster 1, 13.4% in cluster 3 and 13.9% in cluster 3). The "solidaristic" face of this labor market model results from a generous split of the value added generated in the economy, which is exhibited in the highest labor costs among all EU25 economies.

Nevertheless, the emergence of a coherent feature, which is an attempt to implement the principle of social justice in the area of the labor market in all countries concerned and avoiding the development of a two-tier labor market, highlights the similarities to the inclusive labor market model, described in terms of a well-developed system of initial skills formation, the balance of power between capital

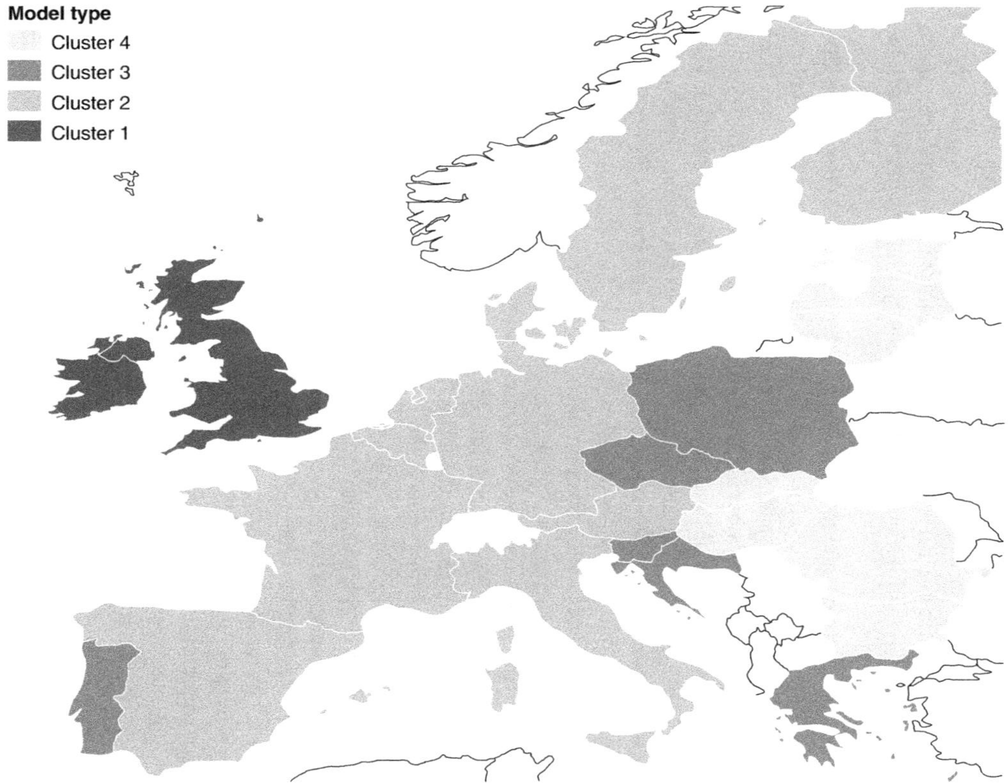

Map 5.1 Models of capitalism in the European Union: labor market and industrial relations

Source: Authors' elaboration.

and labor, work integration policies and employment integration policies aimed to sustain high employment and encourage the unemployed back into the labor market (Coats, 2011). It seems that the choice of the logic of sustainable development based on the elements of social solidarism and industrial democracy made in this cluster entailed a trade-off with slightly lower labor productivity and high labor costs, even if compared to the Anglo-Saxon model.

Cluster 2 is the most heterogenous group of sample countries identified, which can be seen when one inspects Table A5.4 (see Appendix). The institutional distance from other models of the labor market varies largely from one country to another and from cluster to cluster, but one is common for all cluster 2 members: the average distance (be it high or low) of each country from cluster 1, 3 and 4 is of a similar magnitude.

Cluster 3, labeled *statist*, includes two old EU member states, Greece and Portugal (in many studies, both countries are often classified as part of the Mediterranean model, along with Italy and Spain), and four CEE economies: the Czech Republic, Poland, Croatia and Slovenia. The most important characteristic of this cluster is a weak mechanism of "industrial democracy". Low unionization level (19.3% compared to over 38% in cluster 2 and almost 30% in cluster 1) and underdeveloped forms of employee representation (39% in the statist cluster, slightly over 60% in the continental cluster and almost 50% in the Anglo-Saxon cluster) are accompanied by a weakening position of collective bargaining (see Table 5.2). To some extent, the weakness of "industrial democracy" in this cluster results from the underlying state's philosophy related to its function in the industrial relations system. The state, with its administrative apparatus, consistently (which does not always mean "effectively") fulfills its tasks resulting from "exercising power". In turn, social partners increasingly take the attitude of a "petitioner", demanding their rights to become a stakeholder of the policymaking processes.

The highest value of the variable "government intervention in wage bargaining" compared to other clusters (3.3 versus 2.3 for cluster 1 and 2.9 for both cluster 2 and 4) implies that the state autonomously sets minimum wage and adopts wage policies concerning wage taxation. This is equivalent to saying that the social partners are not treated as fully fledged participants in the decision-making process. Governments tend to influence the wages indirectly through price setting, indexation, tax measures and minimum wages (Visser, 2015). This specific form of wage determination results to some extent from the absence of sufficiently representative and recognized trade unions or employer organizations, which could influence the wage dynamics through bilateral social dialogue (Clarke, de Gijsel and Janssen, 2000). Multi-employer collective bargaining, which in most Western economies performs the function of a mechanism of wage moderation, in Poland, Croatia and the Czech Republic remains weak or even absent. In Croatia, despite a relatively high coverage of collective agreements (for 50%–60% of all employees, wages above minimum are determined by such agreements), they are mainly concluded at a company level (Weber, 2016).

The second most important characteristic trait of the statist model is the lowest employment rate among EU25 economies equal to 64.6% (see Table 5.2), which may result from the difficulties that low-skilled employees face while seeking a job. This goes hand in hand with low employment quality. The key to comprehending the underlying reasons should be sought in a relatively high employment rate among precarious workers, in a comparatively large proportion of people working on the basis of fixed-term contracts among employees, and in relatively low labor costs. As a result, the labor productivity in cluster 3 countries is also much lower than in EU14 economies, staying at a very close level to the one exhibited by cluster 4 countries. The highest value of the employment protection index in this cluster should be conceived, therefore, as a derivative of government intervention aimed to reduce the workers' risks associated with possible layoffs.

5.3 Models of capitalism in the labor market and industrial relations in Central and Eastern Europe

As already indicated in the preceding section, CEE11 countries embody two different institutional models, the previously described statist model and a *deregulated model*, which comprises seven CEE countries gathered in cluster 4 (Bulgaria, Estonia, Hungary, Latvia, Lithuania, Romania and Slovakia). The most distinctive institutional traits of this cluster include in particular underdeveloped "industrial democracy" mechanisms, even compared to cluster 3. It is characterized mainly (see Table A5.4 in the Appendix) by the lowest coverage of collective agreements (22.8% compared to 35% in cluster 1, 49% in cluster 3 and 85% in cluster 2) that is accompanied by decentralization of collective bargaining, where the predominant part of negotiations takes place at the company level. Other measures that indicate the lack of "industrial democracy" mechanisms are the lowest union density (12.9%; see Table 5.2 for a comparison with other clusters) and a limited scope of employee representation (39.1%).

Another very important characteristic of the labor market in cluster 4 countries is the smallest share of people employed on contracts with limited duration (13.4%). This, together with low coverage of collective agreements, low employment protection and much lower state interventions compared to the statist model, can be interpreted as indicators of a deregulated labor market. Hiring and firing of employees is very easy and the bargaining power of workers is very low, which limits the usefulness of contracts with limited duration. This trait of the deregulated model makes it similar to the Anglo-Saxon cluster described in the previous section. As shown in Table A5.4 (see Appendix), the institutional distance between cluster 1 and cluster 4 countries is the smallest in comparison with other groups of the sample countries with distinct labor market institutions. Moreover, the institutional proximity to the UK and Ireland is characteristic for almost all CEE11 countries. Similarly, the EU member states classified in cluster 3 exhibit a lower distance to cluster 1 than to cluster 2 countries (however the distance is, on average, larger than for cluster 4 countries). The only exception is Slovenia which, due to a long history of collective bargaining (see section 5.4), resembles slightly more the continental model than the Anglo-Saxon one.

Among other features of the labor market in the deregulated model are those connected to a low quality of work: low employment rate (68.6%) and a small proportion of low-skilled workers in the labor force (45.8%) as well as the highest rate of precarious employees (31.2%). This is also a labor market property that CEE11 countries from the deregulated cluster share with those from the statist one. This commonality points to another essential feature of CEE countries, which refers to the working conditions that were subordinated to the aim of attracting foreign capital.

Countries like Poland, the Czech Republic and Romania consistently pursued the strategies of keeping labor costs low to ensure the inflow of capital via foreign direct investment, what Nölke and Vliegenthart (2009) interpreted as a feature of a "dependent market economy" (see also Chapters 2 and 3). The International Monetary Fund (2013) depicted these economies as the German–Central European Supply Chain Cluster (GCESCC). The GCESCC has expanded since the mid-1990s, when German firms started shifting some parts of their production to Central Europe, either by directly investing there or by purchasing intermediate inputs from the domestic firms. The CEE countries serve as a reservoir of cheap, skilled and flexible labor in this supply chain.

A dependent position of the labor markets in CEE countries in the supply chain concerned entails their increased vulnerability to global economic downturns. When the trade unions are weak and the collective bargaining is decentralized, the protection of workplaces depends on the existing labor law.

The limited state involvement in the industrial relations system set of institutional properties and the resulting pattern of pertinent interrelationships is what distinguishes the "statist" from the "deregulated" CEE11 countries.

A comparison of measures describing the sphere of industrial relations leads to the conclusion that the economies making up cluster 4 have undergone a far-reaching decentralization of the relations between employers and employees, while at the same time the state has not aspired to assume an active role in industrial relations. Violaine Delteil (2015) underlines the lobbying power of foreign investors vis-à-vis public authorities. The investors in Bulgaria and Romania are organized in the chambers of commerce, the Foreign Investors Council or the American Chamber of Commerce, which – benefiting from the diplomatic support – enjoy a very strong bargaining position when negotiating with governments in the host countries. Markku Sippola (2017) found a similar pattern in Latvia, Lithuania and Estonia, where the window of opportunity was widely opened for companies from highly unionized Nordic countries to invest in the sparsely unionized Baltic countries. He believes that these strategies widened the spectrum of "regime shopping", with employers seeking locations where unions are unable to exert their influence (Sippola, 2017).

Bohle and Greskovits (2012) interpret these tendencies as an evidence of the "weak state", which in the bargaining process leaves the door open to instrumentalization of the social dialogue under the pressure from external voices. By the same token, if neither the state nor the social partners in the CEE countries are able to influence the working and wage conditions, either by means of enforcing the existing law or through collective agreements, this is conducive to a wide-ranging deregulation of employment. This in turn brings about a decrease in the quality of employment.

5.4 Evolving models of labor market and industrial relations in CEE11 countries between 2005 and 2014

This section tracks the pace and directions of changes in the institutional architecture of the labor markets and industrial relations in CEE11 countries between 2005 and 2014. The data provided in Table 5.3 (all the data for Croatia and Romania for 2005 were not available) shows that in the analyzed period, most countries followed the path of decentralization in the sphere of industrial relations and deregulation in the labor market. This is reflected in positive changes in the absolute distance from cluster 4 (which is equivalent to a convergence to this cluster) in all CEE economies but Poland, the largest such change being experienced in Slovenia.

The overriding trend that can be observed in most CEE11 countries was a consistent shift of the burden of collective bargaining down the system of industrial relations to the company level – the adjusted bargaining coverage rate dropped from 37.1% in 2005 to 28.0% 2014 on average in the CEE region (see Table A5.6 in the Appendix). This was aimed to make the collective negotiations more flexible and to better match their results to the current economic situation. The trade unions and single employers are increasingly expected to bargain and bilaterally regulate the working and wage conditions. As a result, the union density also dropped significantly, from 19.7% to 13.0%, and the share of workers having a representation in employer-employee negotiations also fell, from 52.1 to 39.3%. The decentralization trend in the collective bargaining has been accompanied by

Table 5.3 Change in the absolute distance from 2014 clusters for each CEE country* and each subspace dimension between 2005 and 2014 (standardized values)

	Cluster 1 Anglo Saxon	*Cluster 2 Continental*	*Cluster 3 Statist*	*Cluster 4 Deregulated*
Bulgaria	0.24	−0.44	−1.55	0.84
Czech Republic	−0.24	−0.03	0.28	0.38
Estonia	−0.01	0.21	−0.15	0.30
Hungary	−0.29	0.53	0.60	1.00
Latvia	0.13	0.05	−0.01	0.05
Lithuania	−0.16	−0.70	0.10	0.04
Poland	−0.38	−0.43	0.31	−0.86
Slovakia	−0.11	0.30	0.70	1.37
Slovenia	1.08	−0.92	1.43	2.10
Median change	***−0.11***	***−0.03***	***0.28***	***0.38***

* Excluding Croatia and Romania, due to non-availability of pertinent data.

Source: Authors' elaboration.

relatively well-developed formal mechanisms of tripartite social dialogue involving trade unions, employer organizations and government representatives. Bohle and Greskovits (2012) claim that tripartite bodies were established with a view to mobilize political support and legitimize social and economic reforms. David Ost (2000) called this phenomenon “illusory corporatism”, since tripartite bodies were used to yield neoliberal outcomes, which weakened the position of labor (see also Chapter 2).

The foregoing process can be partially explained as a derivative of the austerity measures undertaken by the EU member states in response to the global financial crisis of 2008, aimed to improve their fiscal position, which entailed wage reductions and benefit cuts. Moreover, the global financial crisis also forced CEE11 countries, which traditionally relied on attracting foreign investments, to improve their comparative advantage through reducing employees’ bargaining power in wage negotiations. This was especially important as labor costs almost doubled between 2005 and 2014 in the CEE11 region (see Table A5.6 in the Appendix). As a result, in 2014 in CEE11 economies the proportion of employees on work contracts of limited duration stood at 26.7%, 4.9 percentage points higher than in 2005, and the employment protection index dropped from 2.4 to 2.2.

At the level of individual CEE countries, the 2005–2014 period (as evidenced by the data in Table 5.3) saw both the institutional convergence and divergence trends. If we split the CEE11 group into cluster 3 and cluster 4 countries, the emerging picture becomes sharper: the statist countries tend to diverge both from the Anglo-Saxon and the continental model, while deregulated countries exhibited in general a constant institutional distance from the Anglo-Saxon countries and a modest convergence to the continental model – the last trend being a result mainly of rising labor costs throughout the region (see Table A5.6 in the Appendix).

The only exception to the patterns described above is Slovenia, which experienced a large (greater than 1 standard deviation) convergence to the Anglo-Saxon countries and the highest divergence among the CEE economies from the continental model. In 2005 Slovenia was the only country in the region to exhibit a highly coordinated system of collective bargaining. However, as of 2006 the Slovenian government shortened the duration of collective agreements and facilitated more frequent cancellations of the agreed provisions, which for many observers reflected the drift of this country from neo-corporatist traditions (Bernaciak, 2015). As a consequence, a gradual decentralization of the collective bargaining took place and Slovenia institutionally converged by more than 2 standard deviations (see Table 5.3) to the deregulated model of the labor market present in CEE countries. Since then, the dominant form of bargaining in Slovenia has been single-employer bargaining (Stanojević and Claric, 2013). It is worth noting, however, that path dependence mechanisms and underlying informal institutions slowed down the process of institutional transformation, and by 2014 Slovenia was still classified in the statist cluster, where the scope of labor market deregulation is smaller than in cluster 4.

Another interesting case in Hungary, where amendment of the Labor Code during the 2008 global financial crisis unleashed some unexpected risks. The new regulation weakened the position of trade unions while simultaneously empowering works councils with additional rights, which may pave the way to the creation of "yellow" work councils[1] entitled to bargain on collective agreements (Bernaciak, 2015). These changes brought about a clear divergence trend from the Anglo-Saxon model (see Table 5.3), while at the same time the country's institutional distance to the continental model decreased the most in comparison with the rest of the CEE countries.

In the analyzed period, Poland and Lithuania have pursued policies aimed at tightening the state's grip on the labor market and strengthening government's decision-making monopoly in the domain of labor relations, with varying degrees of success. It can be most vividly seen in the case of Poland, which was the only CEE country that experienced an increase in the institutional distance from the deregulated model (cluster 4) between 2005 and 2014 and at the same time a divergence (together with Lithuania) both from the Anglo-Saxon and the continental models.

Worth mentioning is also the case of Latvia, which has undertaken the ambitious challenge of building a system close to the Anglo-Saxon pattern so as to raise the country's competitiveness in the labor market dimension. Again, the data in Table 5.3 seem to confirm this contention, although the positive change in the institutional distance or convergence to the Anglo-Saxon cluster was quite small.

The empirical study carried out in this book ended by 2014. Since that time, however, a number of significant developments and economic policy changes in CEE11 countries have occurred, which may lead to the emergence of new labor market and industrial relations regimes or can change the composition of particular clusters identified in our subspace clustering exercise. After 2014, most of the CEE11 new EU member states – particularly Poland, Romania, Latvia, Slovakia, Hungary and the Czech Republic – recorded a relatively fast economic growth together with an aging society, which resulted in rising employment rates, higher activity rates and lower unemployment. In 2018, among the four best performing EU countries with the lowest unemployment rates, three were from the CEE region: the Czech Republic, Poland and Hungary.

At the same time, several laws on the labor market and industrial relations were implemented in the CEE region. For example, in Lithuania a new national agreement on labor market reforms was signed in 2017, which is supposed to strengthen the social dialogue and more generally the power of social partners in this Baltic country. The new law should also ensure a new, more efficient system of vocational training at the company level and lifelong learning.

In Bulgaria the social partners agreed in 2017 on major reforms concerning the "flexijob" (i.e. flexible and cheap forms of job, responding to high volatility in the labor demand) and the adjustment in the duration of the notice period. In the same year, the Slovenian government embarked on a "mini-labor reform" program with several amendments of important labor laws like the Labor Market Regulation Act.

A new phenomenon that recently emerged in the field of industrial relations is the attempt to merge trade union federations and confederations in several

CEE countries including Slovenia, Latvia and Lithuania. In Hungary, the government accepted the trade unions' request to set up a separate tripartite consultative framework. In Lithuania, the requirements concerning the works councils' establishment were relaxed in 2017.

The foregoing trends in the labor markets in this part of Europe, which are accompanied by changes in industrial relations systems, may be seen as a symptom of a more comprehensive transformation being faced by individual CEE countries in the area of labor market and industrial relations. At this stage, however, it is difficult to prejudge whether the changes concerned will trigger the emergence of new models in this area or whether they will just entail the shifts of individual countries between the existing clusters.

Note

1 "Yellow" works councils are workers' representations dominated or controlled by the employer.

References

Bernaciak, M. (2015). Beyond the CEE "Black Box": Crisis and industrial relations in the new EU member states, Brussels, *ETUI Working Paper 2015.05*.

Bohle, D. and Greskovits, B. (2012). *Capitalist diversity on Europe's periphery*. Ithaca: Cornell University Press.

Clarke, L., de Gijsel, P. and Janssen, J. (2000). *The dynamics of wage relations in the New Europe*. Boston: Kluwer Academic Publishers.

Coats, D. (2011). *Exiting from the crisis: Towards a model of more equitable and sustainable growth*. Brussels: European Trade Unions Institute.

Davoine, L., Erhel, C. and Guergoat-Larivière, M. (2008). A taxonomy of European labor markets using quality indicators: Final report for the European Commission. Rapport de recherche du Centre d'Etudes de l'Emploi n°45, Paris.

Delteil, V. (2015). *The "Tripartism of Political Legitimation" or the (Post-) democratic face of dependent capitalisms: The case of Bulgaria and Romania*. Available at: https://halshs.archives-ouvertes.fr/halshs-01152979 [Accessed 10 Dec. 2018]

Dunlop, T. J. (1958). *Industrial relations system*, New York: Holt.

Eurofound (2016), *Mapping varieties of industrial relations: Eurofound's analytical framework applied*. Luxembourg: Publications Office of the European Union.

Eurofound (2018). *Industrial relations*. Available at: www.eurofound.europa.eu/areas/industrialrelations/index [Accessed 10 Dec. 2018]

European Trade Unions Institute (2012). *Benchmarking working Europe 2012*, Brussels: ETUI.

Furåker, B. (2005). The individual-collective aspect of employment relationships. In: *Sociological perspectives on labor markets*. London: Palgrave Macmillan.

IMF (2013). Multi-country report. German – Central European supply chain – Cluster report, *IMF Country Report No. 13/263*, Washington, D.C.

Kaufmann, B. E. (2010). The theoretical foundations of industrial relations and its implications. *ILR Review*, 64(1).

Nölke, A. and Vliegenthart, A. (2009). Enlarging the varieties of capitalism: The emergence of dependent market economies in East Central Europe. *World Politics*, 61(4).

Ost, D. (2000). Illusory corporatism in Eastern Europe: Neoliberal tripartism and postcommunist class identities. *Politics & Society*. London, 28 Aug.

Salamon, M. (1998). *Industrial relations. Theory and practice*. London: Prentice Hall.

Sippola, M. (2017). *Ideological underpinnings of the development of social dialogue and industrial relations in the Baltic States*, A report commissioned by the Council of Nordic Trade Unions (NFS) on Violations to Trade Union Rights in the Baltic States. Presented at NFS Conference "Employees' Rights in the Baltics", Vilnius, Available at: www.researchgate.net/publication/313934541_Ideological_underpinnings_of_the_development_of_social_dialogue_and_industrial_relations_in_the_Baltic_States [Accessed 10 Dec. 2018]

Sisson, K. (2010). *Employment relations matter* [Electronic version]. Warwick, UK: University of Warwick. Cornell University, School of Industrial and Labor Relations site, Available at: http://digitalcommons.ilr.cornell.edu/articles/29/ [Accessed 12 Oct. 2018]

Stanojević, M. and Claric, M. (2013). The impact of socio-economic shocks on collective bargaining and social dialogue in Slovenia, *CELSI Discussion Papers no.11*, Bratislava.

Tonin, M. (2009). Employment protection legislation in Central and East European countries. *South-East Europe Review*, 12(4), Brussels.

Trigilia, C. (2002). *Economic sociology. State, market and society in the modern capitalism*. Oxford: Blackwell Publishing.

Visser, J. (2015). *ICTWSS data base: Version 5.0*. Amsterdam: Amsterdam Institute for Advanced Labour Studies AIAS.

Weber, M. (2016). Wage determination and employment adjustment in Croatia, *CESifo-Forum*, 1 Mar, Munich.

Weiler, A. (2004). *Quality in industrial relations: Comparative indicators*. Dublin: European Foundation for the Improvement of Living and Working Conditions.

Appendix 5

Table A5.4 Distance from cluster in each subspace dimension (absolute, standardized values)

	Cluster 1 Anglo-Saxon	*Cluster 2 Continental*	*Cluster 3 Statist*	*Cluster 4 Deregulated*
Ireland	0	0.98	0.45	0.09
United Kingdom	0	0.65	1.29	0.53
Finland	1.98	0	1.48	2.18
Belgium	1.99	0	0.77	2.68
Germany	0.77	0	0.06	0.30
Spain	1.32	0	1.21	0.95
Netherlands	1.78	0	0.75	1.11
Denmark	1.86	0	1.61	1.95
Sweden	1.88	0	1.52	1.84
Austria	2.35	0	1.14	2.24
Italy	1.50	0	0.83	1.31
France	2.26	0	1.91	1.70
Croatia	0.78	1.38	0	1.06
Portugal	0.98	0.56	0	0.59
Czech Republic	0.55	1.51	0	0.35
Greece	0.20	0.52	0	0.61
Poland	0.98	2.86	0	1.34
Slovenia	1.05	0.95	0	0.89
Bulgaria	0.09	1.73	1.97	0
Estonia	0.13	1.20	0.39	0
Hungary	0.31	2.14	0.22	0
Latvia	0.46	2.01	0.84	0
Lithuania	0.64	2.79	0.31	0
Romania	0.34	0.57	1.59	0
Slovakia	0.33	2.30	0.11	0

Source: Authors' elaboration.

Table A5.5 Measures for cluster distinction in order of importance

Anglo-Saxon	*Continental*	*Statist*	*Deregulated*
adjcov	adjcov	ud	adjcov
emplidur	lowskill	adjcov	emplidur
ud	labcost	labprod	precemp
labprod	precemp	anyrep	lowskill
anyrep	neets	precemp	ud
govint	level	lowskill	anyrep
lowskill	lump	emprat	ownaccwork
precemp	labprod	labcost	govint
labcost	ownaccwork	emplidur	emprat
emprat	emplidur	ownaccwork	lump
lump	emprat	govint	labprod
neets	tc	ri	neets
ownaccwork	ud	level	level
avewoho	anyrep	neets	labcost
ri	ri	lump	tc
tc	avewoho	tc	ri
empprot	govint	empprot	empprot
level	wc_rights	avewoho	avewoho
wc_rights	empprot	wc_rights	wc_rights

Source: Authors' elaboration.

Table A5.6 Change in value of variables between 2005 and 2014 (average for CEE11 countries)

	2005	*2014*	*Change between 2005 and 2014*
adjcov	37.1	28.0	−9.2
govint	2.7	2.7	0.0
level	1.4	1.4	0.0
ri	1.0	0.9	−0.1
tc	1.7	1.4	−0.2
ud	19.7	13.0	−6.7
wc_rights	1.3	1.2	−0.1
ownaccwork	9.5	9.3	−0.1
labcost	5.5	9.9	4.5
labprod	61.8	71.8	10.0
avewoho	40.6	39.7	−0.8
precemp	25.6	27.7	2.2
neets	13.3	12.2	−1.1
lowskill	43.0	43.7	0.6
emprat	66.7	69.1	2.4
emplidur	21.8	26.7	4.9
lump	3.5	4.9	1.5
empprot	2.4	2.2	−0.2
anyrep	52.1	39.3	−12.8

Source: Authors' elaboration.

6 Financial intermediation

Bożena Horbaczewska

Introduction

The most important function of the financial intermediation system (or financial system, in short) in every country is to provide funds needed to finance the operations and investment projects of firms. Despite the ongoing process of globalization of financial markets, the institutional architecture of financial systems differs among countries. The traditional distinction between a financial system based on the banking sector and one based on the capital market is still visible. Any financial system observed in practice is an amalgam, in varying proportions, of these two polar cases. The institutional architecture of a country's financial system is of great importance to enterprises and other entities in the economy, since it determines the time horizon for investment in particular and economic decisions in general. At the same time, it defines coordination mechanisms both in the financial intermediation and in other sectors of the economy (e.g. financing of research and development [R&D]; see Chapter 8).

A distinction between a *market-based system* and a *bank-based system* is well established in the pertinent literature. Coates (2000) proposed an approach in which he discriminated between (among others) market-led capitalism, where the main mechanism of coordination is the market, including the capital market; and state-led capitalism, where the coordination mechanism is centralized, with the banking system as the primary source of funding.

In his study of the financial intermediation area, Amable (2003) allocated the sample of Western European EU member countries into four clusters, exhibiting similar values of the institutional measures selected to best depict this area. Countries classified in the first cluster display a decentralized financial system, in which the securities market plays a pivotal role, the system of venture capital financing is well developed, mergers and acquisitions are very common and the concentration of ownership is low. The capital market is crucial for institutional investors, particularly for pension funds. This model of financial intermediation, based on the capital market, is characteristic of the Netherlands and the United Kingdom.

The remaining EU countries were classified by Amable into three distinct groups (clusters 2 through 4), notwithstanding the fact that all of them featured a bank-based financial system. Cluster 2 comprised Belgium, Denmark, Sweden

DOI: 10.4324/9780429056901-8

and Greece, in which banks perform a somewhat "passive" function by investing a large part of their assets in bonds and shares. Ownership and control over enterprises is concentrated and family ownership plays a crucial role. The second group (cluster 3) included small countries (Finland, Norway, Ireland) with extensive banking activities usually performed by foreign banks. The last group (cluster 4) displayed the characteristics that made it the closest to the ideal of a bank-based financial system – in Germany, Austria, France, Italy, Portugal and Spain the value of loans to gross domestic product (GDP) ratio is high, and the share of insurance companies among institutional investors is quite significant. Ownership is concentrated, and the state is a relatively important stakeholder, especially in its function of controlling large corporations.

Hall and Soskice (2001) put forward their general dichotomic typology encompassing the *coordinated-market economies* (CME) and *liberal-market economies* (LME). They pointed out that the Anglo-Saxon (or LME) economies represent a liberal, market-driven model of capitalism with a homogeneous, capital market-based financial system. On the other hand, the remaining European economies embodying the CME variety of capitalism are very diverse in terms of the institutional architecture supporting their financial intermediation systems. Moreover, as argued by Amable (2003), it would be an oversimplification to just contrast the capital market-based and bank-based financial system (or in more general terms, the Anglo-Saxon model with the remaining models of capitalism). In his view, even countries with market-based financial systems are not homogeneous. They differ, among others, in the degree of concentration in the banking system.

Knell and Srholec (2007) embarked on a comparative analysis of three institutional areas in 51 economies, including most of the former socialist countries. Variables determining entry and exit costs, transfer of ownership rights and size of the capital market in relation to bank loans were selected to describe the area called "business regulations". Many of the post-socialist countries in their sample maintained a strong bureaucracy even after the collapse of central planning (with the exception of Lithuania, Hungary and Estonia). Ukraine, Slovenia and Croatia seemed to be countries with overwhelming strategic coordination. Estonia, on the other hand, was described as the most liberal economy.

There is a widespread consensus among economists that the prevailing pattern of the financial system in Europe tends to be bank-based, although there are significant dissimilarities between countries. The main source of capital for firms in CEE countries is bank loans, granted mostly by foreign banks. National capital markets have not become important sources of capital for enterprises and remain relatively underdeveloped in comparison with their Western counterparts. However, this applies only in a limited extent to Poland, as the capital market in this country experienced a remarkable expansion which changed the nature of the entire financial system (Ozsvald, 2014).

Farkas (2011) carried out a cluster analysis in five institutional areas singled out by Amable (2003) for a group of 25 new and old EU member countries. In her study, ten new EU members from the CEE region were allocated to the same cluster, which was characterized by a considerable homogeneity compared to other clusters. Against the backdrop of Western European economies in the sample, both the banking system and the capital market in CEE countries were found to be less developed, although the banking system was relatively more advanced and sophisticated. Simultaneously, the banking concentration was higher than in the old European countries.

In yet another study, the same author concluded that the system of financial intermediation which emerged in the new EU countries from Central and Eastern Europe is most akin to a pattern based on banks in the Continental model, but at a definitely lower level of development (Farkas, 2013).

6.1 Measurement of institutions in financial intermediation

Amable (2003) argued that the most appropriate measures to describe the institutional area of financial intermediation include, inter alia, the size of the capital market (as a proportion of GDP) and the value of bank loans to enterprises (as a percentage of GDP). In his study, he separated countries in which the capital market plays a significant role from those that mostly use the banking sector as the source of funding. Hall and Soskice (2001) proposed another institutional measure: the scope of investors' protection. In their view, this is one of the elements of corporate governance, and by the same token an institution shaping the relations between participants of the capital market. In liberal market economies, problems of corporate governance are solved by market mechanisms. In coordinated market economies, non-market interactions between economic agents are the main pillars of the coordination mechanism, supported by strong links between managers, technical staff and banks; as a result, more complete and reliable information on enterprises is made available, thus mitigating the problem of information asymmetry and the "corporate veil". Much the same conclusions were arrived at by Vitols (2001). Ozsvald (2014) examined the significance of the state as the owner of firms, which is of particular historical relevance in the CEE11 countries as part of their command-economy legacy and in broader terms, their path-dependence record. Between 1945 and 1989, the state was the owner of all or most of the economic entities. The transfer of ownership into private hands has gradually followed since 1990 as a result of privatization. Although its direction used to be quite similar in the CEE countries, the process of ownership transformation reached divergent stages in individual countries. The role of venture capital financing has been marginal in these countries (McGee, 2007), unlike in the incumbent EU member states where it was quite significant (Oehler et al., 2007). As a result of reforms of the financial intermediation system related to the EU accession, various types of funds, including pension funds, have been gaining in importance as entities operating in the financial sector (Ozsvald, 2014).

The inquiry into the intricacies of institutional architectures of the financial system was made possible thanks to the inclusion to the analysis of many variables that reflect various aspects of key interrelationships prevalent within this sector. These variables describe first of all the significance and the most essential features of two basic sources of financing in the economy (the capital market and

Table 6.1 Data sources

Variable name	*Variable description*	*Data source*
SMC	Stock market capitalization to GDP (%)	World Bank
STTV	Stock traded total value to GDP (%)	World Bank
DMBA	Deposit money banks' assets to GDP (%)	World Bank
BAC-5	Five largest banks' assets concentration (%)	World Bank
DCPSB	Domestic credit to private sector by banks to GDP (%)	World Bank
PPR	Protection of property rights over financial assets	Fraser Institute
Hstat	Measure of competition in the banking market	World Bank
GEI	Government enterprises and investment (% of all)	Fraser Institute
CGandSOE	Credit to government and state-owned enterprises to GDP (%)	World Bank
PFA	Pension funds' assets to GDP (%)	World Bank

Source: Author's elaboration.

the banking system) while at the same time allowing for the role of the state and other actors operating in the financial sector.

Based on the results of the foregoing studies, a dataset of ten institutional measures, including both input and output variables, was created for the purpose of the present empirical exercise. Similar to other institutional areas scrutinized in our study, the data were collected for the two edges of the time bracket concerned (i.e. for 2005 and 2014 or for the latest available record, but not prior to 2010). A description of all these measures together with data sources are provided in Table 6.1. They encompass variables describing the relative size of the capital market, measured by its capitalization (SMC) and turnover (STTV), and the relative value (DMBA) and concentration (BAC-5) of banking assets, as well as the value of loans to the private sector (DCPSB). Still other yardsticks selected here give account of the level of legal protection for investors (PPR) and competition on the banking services market (Hstat). They also measure the government involvement in the ownership of enterprises (GEI) and the relative size of loans they have received (CGandSOE). In addition, the relative size of pension funds is scrutinized (PFA).

6.2 Models of financial intermediation in the European Union

All variables defined above, describing the institutional characteristics of the financial system in the sample countries, were used to identify the clusters of countries involved revealing similar modes of financing for enterprises. The ORCLUS algorithm has found two such clusters (see Map 6.1).

Denmark, the Netherlands, Spain, Sweden and the United Kingdom constitute cluster 1. In these countries the capital market is the major source of financing, and hence we label it, following Coates (2000), a *market-based model* of financial

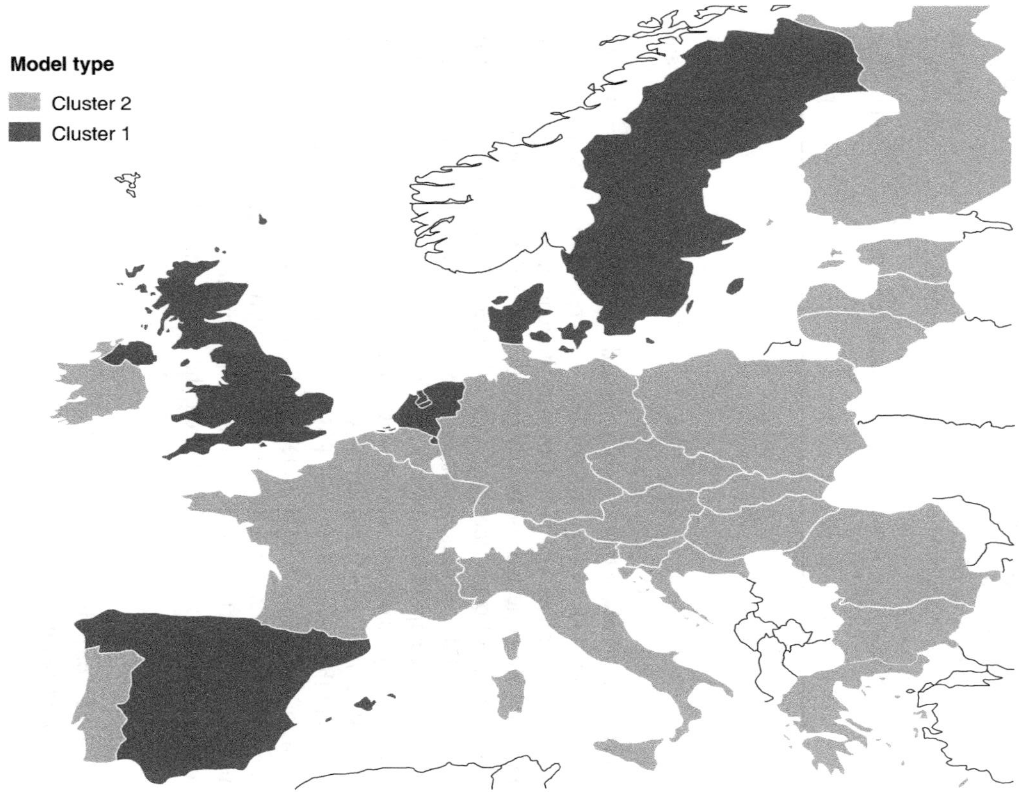

Map 6.1 Models of capitalism in the European Union: financial intermediation

Source: Author's elaboration.

intermediation. The remaining 20 EU member states (nine EU14 countries and all CEE11 economies) make up cluster 2, which we labeled a *bank-based model.* A more in-depth analysis, however (see below), shows that – similar to the findings established by Amable (2003) – this cluster is not as homogeneous as cluster 1.

At this stage of our analysis, the mean values for all variables in both clusters were calculated (Table 6.2). This allows highlighting noteworthy differences in the values of pertinent variables in clusters 1 and 2. It is worth noticing that the most significant dissimilarities between the clusters relate to variables inherent in the capital market. In the case of the relative value of capitalization (SMC), the mean value for cluster 2 reaches almost 30%, while for cluster 1 it amounts to nearly 87%. An even greater discrepancy is a feature of the relative turnover on capital market (STTV) – the mean value of this gauge for cluster 2 equals 14.5%, and for countries with market-based systems it reaches almost 62%. In the case of pension funds' assets (PFA), it goes to 12% and 78%, respectively. Further analyses show that from the group of variables describing the capital market, SMC and STTV proved to be most important for the identification of cluster 1, whereas for cluster 2 the most important was the PFA variable (see Table A6.5 in the Appendix). It can be concluded that the relative share of the capital market for financing firms' activities is about four times higher in the market-based cluster compared to cluster 2.

Regarding the banking sector, the pertinent disparities tend to be smaller. The level of bank loans' financing (DCPSB) totals almost 140% in cluster 1 and is lower by half in cluster 2. Quite a similar pattern holds in terms of banking sector assets (DMBA). However, the level of concentration of these assets (BAC-5) is comparable in both clusters. The DCPSB and DMBA variables are of the utmost importance as cluster 2 identifiers (Table A6.5). The mean value of the indicator depicting protection of property rights (PPR) is higher in market-based financial systems. This variable, together with the measure describing the competition in the banking sector (Hstat), were found to be the least important as determinants of cluster 1 (Table A6.5).

Table 6.2 Cluster-average values for all variables

	Cluster 1	*Cluster 2*
SMC	86.8	29.6
STTV	61.9	14.5
DMBA	153.9	87.5
BAC-5	87.9	81.3
DCPSB	137.9	70.0
PPR	7.8	6.2
Hstat	0.5	0.7
GEI	17.1	17.6
CGandSOE	10.0	12.6
PFA	77.8	11.7

Source: Author's elaboration.

The last finding in this part of our study may seem unexpected: the mean values for the role of the state (GEI as well as CGandSOE) in both clusters are comparable. However, it is not surprising that they are slightly lower in the market-based cluster. These two variables are not important for distinguishing the models of capitalism in the area of financial intermediation (Table A6.5).

Summing up the foregoing discussion, the institutional architecture of financial systems differs significantly between the two clusters. The differences concerned relate primarily to capital market institutions. In cluster 2, the respective indicators make up on average only about a quarter of the level recorded in countries with the market-based financial system. In the case of banking sector institutions, the values of pertinent institutional measures reach on average two-thirds of cluster 1 values. It may be inferred, therefore, that in countries found in cluster 1 in our study, which embody a market-based financial intermediation system, both the capital market and the banking sector are more developed. Nonetheless, the former plays a leading role.

In Table A6.4 (see the Appendix), the distances from clusters for all 25 EU countries have been calculated. Cluster 1, which includes Sweden, Denmark, Spain, the United Kingdom and the Netherlands, is homogeneous in this regard, and hence we can conclude that the countries share similar institutional characteristics. Based on our earlier analysis in this section, it may be argued that this is primarily a function of well-developed institutions of the capital market and the banking system.

In fact, while scrutinizing variables that depict the institutional architecture in the capital market segment, we came to the conclusion that the largest capital market (in relative terms) operates in the United Kingdom. Market capitalization (SMC), the value of turnover (STTV) and assets of pension funds (PFA) are above the cluster 1 average. The values of variables describing this segment for other countries are close to the average values for this cluster. Denmark has the smallest capital market, but relative values of bank assets and loans granted are the highest. A high level of bank concentration (BAC-5) is typical of Sweden and the Netherlands. It must be emphasized, however, that the institutional differentials between the fellow countries are genuinely small. This implies that both the capital market and the banking sector in cluster 1 turn out to be homogenous.

The most puzzling country in this group is Spain. It features both a fairly large capital market (SMC) and a relative stock market turnover (STTV), which is the same as in the United Kingdom. Only the PFA has little significance. Spain's banking sector is quite similar compared to the other countries in the market-based cluster, with all pertinent indicators being either slightly below or above the cluster average. The significant difference between Spain and other "market-based countries" occurs in the case of the state's share in ownership (GEI) and financing provided to government and state-owned enterprises (CGandSOE). The cluster 1 average for the CGandSOE variable amounts to 10%, whereas its value for Spain exceeds 26%. At the same time, however, the government share in ownership (GEI) in this country is relatively the smallest – much below the average in this cluster. Thus, the most distinctive feature of the Spanish financial system is a relatively small government share in ownership and a very high level of lending to the state and state-owned enterprises.

These findings are not compatible with the results obtained by Amable (2003). While the UK and the Netherlands were found in his study to be examples of financial intermediation systems with the dominant role of the market, Sweden and Denmark represented financial systems with the leading role of banks. In turn, Spain was regarded as a country with a financial system most akin to that based on banks. These dissimilarities are probably partly due to changes in the financial intermediation area that have taken place in these countries since the time of Amable's analysis. Another possible underlying reason is a more comprehensive set of variables used in the present research.

Unlike in other institutional areas examined in our study, cluster 2 is not homogeneous (distances from clusters are distinct from zero). Actually, the whole cluster 2 is heterogeneous, characterized by a lack of clear-cut similarities among the countries involved. The countries for which the distance from cluster 2 is the smallest (Greece, Germany, Croatia and the Czech Republic) do not show any similarity at the level of source data, except for the variable describing the concentration of assets in the banking sector (BAC-5 values range from 76.52 to 99.9). However, these are the typical values for other countries too. In the case of eight economies (Ireland, Belgium, Portugal, Italy, Austria, Lithuania, Slovakia and Bulgaria), the distance from cluster 2 is slightly larger (0.11–0.20), but there is also a lack of similarity at the level of source data for this group. A similar range of values of the BAC-5 variable does not mean anything significant here; the same conclusion can be drawn based on a scrutiny of the data on the relative value of bank loans (DCPSB). Further analysis of the source data also remains inconclusive. This only confirms our claim that cluster 2 displays many symptoms of heterogeneity.

Under these circumstances, it seems legitimate to examine the distance from cluster 1 for all those countries that have not been assigned to that cluster. This is a good reason to split the cluster concerned into subgroups, based on the value of calculated distances from cluster 1 and on expert knowledge of each country's institutional characteristics.

Cluster 2 includes, inter alia, nine incumbent EU member states. However, they do not form a cohesive group in terms of their institutional architecture. One can certainly argue that their inner resemblance may be mostly derived from the lack of similarity to cluster 1. Notwithstanding this immanent heterogeneity, it can be noticed that the distances from cluster 1 for Ireland, Belgium, France, Portugal and Greece are relatively small in comparison with other cluster 2 countries (less than 1 standard deviation). We can label this set of countries subgroup 2A, to distinguish it from subgroup 2B, consisting of countries for which the distance from cluster 1 is longer (between 1 and 2 standard deviations); those countries are Finland, Germany, Italy, Austria and one CEE11 country, Croatia. The remaining 10 countries, including all CEE11 economies except Croatia, are located at the greatest distance from cluster 1 (between 2 and 3 standard deviations), making up subgroup 2C.

These subgroups are characterized by smaller mean values of pertinent variables compared to cluster 1. This applies in particular to gauges describing the significance of the capital market as a source of funds to enterprises (SMC). Namely, the average relative value of stock market capitalization in cluster 1 approaches 87%, while in subgroup 2A it amounts to 54%, in subgroup 2B to 39%, and in subgroup 2C to only 13%. A similar pattern prevails in case of the DMBA variable, describing the relative value of banks' assets (154%, 116%, 108%, and 63%, respectively) and DCPSB, or the relative value of credit to the private sector (138%, 96%, 84%, and 50%, respectively). The last two variables render the role of the banking sector in providing financing to the economy.

The three variables discussed above have been indicated as the most important determinants for cluster 1 identification by the ORCLUS algorithm. The fourth was the BAC-5, which shows the concentration of assets in the banking sector. Its average relative values in the three subgroups are quite similar, although for the CEE11 countries the value in question is slightly lower (76% for subgroup 2C, compared to the 80%–90% range for cluster 1 and subgroups 2A and 2B).

This supports the aforementioned conjecture that countries belonging to cluster 2 feature less developed (in terms of relative values) capital markets and banking sectors. However, this finding refers in a larger degree to the capital market. It is also clearly visible that the CEE11 countries lag far behind their Western European peers in terms of using the capital market and the banking sector as the intermediary vehicles for financing the economic activity.

Countries relatively close to cluster 1, denoted subgroup 2A, represent vastly different institutional arrangements. Ireland, Belgium and France have relatively strong capital market institutions and a moderately developed banking sector. Portugal and Greece are economies in which the banking sector plays the most prominent role in the institutional architecture of the financial intermediation system, and in this respect, they are the closest to cluster 1. The capital market in those countries is of minor importance.

Based on the available source data, it may be argued that there are two countries in subgroup 2B (Finland and Germany) with relatively well-developed institutions of the capital market and two countries (Italy and Austria) in which these institutions are relatively weak. On the other hand, the relative value of banks' assets (DMBA) and the relative value of domestic credit to private sector (DCPSB) variables are comparatively very high in the latter countries. This translates into a prominent role of the banking sector (albeit smaller than in cluster 1) as a source of financing firms' operations and investment.

6.3 Models of financial intermediation in CEE countries

Given the results of our empirical exercise, all CEE11 countries were assigned to cluster 2 by the ORCLUS algorithm (i.e. they exhibit a *bank-based* financial system). More specifically, they were found to constitute a separate subgroup within cluster 2, named subgroup 2C. The only exception is Croatia, classified into subgroup 2B.

Table A6.5 (see Appendix) contains the set of most important variables that distinguish countries classified in cluster 2 (including the CEE region). These are primarily measures describing the banking sector (DCPSB, DMBA, Hstat). It might seem that the key variable relating to the capital market should be, principally, its capitalization (SMC). However, this is not the case here: the SMC indicator is of minor importance; instead, turnover on the capital market (STTV) and assets of pension funds (PFA) are more significant.

As for the capitalization of the stock exchange (SMC), only two CEE11 countries boast an index higher than the average for cluster 2 (which equals 29.6%; see Table 6.2): Croatia by 7.4 percentage points and Poland by 4.8 percentage points. In Poland, the relative value of capital market turnover (STTV) is the highest within the CEE11 group, albeit it stays below the average for this cluster (equal to 14.5%) by 2.5 percentage points. In Hungary and the Czech Republic, the STTV yardstick reaches only 6.3% and 5.4%, respectively, while in the remaining CEE11 countries it is close to 1% and even less. The pension fund assets ratio (PFA) in only three CEE11 countries (Croatia, Latvia and Estonia) exceeds the cluster 2 average. This implies that the significance of the capital market as a source of financing for enterprises is limited in the group of CEE11 countries.

The concentration of banking sector assets (BAC-5) is higher than the cluster 2 average in only three countries (Lithuania by 17.1 percentage points, Estonia by 15.9 percentage points and Slovakia by 7.7 percentage points). According to Table A6.5 (see Appendix), the domestic credit to private sector (DCPSB) and domestic money banks' assets (DMBA) variables were the most important determinants for cluster 2 identification. In both cases, Croatia is the top performer among the CEE11 countries. In terms of DMBA, it is the only country in this group to exceed cluster 2 average (by 12.4 percentage points). In the remaining CEE11 economies, the value of this variable ranges between 44.5% (Romania) and 79.9% (Slovenia). Only Croatia and Estonia reached the DCPSB value at a level close to the average for cluster 2 (i.e. 70%). As a general conclusion, it can be inferred that the banking sector in the CEE11 countries is smaller in relative terms than in the EU14 countries found in this cluster. Hence, it may be deemed a less important source of funding compared to Western Europe and underdeveloped against this benchmark.

Regarding the state as owner and borrower, its role in CEE11 countries is bigger than generally is the case in cluster 2. Thus, the largest share of state ownership, in relation to cluster 2 average (17.6%), was recorded in Slovenia (26%), Hungary (25%) and Poland (23%), and the smallest in Lithuania (10%) and Bulgaria (15%). Loans to the state and state-owned enterprises (CGandSOE) significantly exceed the cluster 2 average (12.6%) in Croatia (29%), Slovenia (19%), the Czech Republic (18%) and Hungary (17%). On the other hand, in Estonia and Lithuania, CGandSOE values are negligible (close to 1% in both cases). The general observation that can be made is that in the CEE11 countries, the state's share in ownership is higher than the average for cluster 2. However, this does not result in a larger share in the value of loans granted – the mean CGandSOE for CEE11 is close to the average for cluster 2. This may be due to the overall lower relative value of loans from the banking sector, discussed above.

While interpreting the empirical results of our study, it should not be overlooked that within the group of CEE11 countries the discrepancies in the value of variables describing the banking sector are smaller than in the case of measures related to the capital market. Yet, it is not only the range that matters; also the relative levels of indicators depicting the banking sector surpass as a rule a half of the cluster 2 average. At the same time, the behavior of variables relevant for the capital market was different – in case of the SMC gauge, only four countries have reached a half of the cluster 2 average, and with respect to the STTV yardstick, just one (Poland). This points again to underdevelopment (relative to the EU14 countries) of capital market institutions and some time lag in the development of the banking sector in CEE11 countries. These results are consistent with the conclusions arrived at by Farkas (2011, 2013).

The foregoing analysis of the institutional architecture in the area of financial intermediation in CEE11 countries leads to the conclusion that there is a good deal of complementarity between the capital market and the banking sector. However, the latter is definitely more important as a provider of funds: it is more advanced and more institutionally embedded in CEE11 economies.

In developed market economies, equity has been raised through the market mechanism, whose most essential institutional component is the stock exchange. Seen from the historical perspective, the capital market institutions in CEE11 countries are only in the early stage of development. The state, society and economic agents have been learning the new rules of the game. If so, the capital market cannot play a significant, let alone a key role as a source of financing for economic entities, which has been unequivocally corroborated by the results of our empirical study.

Based on our discussion so far, it may be inferred that the financial systems of CEE11 countries in 2014 were underdeveloped relative to the old EU members. The largest gap was seen in the level of development of capital market institutions. It cannot be denied that such institutions have been established in every CEE11 country, but their macroeconomic importance in individual countries vastly differs, from noticeable and even significant (as in Poland and Croatia) to quite symbolic (as in Slovakia). In turn, the banking sector, which is both more advanced and plays a much more prominent role in the CEE11 economies compared to the capital market, also looks underdeveloped vis-à-vis Western European countries. Nevertheless, the development gap of the latter toward the EU14 is not so spectacular, while the institutional diversity of the banking sector within the CEE11 group (compared to the capital market segment) tends to be much smaller.

It may be concluded that the CEE11 countries do not form a cohesive, uniform group, as they differ in the level of development of both segments of their financial systems and in terms of the institutional arrangements adopted. Relative similarities occur in the sphere of property rights protection and concentration of banking sector assets. Another salient feature is the crucial role of the state as owner and borrower. It may be contended, therefore, that the CEE11 economies do not exhibit any clear-cut pattern of financial intermediation or a distinct institutional architecture compared to their Western European peers.

6.4 Evolving models of financial intermediation in CEE countries between 2005 and 2014

As the CEE11 countries joined the European Union in the recent past, being on their road from the centrally planned economy system to a market-based one, it is obvious by itself that they are still at an early stage of constructing and transforming their financial systems. The question arises whether the EU membership affected the institutional architecture of the financial intermediation area in these countries (and if so, to what extent and how). In our view, the EU membership has accelerated the institutional convergence process, which is reflected in the results of our empirical study. Table A6.6 (see Appendix) provides information on the changes in the average value of variables depicting the area concerned in CEE11 countries between 2005 and 2014.

The relative decline in the average ratios showing the stock market capitalization (SMC) and turnover (STTV) was quite substantial (by 5.1 percentage points and 4.1 percentage points respectively), but the variables concerned ranked among the least important in terms of cluster 2 determination. The decline may be interpreted to some extent as an effect of the global financial crisis. However, a closer look at the source data reveals widely diverging trends in individual CEE11 economies. In Poland and Croatia, the level of the SMC indicator rose (from 28% to 34% and from 27% to 37%, respectively); in Slovakia and Bulgaria it remained roughly unchanged; and in the remaining seven countries it dropped, including a dramatic fall (from 35% to 9%) in the extreme case of Estonia. In this last country also, the STTV value plummeted the most (from 12% to 1%). On the other end of the spectrum, in Poland – as the only CEE11 country – the STTV recorded growth (from 8% to 12%). It may be concluded, therefore, that this was the time when in most CEE11 countries capital markets lost in importance as a source of capital for the corporate sector, the only exception being Poland. In fact, this was a part of a broader trend – between 2005 and 2014 as many as 23 EU countries in our sample experienced a drop in the value of at least one of the two variables examined here (except for Poland and Ireland). This finding seems congruent with the conjecture that the global financial crisis has adversely affected the importance of capital markets as a source of capital for firms across the entire European Union.

The variable, whose average value for the CEE11 countries also went down during the period considered, was the protection of property rights (PPR). All countries except Poland experienced a downward trend in the level of this indicator. The changes in question tended to be small, and only in Hungary did the fall turn out to be significant, as the PPR plummeted by almost a half.

During the period examined, six out of ten indicators in our dataset displayed an upward trend instead. The most impressive growth took place in the average level of pension fund assets (PFA) which more than doubled (from 3.9% to 9.4%). This was the result of its rise in nine CEE11 countries (especially in Slovenia, from 0.01% to 6.27%, and Latvia, from 1.25% to 14%). In Poland the value of this variable remained unchanged, while in Hungary it fell by almost a half. It should be emphasized that the PFA value increased in all but one EU14 country (Finland). It is worth reminding in this context that PFA is the third most important variable determining cluster 2.

The average value of the index showing concentration of assets in the banking sector (BAC-5) augmented. The biggest hike took place in Slovakia (from 76% to 89%). Only in Poland and Romania did the gauge involved fall, by 3 percentage points (from 75% to 72%). Simultaneously, the relative value of banks' assets (DMBA) went up in all CEE11 countries by 15.5 percentage points (see Table A6.6 in the Appendix). Similarly, the behavior of the DCPSB variable, showing the relative value of credit to the private sector, followed the patterns established by the two aforementioned indicators describing the evolution of the banking sector and its macroeconomic role in CEE11 countries in the 2005–2014 period. In particular, DCPSB grew in eight CEE11 countries (it doubled in Poland), declined only in Latvia (from 65% to 51%) and stayed roughly unchanged in Hungary and Lithuania. Based on this part of the discussion, it may be argued that between 2005 and 2014 the banking sector in the CEE11 region experienced its own development and saw its role strengthened in the national economies concerned, while at the same time enhancing its institutional infrastructure. It should be stressed in this context that DCPSB and DMBA were found to be the most important institutional measures for cluster 2 identification.

The government participation in ownership (GEI) increased slightly (by 1.2 percentage points) for the whole group of CEE11 countries. Practically it did not change only in Croatia; in four countries it went down (the most in Lithuania and Latvia, from 16% to 10% and from 28% to 19%, respectively); and it grew in the rest of the group (the most in Slovenia – threefold). In the wake of ownership transformations, small changes in the level of lending to state and state-owned enterprises (CGandSOE) followed. The biggest shift took place in Slovenia, where the CGandSOE yardstick rose from 0.05% to 19.44%. This variable fell in Slovakia, Latvia and Lithuania. A more in-depth analysis of this variable at a country level shows that the policies in various CEE11 countries with regard to state ownership and its financing have taken different paths. The privatization of state property was a common practice in these countries in the 2005–2014 period; as a matter of fact, one can even speak of a reversal of the privatization trend. In addition, a similar trend was revealed in cluster 1, where the state's share in ownership was also on the rise.

Thus, when analyzing changes taking place at the aggregate level of the whole CEE11 group, it can be noted that variables describing the significance of the capital market have clearly experienced a downward trend. Although pension funds' assets increased, this change does not have to go hand in hand with the development of the capital market. In contrast, the banking sector has grown significantly, as has the role of the state in the economy.

The transformation of the institutional architecture in the financial sector of each CEE11 country has been a derivative of multiple factors both on the capital market and in the banking sector. As a result, between 2005 and 2014 individual CEE11 countries experienced changes, of different scope and directions, in the absolute distance from cluster 1 and cluster 2. Table 6.3 gives an account.

The CEE11 countries, as a group, converged to the institutional patterns existing in those Western European countries, which were identified as part of cluster 1, representing the market-based model. As a matter of fact, the change concerned was, on average, far from being large (0.15), yet noticeable. At the same time the CEE11 economies witnessed the convergence trend toward cluster 2, which was slightly more sizeable compared to cluster 1; it amounted to 0.23 on average. Given other results of our empirical study discussed earlier in the chapter, it may be argued that the above convergence tendencies were in aggregate a derivative of a rising macroeconomic importance of the banking sector in CEE11 countries which outweighed the opposite trend occurring in the capital market, whose relative role as a source of financing diminished between 2005 and 2014.

Six out of 11 countries in the CEE region (Bulgaria, Croatia, the Czech Republic, Poland, Slovakia and Slovenia) experienced a parallel institutional convergence to both clusters. Four of them (apart from the Czech Republic and Poland) cut short the distance toward cluster 1 more than to cluster 2. The most essential change that occurred in Bulgaria over the 2005–2014 period was a growing importance of the banking sector in the economy. The changes in the Bulgarian capital market were small, yet the value of pension funds' assets recorded a sizeable growth. Croatia, which was classified in subgroup 2B (close to Germany and Italy; see Table A6.4), developed its capital market, strengthened the position of the banking sector, downsized the role of the state and saw the fastest development of pension funds in the CEE11 group. In addition, it maintained high competitiveness of the banking sector, much in line with the patterns typical of cluster 1. In Slovakia, the macroeconomic importance of the capital market remained very

Table 6.3 Change in absolute distance from 2014 clusters for each CEE11 country and each subspace dimension between 2005 and 2014 (standardized values)

	Cluster 1	*Cluster 2*
Bulgaria	0.51	0.03
Croatia	0.81	0.55
Czech Republic	0.15	0.36
Estonia	−0.24	0.49
Hungary	−0.19	0.76
Latvia	−0.13	−0.29
Lithuania	−0.14	0.17
Poland	0.01	0.37
Romania	0.33	−0.19
Slovakia	0.27	0.17
Slovenia	0.46	0.23
Median change	***0.15***	***0.23***

Source: Author's elaboration.

similar in 2005 and 2014, but all indicators describing the banking sector went up – in particular, the concentration of banks' assets. The stock market capitalization ratio in Slovenia decreased significantly, while all variables describing the banking sector augmented.

The Czech Republic and Poland, although they got closer to both clusters, reduced the institutional distance proportionally more (and to a similar extent) toward the bank-based model. In case of the Czech Republic, this was due to a growing significance of the banking sector as a source of funds, while the role of the capital market diminished. At the same time, pension funds doubled their assets. In case of Poland, by 2014 the distance to cluster 1 remained virtually unchanged. Simultaneously, the changes witnessed in the banking sector as a source of funds for the economy entailed Poland's convergence toward cluster 2.

Romania narrowed the institutional gap to the market-based model, while at the same time moving away from cluster 2. As in most countries of the region, the macroeconomic significance of the capital market diminished there, which was accompanied by a considerable rise in the importance of the banking sector.

The four remaining CEE11 economies (Estonia, Hungary, Latvia and Lithuania) experienced changes in the institutional architecture of their financial systems that unleashed the institutional divergence from the market-based model. Estonia witnessed a growth trend in the importance of the banking sector and that of the state in the macroeconomy, coupled with a departure from market-based institutional arrangements. Hungary, due to a limited and descending role of the capital market, moved away from the institutional patterns embedded in cluster 1 countries. In this country, the role of the state as owner increased markedly; at the same time, the banks' assets concentration index went up. Overall, Hungary recorded the largest convergence to cluster 2 in the CEE11 group. The prevailing pattern of changes in the institutional architecture of Lithuania's financial system resembled the evolution path in the countries discussed above: it combined a downward trend in the significance of the capital market as a source of financing to economic entities and the enhanced position of the banking sector. Similar to Estonia, the macroeconomic importance of pension funds in Lithuania increased, but the role of the state in the economy (as owner and borrower) diminished significantly.

Latvia is the only CEE11 country that saw its distance to both the market-based and the bank-based clusters grow between 2005 and 2014. It is worth reminding in this context that by 2014 this country was the most institutionally distant from cluster 1 in the whole sample while at the same time revealing the largest gap to cluster 2 among the CEE11 countries (see Table A6.4 in the Appendix). This was a derivative of multiple factors, the most crucial being the dramatic contraction of the stock market turnover (by 80%) and a deep decline (by 70%) in stock market capitalization. Even more important, however, was a sizeable fall in the level of credit to the private sector. The main underlying reason was the deep economic recession suffered in 2008–2009 and the crisis in the banking sector, which was slightly mitigated due to restructuring measures implemented in this sector. All the foregoing changes in the institutional architecture of financial intermediation were effectively conducive to a departure of Latvia from the convergence path toward the pertinent patterns prevalent in other EU member states.

As a general conclusion summarizing this part of the discussion, it may be argued that changes in the institutional architecture of the financial intermediation area in CEE11 countries have brought them closer to the patterns established in the incumbent EU countries – seen both in cluster 1 and in cluster 2. Yet the scope of the convergence process tended to be quite meager, with a slight edge of this trend with regard to cluster 2. The convergence trend toward both clusters was mainly due to a declining role of the capital market, a growing importance of the banking sector and an increased share of the state in ownership.

Contrary to widespread initial expectations, the role of the capital market and its institutions in 2005–2014 diminished in CEE11 economies. Over the same period, the banking sector expanded, strengthening its function of a primary source of funds for the corporate sector and the state. Simultaneously, the importance of the state as owner and the value of loans granted to government and state-owned enterprises augmented. The rising financing needs being, inter alia, a derivative of economic development have been increasingly met by banks rather than by a stock exchange. This brought the countries of the CEE11 region closer to the bank-based model.

Still, the above conclusion calls for some fine-tuning. As a matter of fact, banks operated in CEE11 countries before the EU accession, and even prior to the establishment of capital market institutions (i.e. since the outset of systemic transformation). Hence, they had worked out necessary procedures, transplanted good practices from the Western world, designed and put in motion new institutions and established cooperation with both private firms and the government. In the years that followed the start of systemic transformation, the development of the banking sector in Central and Eastern Europe seems to have been correlated with economic growth. Financing by banks is a well-known way to raise funds in CEE11 economies. In contrast, the capital market and its institutions, with their very short historical record in these economies, had to be learned and internalized virtually from scratch (including a very crucial factor of gaining trust by capital market participants). Altogether, the analysis carried out in sections 6.2 and 6.3 revealed a picture of small and undeveloped capital markets in most of the CEE11 countries (including a lack of well-rooted institutions), which perhaps do not mean anything else than just prestige. This makes plausible a conjecture that the banking sector might have been a preferred option when looking for sources of funds. It may be also argued that the development of the banking sector as a primary source of financing in many CEE economies might have simultaneously extinguished incentives for the expansion of the capital market. As a result, its importance remained small and even diminished. If this is the case, without any additional stimuli provided by the national governments or implemented at the EU level, weak institutions of the capital market will remain persistently weak and insignificant in the CEE11 economies.

There are two exceptions to this general pattern, however, among the CEE11 countries: Poland and Croatia. The relative size of both the capital market and the banking sector has significantly grown there. It goes without saying that the role performed by the capital market in these countries has been relatively small so far, yet growth tendencies are clearly visible. In contrast, in other CEE11 countries, with a rising macroeconomic importance of the banking sector, the role of the capital market as a source of funds for the macroeconomy has been on the decline.

The relative underdevelopment of the financial system in CEE11 countries is to a large extent a part of the command-economy legacy; simultaneously, it may be explained as a function of time (i.e. in terms of the early stage of the emerging capitalism in these countries). In our view, membership in the European Union has accelerated the convergence process of this institutional area to the standards developed in Western Europe. This process is likely to continue in the years to come, but in the aftermath of the global financial crisis it is difficult to foretell exactly where it will lead. As a starting logical premise for any viable projection regarding the prospective development of financial intermediation in the CEE region, it seems advisable to recall one of the key findings of our research discussed in this chapter, namely that in the 2005–2014 period the institutional convergence process led the CEE11 countries more toward the bank-based model than toward the market-based model of financial intermediation.

References

Amable, B. (2003). *The diversity of modern capitalism*. Oxford: Oxford University Press.

Coates, D. (2000). *Models of capitalism. Growth and stagnation in the modern era*. Cambridge: Polity Press.

Farkas, B. (2011). The Central and Eastern European model of capitalism. *Post-Communist Economies*, 23(1), pp. 15–34, doi:10.1080/14631377.2011.546972

Farkas, B. (2013). Changing development prospects for the Central and Eastern European EU member states, *MPRA Working Paper, 48172. Paper presented at the 2nd annual SPERI conference*, University of Sheffield, UK, 1–3 July.

Hall, P.A. and Soskice, D. (2001). An introduction to varieties of capitalism. In: *Varieties of capitalism. The institutional foundations of comparative advantage*. Oxford: Oxford University Press.

Knell, M. and Srholec, M. (2007). Diverging pathways in Central and Eastern Europe. In: D. Lane and M. Myant, eds. *Emerging varieties of capitalism in post-communist countries*. Basingstoke: Palgrave Macmillan.

McGee, R. (2007). Venture capital in European transition economies: A scoring system. In: G.N. Gregoriou, M. Kooli and R. Kraeussl, eds., *Venture capital in Europe*. Oxford: Elsevier Finance.

Oehler, A., Pukthuanthong, K., Rummer, M. and Walker, T. (2007). Venture capital in Europe: closing the gap to the U.S. In: G.N. Gregoriou, M. Kooli and R. Kraeussl, eds., *Venture capital in Europe*. Oxford: Elsevier Finance.

Ozsvald, E. (2014). Corporate governance in Central Eastern Europe – A comparative political economy approach, *Grincoh Working Paper Series, No. 7.03*.

Vitols, S. (2001). Varieties of corporate governance: Comparing Germany and the UK. In: P.A. Hall and D. Soskice, eds., *Varieties of capitalism. The institutional foundations of comparative advantage*. Oxford: Oxford University Press.

Appendix 6

Table A6.4 Distance from cluster in each subspace dimension (absolute, standardized values)

	Cluster 1	*Cluster 2*
Sweden	0	1.01
Denmark	0	0.80
Spain	0	1.09
United Kingdom	0	2.08
Netherlands	0	4.10
Ireland	0.69	0.19
Belgium	0.71	0.12
France	0.73	0.34
Portugal	0.79	0.17
Greece	0.89	0.03
Finland	1.01	0.29
Germany	1.26	0.04
Croatia	1.36	0.10
Italy	1.50	0.14
Austria	1.73	0.17
Estonia	2.08	0.23
Slovenia	2.24	0.29
Lithuania	2.25	0.17
Czech Republic	2.26	0.02
Slovakia	2.31	0.12
Poland	2.46	0.28
Hungary	2.58	0.31
Bulgaria	2.70	0.13
Romania	2.78	0.27
Latvia	2.91	0.46

Source: Author's elaboration.

Table A6.5 Measures for cluster distinction in order of importance

Cluster 1	*Cluster 2*
DMBA	DCPSB
SMC	DMBA
DCPSB	PFA
BAC-5	Hstat
STTV	STTV
GEI	CGandSOE
PFA	SMC
CGandSOE	BAC-5
PPR	GEI
Hstat	PPR

Source: Author's elaboration.

Table A6.6 Change in value of variables between 2005 and 2014 (average for CEE11 countries)

	2005	*2014*	*Change between 2005 and 2014*
SMC	23.2	18.1	−5.1
STTV	9.7	5.6	−4.1
DMBA	52.7	68.2	15.5
BAC-5	76.4	77.9	1.5
DCPSB	46.5	54.1	7.6
PPR	6.3	5.6	−0.7
Hstat	0.6	0.7	0.1
GEI	16.5	17.7	1.2
CGandSOE	10.0	10.8	0.8
PFA	3.9	9.4	5.5

Source: Author's elaboration.

7 Social protection system

Piotr Maszczyk

Introduction

The aim of this chapter is to present the results of empirical analysis of the social protection system in 25 European Union (EU25) countries. According to Amable (2003), the social protection system ranks among the most important parts of not only the whole institutional architecture of a country but also its economic policy designed according to the political economy rules.

While analyzing the menu of possible institutional arrangements in the organization of the social protection system, some key elements have to be underlined. First, the most essential factor which influences the institutional architecture of this area is path dependence, mostly due to historical, political, demographic and cultural determinants, which differ substantially even in a relatively homogenous group of Central and Eastern European EU new member states (CEE11). Hence, it is much harder – compared to the remaining institutional areas covered by our study – to identify clusters as a function of clear-cut institutional similarities among the countries involved, because in the case of the social protection system these are endogenous or domestic factors that play the most vital role. To some extent, each country in the analyzed group could form its own cluster, or alternatively the whole sample combining "old" and "new" EU member states could be classified into two undifferentiated clusters.

Second, the foregoing peculiarity makes this institutional area a "non-tradeable" sector par excellence, as it was designed and has evolved without a substantial influence of exogenous or external factors.[1] This also implies that the social protection system contrasts in this respect with some other institutional areas involved, such as product market competition or the labor market and industrial relations, which in essence are "tradeables".

Third, the institutional architecture of a social protection system, especially the scope of government involvement, has constantly evolved in line with economic development, demographic trends and technological changes and – most of all – revisions in the prevailing values in the society and commonly shared beliefs on a desirable level of solidarity and a welfare state (Amable, 2003). Certainly, some changes are common for the whole analyzed group. A steady increase of public

DOI: 10.4324/9780429056901-9

and private spending on healthcare and the pension system (due to demographic changes) and fluctuations of unemployment compensation as a function of booms and busts are most likely the most visible symptoms of those kinds of shifts.

Fourth, as we know from the trailblazing book by Amable (2003), it is not easy to define whether a given set of institutions meets the efficiency criteria. The right approach to the evaluation of this dimension should always involve an additional qualifier: "efficient for whom?" It is not easy to settle in favor of which group a given change was introduced, even in the case of product market competition, financial intermediation or knowledge creation areas. Is it better to have the labor market institutions that would maximize the participation rate, or rather to design them in the way that would ensure the supply of a required number of skilled and cheap workers, with unemployment mitigating the wage hike expectations and diminishing the negotiation power of the labor force? The first scenario is obviously better for the society as a whole, whereas the second alternative would be most welcome by foreign investors in particular and employers in general. In the case of the social protection system, with its large component of political economy and public choice decisions, such judgment (in whose favor a particular change was designed) seems almost impossible. According to Amable (2003), the final shape of an institution is always an outcome of political compromise between various groups of vested interests who try to enforce the most desirable (for the interests concerned) conformation of that institution, no matter its efficiency for the economy as a whole. In the social protection system, it is easy to mask such strategy, because it is difficult to measure the efficiency of institutions in this area. As a result, the entire social protection system is vulnerable[2] to the lack of efficiency and thus complementarity, both internal and external (see Chapter 1). Moreover, as the institutional change requires (according to Amable) the support of vested interests powerful enough to enforce such change, the situation in which the shape of the whole institutional area – seen from the complementarity perspective – is suboptimal could be sustainable in the medium or even the long run.[3]

It is worth stressing that the foregoing mechanism is typical of both "old" and "new" EU member states. A direct support for children in the families can be conceived as a novel institutional vehicle in Poland (see endnote 3) and in the CEE region, but it has a long record in Germany and in Western Europe in general. Leaving aside its efficiency (assuming roughly the same relative level of spending under this heading, in 2005 in Germany the fertility rate was lower by more than 0.4 points compared to Sweden and by over 0.6 points compared to France, and in 2014 these differences did not essentially change),[4] the mechanism of a direct support for children seems to be long-lasting.

In view of the persistency of the above-described mechanisms in the whole analyzed sample (EU25), mostly input variables were considered for analytical and classification purposes in the social protection domain. Given all the aforementioned objections, the most important distinction between various models of the social protection system is a function of the type of risks which the citizens of a country are protected against by the government, and the scope of this protection

(Amable, 2003). Seen from this angle, there are six major areas to which government spending is channeled: healthcare, housing, pensions (and more generally, elderly people), sick and disabled persons, families and the unemployed. As the housing market is discussed in more detail in Chapter 9, there are five such areas remaining. The relative weight of each risk can be calculated using two different measures. The first measure is the share of a particular category of public spending in total public expenditure. Using this yardstick, one can assess the relative importance of a given area for the public sector. The second gauge compares the amount of public expenditure in the area involved with gross domestic product (GDP), which points to the relative macroeconomic significance of this area. To complete the picture, some other indicators that emphasize the most salient features of the tax system in a country (the relative burden of taxation, the main sources of tax revenues and the top personal income tax rate) are taken into consideration. Once again, it must be stressed that the way the existing system actually protects people against a given risk (output variables) is not accounted for – mostly due to the political economy peculiarities mentioned earlier.

The above-described set of measures led Amable (2003) to the conclusion that the dispersion of institutional characteristics in the social protection area in the group of countries examined in his study (mostly developed, at least medium-sized European economies as well as the United States, Canada, Australia, Japan and South Korea) can be explained by three principal factors or indicators. The first is the ratio of benefits to total public expenditure and to GDP. These variables, according to Amable, enable a distinction between countries with a well-developed social protection system and those in which this area is (financially) underdeveloped. Amable indicated that this factor explains approximately 60% of institutional variance in the social protection systems in his sample (2003). The second factor draws on a comparison of the relative level of public expenditure targeted at families with the relative level of public spending directed to the elderly. The third indicator boils down to a relative amount of public money channeled to the healthcare system or the ratio of that expenditure to total public expenditure and to GDP.

Based on these findings, Amable identified five European clusters or models of the social protection system (2003). His first cluster consisted of four countries (Sweden, Denmark, Finland and Norway) with a high ratio of benefits and social spending to both total public expenditure and GDP. Additionally, all countries in this cluster concentrated social spending on families and displayed a high ratio of income tax revenue to GDP. The second cluster contained Ireland and Australia and was characterized by a relatively low level of public spending on social protection and a low ratio of consumption tax revenue to total tax revenue. The third model embraced the United Kingdom, the Netherlands, Spain and Portugal. It was similar to the first cluster, but it exhibited a lower relative level of social spending and benefits. The last two clusters encompassed Italy and Greece (with a generally low level of social spending and concentration on elderly people and pensions), and France, Germany, Austria, Belgium and Switzerland, respectively.

Boeri (2002) in his earlier work compared the performance of the four identified models of social policy (Mediterranean-Southern, Continental, Anglo-Saxon and Nordic) in terms of meeting three objectives of this policy:

- Reduction of income inequality and poverty;
- Protection against uninsurable labor market risk;
- Reward to labor market participation.[5]

Protection against uninsurable labor market risk can be provided either by employment protection legislation (EPL), which to some extent safeguards workers against firing, or by unemployment benefits (UB). The differences between these two mechanisms are clear: EPL protects those who already have a job and does not impose any tax burden, whereas UB provide insurance to the population at large and are typically financed by a tax on those who work. Thus insiders, those with a stable and regular job, typically prefer EPL to UB. The four European social policy models vastly differ in their design and institutional traits. The Mediterranean model is characterized by very strict employment protection regulations and quite low coverage of unemployment benefits. On the opposite side of the spectrum, the Nordic model provides unemployment benefits which are both generous and comprehensive, but the strictness of the EPL is quite low. The Continental model provides generous unemployment benefits too, but its EPL is stricter. Finally, the Anglo-Saxon model ensures comparatively less protection than its peers, with a far lower EPL strictness but as much unemployment insurance as the Continental and Nordic models.

Applying the methodological framework introduced firstly by Boeri (2002) and then Amable (2003), Sapir (2006) proposed his classification of the European social models, varying in their most salient features and performance in terms of efficiency and equity. He argued that models that are not efficient are not sustainable and must be reformed. According to his calculations, the combined GDP of countries embodying inefficient social models accounted for two-thirds of the entire EU and 90% of the Eurozone. The four models singled out by Sapir covered four different geographical areas. The Nordic countries (Denmark, Finland and Sweden plus the Netherlands) featured the highest levels of social protection expenditures and universal welfare provision. There was extensive fiscal intervention in labor markets based on a variety of "active" policy instruments. Strong labor unions ensured highly compressed wage structures. The Anglo-Saxon countries (Ireland and the United Kingdom) featured relatively large social assistance of the last resort. Cash transfers were primarily targeted at people in the working age. Activation measures were important as well as schemes conditioning access to benefits to full-time employment. On the labor market side, this model was characterized by a mixture of weak unions, comparatively wide and increasing wage dispersion, and a relatively high incidence of low-pay employment. The Continental countries (Austria, Belgium, France, Germany and Luxembourg) relied extensively on insurance-based non-employment benefits and old-age pensions. Although their membership was on the decline, unions remained strong as regulations extended the coverage of collective bargaining to non-union situations. Finally, the Mediterranean countries (Greece, Italy, Portugal and Spain) concentrated their social spending on old-age pensions and allowed for a high segmentation of entitlements and status. Their social welfare systems typically drew on employment protection and early retirement provisions to exempt segments of the working-age population from participation in the labor market. The wage structure was, at least in the formal sector, covered by collective bargaining and strongly compressed.

According to Sapir, both the Continental and the Anglo-Saxon countries seemed to face a trade-off between efficiency and equity. While the former enjoyed far more equity but exhibited relatively lower efficiency, in the latter the opposite pattern was true – there was relatively more efficiency and less equity. The Continental model countries were reasonably successful in mitigating poverty yet nevertheless were blighted with high unemployment, especially in terms of job creation. Socially the model was fractious, splitting highly taxed workers ('insiders') against a growing population of welfare recipients ('outsiders'), who despite being adequately cared for by the state might have lacked a measure of social inclusion that employment provides. The Mediterranean countries apparently faced no such trade-off: their citizens lived in a social system that, according to Sapir, delivered neither efficiency nor equity. These countries were generally unsuccessful in both combating poverty and unemployment. Traditionally social security was provided by social insurance funded by contributions from workers, with minimal benefits being offered to the unemployed or people with childrearing or caring responsibilities. By design, the family consequently has a strong role in social welfare, headed by a male breadwinner with strong job security. The paternalistic Mediterranean model has been criticized by Sapir not just for providing poor outcomes in terms of fixing unemployment and poverty, but also for not addressing long-term issues around sustainability, such as financing pensions and addressing falling fertility among women unable to survive without adequate government support. In the Nordic countries there was no efficiency-equity trade-off either; according to Sapir, they appeared a bit successful in combining the impossible (i.e. a good economic performance without economic incentives distorted by high tax wedges or generous social security systems).

Regarding the reduction of income inequality and poverty, Sapir found that the extent of redistribution effected via taxes and transfers was the highest in the Nordic countries (with 42% reduction of inequality) and the lowest in the Mediterranean countries (35% reduction), with the Anglo-Saxon and Continental countries in the middle (39% reduction).

He also pointed out that rewards to labor market participation varied a great deal across the four European social models. Employment rates were far higher in the Nordic and Anglo-Saxon countries (72% and 69% in 2004, respectively) than in the Continental and Mediterranean economies (63% and 62%, respectively), with much of the disparity being attributable to differences at the two ends of the age spectrum. For workers aged 55–64, the employment rate was considerably higher in Nordic (56%) and Anglo-Saxon (53%) countries than in Continental (34%) and Mediterranean (40%) states. For workers aged 15–24, the unemployment rate was significantly lower in Nordic (13%) and Anglo-Saxon (10%) countries than in Continental (17%) and Mediterranean (22%) economies.

Yet another typology of welfare capitalism which is worth mentioning is the proposal put forward by the Danish sociologist Esping-Andersen (1990).[6] In his view, such typology should rely on three criteria:

- The capacity for de-commodification of social rights, which captures the degree of independence from market which is necessary to people for protecting their livelihoods;
- The impact of redistribution on social stratification (status or class inequality) and thus its contribution to the reproduction of the existing institutional context;
- The respective contributions of the state, the market and the family to the financing of social protection.

Based on his analysis of social protection systems in 18 industrialized countries, Esping-Andersen identified three types of welfare-state models, which are characterized by a specific post-industrial employment trajectory. *Liberal regimes* (the United States, Canada, Australia, Ireland and New Zealand; the UK was indicated to be close to this model) are characterized by modest means-tested assistance and targeted at low-income, usually working-class recipients. The strict entitlement rules of such assistance are often associated with stigma. This model of welfare state encourages market-based solutions to social problems – either passively, by guaranteeing only a minimum, or actively, by means of directly subsidizing private welfare schemes. *Conservative regimes* (Germany, Italy, Finland, Japan, Switzerland and France) are typically shaped by traditional family values and tend to encourage family-based assistance dynamics. Social insurance in this model typically excludes non-working wives, and family benefits encourage motherhood. State assistance will typically only step in when the family's capacity to aid its members is exhausted. *Social democratic regimes* (mostly Scandinavian countries as well as Austria, Belgium and the Netherlands) feature universalistic systems that promote equality of high standards rather than equality of minimal needs. This implies de-commodifying welfare services, reducing the division introduced by market-based access to welfare services and pre-emptively socializing the costs of caring for children, the aged, and the helpless, instead of waiting until the family's capacity to support them is depleted. This in turn results in a commitment to a heavy social service burden, which introduces an imperative to minimize social problems, thereby aligning the system's goals with the welfare and emancipation (typically via full employment policies) of those it supports.

The classification brought into scholarly circulation by Esping-Andersen gave birth to a large number of empirical studies, which applied his methodology for different groups of countries and time brackets (see, e.g., Wood and Gough, 2006; Fenger, 2007; Rudra 2007, 2008).

Other typologies refer mostly to labor market institutions. Worth referencing in this context is the study by Estevez-Abe, Iversen and Soskice (1999), who extensively used the concept of internal and external complementarity of social protection system institutions, primarily with the knowledge sector. The authors pointed out that "social protection does not always mean 'politics against markets'". They argued that social protection rescues the market from itself by preventing market failures. They rejected the thesis, well established in the literature, that protection of employment and income is seen as reducing workers' dependence on the market and employers. They also claimed that employment and income protection can be seen as efforts aimed to increase workers' dependence on particular employers as well as their exposure to labor market risks. Moreover, in their view social protection often stems from the strength rather than the weakness of employers. The key argument behind this claim is the link between social protection and the level and composition of skills. In a modern economy, skills are essential for firms to compete in international markets, and depending on a particular product and market strategy involved, they rely on a workforce with a certain combination of firm-specific, industry-specific and general skills. To be cost-efficient, firms need workers who are willing to make personal investments in these skills. And if enterprises want to be competitive in product markets that require an abundance of specific skills, workers must be willing to acquire these skills at the cost of increasing their dependence on a particular employer or group of employers. As investment in specific skills increases workers' exposure to risks, only by insuring against such risks can firms satisfy their need for specific skills.

The present chapter consists of four parts that follow the introductory section. In section 7.1, the set of institutional measures is presented that best describes the environment of the social protection system in 25 EU countries. In section 7.2, based on the indicators selected, the results of subspace clustering are provided for the institutional area involved in the European Union. Section 7.3 sheds a more in-depth empirical light on the emerging models of capitalism in the social protection area in the CEE11 countries. The chapter concludes with an empirical analysis of institutional changes in social protection systems in Central and Eastern Europe that occurred between 2005 and 2014 (section 7.4).

7.1 The dataset

The overriding objective of this section is to select a set of indicators that will best describe the institutional environment of the social protection system in CEE11 and EU14 countries. The chosen set of indicators is to be used for further analytical purposes, such as cross-country comparisons aimed to allow for discrimination between the models of capitalism emerging in 11 CEE countries and 14 Western European countries being analyzed.

Taking into consideration previous empirical studies on the institutional diversity in the social protection system and based on the data provided by Eurostat, a dataset of 17 institutional measures was created encompassing mostly input variables. The data were collected for 2005 (the initial year of our study) and for 2014 or the latest available record, but not prior to 2010. A description of all indicators involved together with the respective data sources can be found in Table 7.1.

Table 7.1 Data sources

	Variable name	*Variable description*	*Data source*
1	BtE	Benefits to total expenditures ratio	Eurostat
2	BtGDP	Benefits to GDP ratio	Eurostat
3	GHtE	Public expenditures on healthcare to total expenditures ratio	Eurostat
4	GFtE	Public expenditures on families to total expenditures ratio	Eurostat
5	GOAtE	Public expenditures on old age people to total expenditures ratio	Eurostat
6	GUtE	Public expenditures on unemployed people to total expenditures ratio	Eurostat
7	GSDtE	Public expenditures on sick and disabled people to total expenditures ratio	Eurostat
8	GHtGDP	Public expenditures on healthcare to GDP ratio	Eurostat
9	GFtGDP	Public expenditures on families to GDP ratio	Eurostat
10	GOAtGDP	Public expenditures on old age people to GDP ratio	Eurostat
11	GPTGDP	Public expenditures on pensions to GDP ratio	Eurostat
12	GSDtGDP	Public expenditures on sick and disabled people to GDP	Eurostat
13	GUtGDP	Public expenditures on unemployed people to GDP	Eurostat
14	ITtTR	Income taxes revenue to total tax revenue ratio	Eurostat
15	VATtTR	Value-added taxes revenue to total tax revenue ratio	Eurostat
16	TRtGDP	Total tax revenue to GDP ratio	Eurostat
17	TPIT	Top personal income tax rate	Eurostat

Source: Author's elaboration.

Given the peculiarities of the institutional area in question as well as the availability of data provided by OECD, ECB and the World Bank, the indicators selected for this part of our empirical exercise mostly describe the absolute (variables 8–13) and relative (variables 3–7) importance of particular risks, against which the society is protected by the government. In turn, the ratio of benefits to total government expenditure and especially the ratio of benefits to GDP (variables 1–2) will be interpreted as a proxy for the type of a coordination mechanism prevalent in the social protection system. The higher the absolute and relative weight of benefits (their ratio to total government spending and to GDP), the more important is the market (private) mechanism of coordination. In other words, under such a scenario the government would mostly distribute money among eligible members of the society rather than directly financing the collective consumption of public goods and services (or private yet perceived as merit goods). By the same token, the administrative (bureaucratic) mechanism of coordination would be used on a smaller scale.

Another category of public expenditure on social protection which calls for an additional comment is "assistance for families" (variables 4 and 9). Under this heading, the government could be involved in supporting the education system through direct financing of a public network of full-time nurseries and kindergartens while at the same time channeling some benefits to families (whose relative significance would then be smaller). Under an alternative scenario, the government would only distribute financial assistance to families without a direct involvement in financing and distributing the preschool education. In that case, the relative importance of benefits would be much larger.

It is also worth noting that indicators 14–17 are, respectively, employed to discriminate between the progressive vs. regressive tax systems and thus to address the question whether households with higher incomes pay higher taxes (the dominant role of personal income tax – variables 14 and 17) or whether the tax burden is mostly placed on households with lower income (the dominant role of value-added tax – variable 15). Variable 16 measures the absolute tax burden and thus could be treated as a proxy for government involvement in the process of income redistribution in the economy.

7.2 Models of social protection system in the European Union

The analysis of the data gathered on institutional measures with the ORCLUS subspace clustering algorithm made possible to identify two distinct clusters of countries within the EU14 group that share a set of institutions that are described by similar indicators, in terms of their value and order of importance. This implies a substantially different result, compared to the findings established by Amable or Esping-Andersen in their studies. The two Western European clusters were labeled the *generous benefits model*, prevalent in most EU14 countries as well as in Slovenia and Croatia (cluster 1), and the *high taxes and public consumption model*, to be found only in Denmark and Sweden (cluster 2). Apart from these two models, the third cluster, comprising most of the CEE11 countries, was identified and named the *private mode of coordination model* (cluster 3). The spatial distribution of these three models across the European Union is depicted on Map 7.1 while the institutional characteristics of each model are provided in Table 7.2. The following is a short description of the two Western European models of social protection system identified in our empirical study.

The *generous benefits model* can be traced in the Anglo-Saxon countries (the United Kingdom, Ireland), some of the Nordic states (Finland), some of the Benelux countries (Belgium, the Netherlands), continental (Germany, Austria) and all Mediterranean countries (Spain, Portugal, Greece and Italy), as well as in two CEE economies (Croatia and Slovenia). It is characterized[7] mostly by the up-close ratio of public expenditures on elderly people to both total public expenditures and GDP (GOAtE of 20% in comparison with 18% in cluster 2 and GOAtGDP of 10% in comparison with 8% in cluster 3) coupled with moderate values for total tax revenue to GDP ratio and income tax revenue to total tax revenue ratio (TRtGDP of 26% in comparison with 45% in cluster 2 and 20% in cluster 3; ITtTR of 28% vs. 52% in cluster 2 and 20% in cluster 3). It is worth stressing that the ratio of public expenditures directed to families to both total public expenditures and GDP is relatively low in this group (GFtE of 4% and GFtGDP of 2% in comparison with 7% and 4%, respectively, in cluster 2). Moreover, what is characteristic for this model of social protection is an extraordinarily high ratio of benefits to

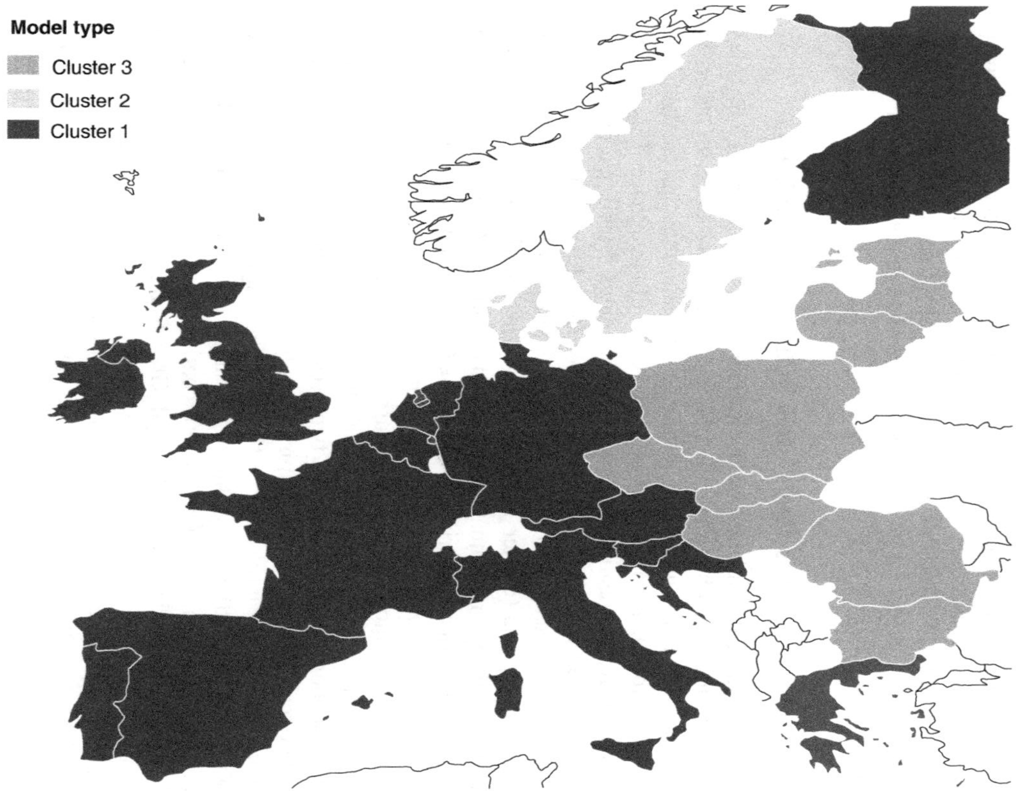

Map 7.1 Models of capitalism in the European Union: social protection

Source: Author's elaboration.

Table 7.2 Cluster-average values for all variables

	Cluster 1 Generous benefits	*Cluster 2 High taxes and public consumption*	*Cluster 3 Private mode of coordination*
Benefits to total expenditures ratio	0.42	0.34	0.36
Benefits to GDP ratio	0.18	0.16	0.12
Public expenditures on healthcare to total expenditures ratio	0.15	0.15	0.12
Public expenditures on families to total expenditures ratio	0.04	0.07	0.03
Public expenditures on old age people to total expenditures ratio	0.20	0.18	0.20
Public expenditures on unemployed people to total expenditures ratio	0.03	0.04	0.01
Public expenditures on sick and disabled people to total expenditures ratio	0.06	0.09	0.06
Public expenditures on healthcare to GDP ratio	0.08	0.08	0.04
Public expenditures on families to GDP ratio	0.02	0.04	0.02
Public expenditures on old age people to GDP ratio	0.10	0.10	0.08
Public expenditures on pensions to GDP ratio	0.09	0.09	0.07
Public expenditures on sick and disabled people to GDP	0.02	0.04	0.01
Public expenditures on unemployed people to GDP	0.02	0.02	0.00
Income taxes revenue to total tax revenue ratio	0.28	0.52	0.20
Value-added taxes revenue to total tax revenue ratio	0.19	0.20	0.25
Total tax revenue to GDP ratio	0.26	0.45	0.20
Top personal income tax rate	0.48	0.56	0.20

Source: Author's elaboration.

total expenditures, which by 8 and 6 percentage points exceeds the levels recorded in clusters 2 and 3, respectively. A similar pattern holds for benefits to GDP ratio, which is the highest in the generous benefits cluster surpassing by 2 and 6 percentage points, respectively, similar indicators in clusters 2 and 3. Finally, cluster 1 countries exhibit a lower average ratio of public expenditure on sick and disabled people to both total public expenditure and GDP compared to cluster 2 (GSDtE of 6% vs. 9%; GSDtGDP of 2% vs. 4%).

It can be noted that the most distinctive feature of the social protection system in countries identified by the ORCLUS algorithm as the generous benefits cluster is a high ratio of benefits to both total public expenditure and GDP (see Table A7.5 in the Appendix). The systems prevalent in these countries are based mostly on transfer payments or redistributive allocation of public expenditure among members of the society rather than on a direct provision of public goods and services needed by particular social groups. Worth emphasizing is also the fact that social transfers are targeted mostly at elderly people and only in limited proportions at families and sick and disabled people. The relative tax burden in these countries tends to be substantially lower compared to the high taxes and public consumption cluster yet higher than in the private mode of coordination model of social protection. The ratio of personal income tax to total tax revenue is also substantially lower. The major source of tax revenues in countries making up this cluster are indirect taxes, mostly the value-added tax. Although a high ratio of benefits to GDP indicates that the dominant mechanism of coordination in the generous benefits model is government-based, it simultaneously shows that rather than directly providing or outsourcing the provision of public goods and services, countries in this group stay surprisingly passive when it comes to deciding how to spend public money.

On the other hand, the institutional structure of the tax system and social protection seems to be coherent in this cluster. The major source of government revenues is personal income tax, with the top rate being relatively high (though lower by 0.6 percentage points compared to high taxes and public consumption cluster). Additionally, a relative importance of the value-added tax in this cluster is even lower than in the private mode of coordination model (by 0.06 percentage points). The government in this way redistributes incomes between social groups with different income levels, thus influencing the original market distribution. This is equivalent to saying that the coordination mix (the contribution of different mechanisms/modes of coordination) prevailing in this cluster preserves the dominant element of government (bureaucratic mode), yet with a far greater component of market mechanism, compared to the high taxes and public consumption cluster.

The *high taxes and public consumption* cluster has been found only in Sweden and Denmark. The differences – compared to the previous cluster – are concentrated mostly in the architecture of the tax system (see Table A7.5 in the Appendix). High taxation, both in relative and absolute terms, distinguishes these two countries from the generous benefits cluster. The top income tax rate in the former is higher than the average in the latter by 8 percentage points. It is interesting to note that the ratio of benefits to total public expenditure in Sweden and Denmark is lower not only relative to cluster 1 but also to cluster 3. This finding seems to contradict the conclusions arrived at by Amable in this respect. At the same time, the ratio of benefits to GDP is only slightly higher in comparison with the CEE11 average (cluster 3) and still lower compared to the generous benefits cluster. Hence the protection from various risks in the high taxes and public consumption cluster countries takes place through the collective consumption rather than direct public financial support. Public expenditures in this cluster are targeted mainly at families (the respective share indicator is twice as high as in both cluster 1 and cluster 3) and at sick and disabled people. A higher relative weight of these two categories of public spending can be traced in both their ratio to total public expenditures and to GDP. On the other hand, the ratio of expenditures on old-age people to total public expenditures in these countries is 2 percentage points lower than in the generous benefits and private mode of coordination clusters. Simultaneously, the ratio of this category of public expenditure to GDP exceeds the levels recorded in cluster 3 and is on a par with cluster 1. This implies that the absolute significance of this sphere in Sweden and Denmark is on average the same as in other old EU member states. Nonetheless, the relative importance of this type of risk is lower due to a higher incidence of other risks.

The coordination mix in the high taxes and public consumption cluster, bearing in mind both the ratio of benefits to total expenditure and the structure of tax revenues, relies predominantly on a government-led mechanism of coordination, with only a minor role of market-based coordination. Seen from this angle, the governments of Denmark and Sweden levy high personal income taxes, but rather than just redistributing income through transfer payments, they spend their tax revenues on the provision of public goods and services.

The future evolution of the institutional architecture of the social protection system in old EU member states is hardly predictable. As a derivative of the projected demographic changes, one can expect the augmenting proportion of transfer payments directed to elderly people and a declining relative weight of other social spending. It is worth pointing in this context to a trade-off existing between the public assistance to families and to old-age people. The higher the share of public expenditure allocated to the latter, the lower is the proportion of social transfers the government can allocate to the former. As a derivative, the more painful become the consequences of demographic changes. Given the growing number of old-age members of the society (who are simultaneously voters), and bearing in mind the implications of the public choice theory, it seems extremely difficult to rechannel public assistance to families. Such a shift is likely to be rejected by the majority of voters, and hence there will not emerge a viable coalition powerful enough to impose this change. This scenario appears to be particularly realistic in view of the fact that at least in some countries in the generous benefits cluster (e.g. Germany), the positive effects of direct financial assistance to families are very limited (as was pointed out in the introduction to this chapter). It seems, therefore, that without deeper changes in informal institutions, targeting public expenditures at families is not a winning proposition as it will bring only very modest results. Since such changes are hardly feasible to be implemented in a top-down manner (particularly in the short run), the negative externalities triggered by adverse demographic trends (e.g. a shrinking stock of the labor force) will be minimized – or at least alleviated – thanks to a rising number of young migrants with selected skills and qualifications. As a result, it is reasonable to expect a growing relative level of public spending directed to young families with children.

Second, in line with a radical technological change, which will be conducive to a substantial fall in labor demand, especially for unskilled workers, in the next 20–30 years one can envision a rise in the value of welfare benefits relative to both total public expenditure and GDP. It may be argued that this adverse labor market trend can be to some extent offset by strong informal institutions, characteristic of most societies in the European Union. As a matter of illustration, the commonly shared values in Western Europe entail a belief that adults should be responsible for their own lives, which puts a downward pressure on the level of benefits channeled to unemployed persons (e.g. social reform of Hartz IV in Germany, or the failure of the referendum on minimum guaranteed income in Switzerland). With a growing number of unemployed and inactive workers, this attitude may change. It is interesting to see how the active labor market policy pursued in high taxes and public consumption cluster countries substitutes to some extent the benefits offered to jobless people. Obviously, the jobless compensation (especially in Denmark) is high in comparison with most generous benefits cluster countries. Still, low unemployment rates (in particular, long-term unemployment rates) push down the relative level of unemployment benefits below the EU14 average. This type of labor market policy (known as *flexicurity*) seems to make the social protection system in this cluster both efficient and fair.

7.3 Models of social protection systems in CEE countries

The CEE region does not differ fundamentally from the rest of the European Union in terms of institutional architecture of the social protection system. The types of risks the government can protect society from are roughly the same (with still a very limited number of migrants and refugees who need public assistance). The mechanisms the government can implement to establish such protection are well-known too.

Nevertheless, the *private mode of coordination* cluster countries differ in many respects from both the generous benefits and high taxes and public consumption models. First, one of the key underlying reasons lies in a much lower benefits to GDP ratio. Although the ratio of benefits to total public expenditure in this cluster is above the respective indicator in the high taxes and public consumption model, the proportion of benefits to GDP stands at only 12%, compared to 16% in that model and 18% in the generous benefits cluster. Similarly, the ratio of almost all types of benefits (the exception being only transfers targeted at elderly people) to total public expenditure tends to be on average substantially lower in the new EU member states in the CEE (excluding Slovenia and Croatia) making up cluster 3. Second, the average ratio of total tax revenue to GDP is by 6 and 25 percentage points lower in this cluster in comparison with the generous benefits and the high taxes and public consumption clusters, respectively. A much lower tax burden becomes even more apparent when we compare the role of various taxes as a source of government revenue. For countries embodying the private mode of coordination model, the major source of tax revenue is the value-added tax (VATtTR equals on average 25% in cluster 3 compared to 20% in cluster 2 and 19% in cluster 1). The relative significance of income tax revenue is much lower in CEE economies (ITtTR amounts to 20% vs. 52% in the high taxes and public consumption cluster and 28% in the generous benefits model). The CEE countries not only have on average less money to spend on social protection, but most of the tax revenues comes from the consumption taxes, which put the tax burden on households with relatively lower incomes.

The foregoing pattern can be to some extent explained by the underdevelopment of tax collection institutions in CEE11 countries, which have it easier to collect indirect taxes, compared to taxes on income (especially personal income). Yet, the path-dependent nature of the mechanism which enhances the economic significance of indirect taxes can be easily recognized. A much lower relative weight of the income tax coupled with a very low top personal income tax rate (20% on average in the private mode of coordination cluster vs. 56% in the high taxes and public consumption and 48% in the generous benefits models) is a derivative of the power of special interests of the richest taxpayers' group. The popularity of flat (proportional) income taxes in the CEE economies is a consequence of a widespread belief that taxes are a kind of in-law robbery and hence there is nothing wrong in not paying them. If a personal income tax must be levied, it should be as low as possible and preferably proportional (rather than progressive). This attitude seems comprehensible in the case of people who gain on such tax policy design (i.e. high-income taxpayers), but this is not the case for the rest of the society. This holds particularly true once we realize that if a personal income tax incidence is relatively low and evenly spread in a society, other taxes must be higher, or else the government would face a hard budget constraint which would push down the level of spending on social protection, for example. In general, underdevelopment of the social protection system in the private mode of coordination cluster may be conceived as a derivative of strong and persistent informal institutions. They tend to constrain the possibilities for a profound tax reform, which would on the one hand increase the burden of income taxes while at the same time would be conducive to higher overall tax revenues, and by the same token to more funds available for public spending.

The coordination mix prevalent in cluster 3 seems to be coherent. A much lower income tax to GDP ratio, compared to both the high taxes and public consumption and the generous benefits clusters, and similarly a low benefits to GDP ratio, indicates that this is the market (private) mechanism of coordination that predominates in the CEE countries. Moreover, even when government takes a more active role in the social protection system, it boils down mostly to transfer payments or one-way, redistributive disbursement of money rather than the provision (through funding or directly producing) of public goods and services (the ratio of benefits to total expenditures for this cluster is above the level recorded in the high taxes and public consumption model). Seen from this perspective, it may be inferred that the social protection systems in cluster 3 meet the criteria of internal complementarity, leaving aside its effectiveness and efficiency. However, as it was pointed out in the introduction to this chapter, in the case of this particular institutional area, it is extremely difficult to measure how efficient is the set of existing social security institutions in protecting the society from undesirable risks. It may be argued, therefore, that the internal complementarity is being met as long as it keeps people supporting the government and the ruling party.

A more in-depth analysis of institutional architecture of the social protection system in the private mode of coordination cluster indicates that only in case of elderly people can the relative level of risk protection be deemed comparable to two other clusters. Obviously, the same ratio of the respective expenditure to GDP as in clusters 1 and 2 (or even higher than in the high taxes and public consumption model) does not necessarily entail the same absolute levels of monetary transfers disbursed to this social group. It is worth emphasizing in this context that in the case of public support for families, sick and disabled people, healthcare or the unemployed, the relative weight of public expenditures under these brackets, measured as a proportion of both total expenditure and GDP, tends to be substantially lower compared to clusters 1 and 2. Again, this fact can be explained mostly by demographic factors within the political economy framework. A growing number (as well as the proportion) of old-age persons in all countries in this cluster puts an upward pressure on the level of transfer payments channeled to this group. This in turn implies that the elderly are likely to gain in importance in the electoral process, which makes it hard to win the election without a considerable rechanneling of public expenditures to this category of voters. In order to change this pattern, a substantial shift in the median voter preferences regarding the hierarchy of social protection goals financed by the general government is needed.[8]

Based on the data provided in Table A7.4 (see Appendix), it is easy to ascertain that in case of five CEE11 countries (the Czech Republic, Poland, Lithuania, Slovakia and Bulgaria) representing the private mode of coordination model, the institutional distance to cluster 1 or the generous benefits model is smaller compared to the high taxes and public consumption model (cluster 2), yet it remains relatively large (only in Poland and Slovakia it does not exceed 0.5 standard deviation). For the rest of the CEE countries in this cluster (Estonia, Latvia, Hungary and Romania), the distance to cluster 2 is smaller compared to the generous benefits model, yet again, only in Hungary it does remain less than 1 standard deviation. Hence, it may be claimed that the institutional architecture of the social protection system in CEE countries significantly differs from the patterns established in both the high taxes and public consumption and the generous benefits models.

As far as the CEE11 outliers are concerned (Croatia and Slovenia), which in our empirical exercise were found to be part of cluster 1 comprising most of the Western EU member countries, at least the status of Slovenia appears to be clear. As it is the second-richest economy in the CEE region (in terms of GDP per capita in purchasing power parity [PPP]), it has managed to join the generous benefits cluster consisting of developed countries. However, the coordination mix, with a strong bias toward the private (market) mode of coordination, places Slovenia next to Greece, Portugal, Spain and Italy, rather than Sweden and Denmark. Much more interesting is the case of Croatia. Although this country is ranked much lower on the development ladder – in terms of GDP per capita in PPP – compared not only to Western European economies but also to the Czech Republic, Poland or Hungary, it succeeded in keeping the benefits to GDP ratio by approximately 2 percentage points above the mean level in the private mode of coordination cluster (a similar pattern holds for Slovenia, but with a 4 percentage points differential). As this variable ranked among the most important measures for the private mode of coordination cluster distinction (see Table A7.5 in the Appendix), Croatia could not have been classified together with the remaining CEE11 countries.

Furthermore, the tax structures in both Croatia and Slovenia differ considerably from the patterns established in the rest of the CEE region. The ratio of total tax revenue to GDP in Croatia is higher by more than 5 percentage points (by more than 2 percentage points in case of Slovenia) compared to the average in the private mode of coordination cluster. Even more remarkable are the pertinent differences regarding the top personal income tax rate. In 2014 it amounted to 47.2% in Croatia and 50% in Slovenia, whereas the average level in the private mode of coordination cluster totaled 20%. It may be contended, therefore, that the coordination mix in both countries included a much larger component – at least compared to other CEE11 countries – of government-led mechanism of coordination.

7.4 Evolving models of social protection system in CEE countries between 2005 and 2014

The model of social protection prevailing in most CEE11 countries reveals in many respects a patchwork nature and hence is highly unstable. The institutional architecture of the social protection area in the CEE states making up the private mode of coordination cluster is non-complementary and ineffective (at least seen from the social perspective), the existing institutions do not protect citizens from major risks and – what is even more important in the long run – do not generate positive externalities to the economy. The CEE11 economies, in which the shrinking labor supply seems to be the most acute challenge, suffer from a lack of economic mechanism that would raise the participation rate, in particular among the older-age cohorts.[9] In many instances, even if the new institutions which have been launched in the social protection area prove moderately successful with respect to their target dimension, they simultaneously give rise to negative externalities in other segments of the economy (e.g. the aforementioned family-oriented program "500 plus" in Poland, which adversely affected the participation rate among women). At the same time, the Polish government lowered the retirement age for both men and women. It goes without saying that the changes concerned were a derivative of public choice considerations as they predominantly served to win the parliamentary elections in 2015.

In a broader sense the patchwork nature of the private mode of coordination cluster in the social protection area is a consequence of the lack of a strategic vision of policymakers in the CEE countries with regard to this institutional domain. Only limited changes (the benefits to total expenditure ratio up by 10 percentage points and the top personal income tax rate slightly down; see Table A7.6 in the Appendix) recorded in the average values of analyzed variables between 2005 and 2014 indicate that neither the EU membership nor the global financial crisis of 2008 substantially reshaped this institutional area. And as is visible in the case of Poland, even if some essential changes have been implemented, they were much more an outcome of current, short-term political considerations rather than an element of a long-term strategic approach. Thus any unambiguous prediction of a possible evolution of the social protection models existing in the CEE11 countries seems very challenging.

The workable scenarios envisioning the most likely directions of social protection systems' evolution in the CEE region should account for a mismatch (or even a clash) between formal and informal institutions. On the one hand, households demanding higher standards of public services (education, healthcare, etc.) will not accept higher taxation and greater state involvement in the economy on the other hand. The pervasive social distrust or a small stock of social capital in CEE countries[10] (including in particular the government-citizens relationships) seems to be the biggest obstacle to change substantially the coordination mix in this institutional area. With the exception of Slovenia and Croatia, the two countries that for the time being proved immune to the policy of cutting taxes (especially income taxes), the rest of the CEE11 group persevered in keeping the tax burden relatively low, combined with a very limited scope of risk protection within their social safety nets. As long as the social attitudes toward the government (bureaucratic) mode of coordination remain negative, there are only small chances to change the current landscape.

Between 2005 and 2014, only in a limited number of CEE11 countries can one trace any kind of institutional convergence of the social protection system toward the generous benefits or high taxes and public consumption models (see Table 7.3). In the case of Bulgaria, the Czech Republic, Hungary and Poland, the distance between these countries and the two clusters encompassing mostly the EU14 member states grew substantially. This was most likely due to varying government responses of individual EU countries to the global financial crisis. In general, the whole EU lowered the level of protection against social risks, yet the scope of cuts in social transfers in CEE countries was much bigger. Croatia, Latvia and Slovenia shortened the distance to both clusters 1 and 2, but far more to the generous benefits model. The case of Slovenia seems to be particularly

Table 7.3 Change in absolute distance from 2014 clusters for each CEE11 country and each subspace dimension between 2005 and 2014 (standardized values)

	Cluster 1 *Generous benefits*	*Cluster 2* *High taxes and public consumption*	*Cluster 3* *Private mode of coordination*
Bulgaria	−1.46	−2.21	1.08
Croatia	0.20	0.05	0.25
Czech Republic	−0.82	−0.70	1.35
Estonia	−0.10	0.23	0.24
Hungary	−0.56	−0.03	0.46
Latvia	0.99	0.16	0.62
Lithuania	−0.40	0.07	1.16
Poland	−0.20	−0.57	0.44
Romania	0.85	−0.95	0.33
Slovakia	0.47	−0.20	0.27
Slovenia	0.54	0.47	−0.52
Median change	***−0.10***	***−0.03***	***0.44***

Source: Author's elaboration.

interesting. This country narrowed the institutional gap to the generous benefits cluster while at the same time experiencing a divergence trend vis-à-vis the private mode of coordination model. Hence, it sounds like a plausible assertion that this CEE country was the only example of a consistent institutional convergence toward the generous benefits model. In the case of Croatia, the second CEE country classified by the ORCLUS algorithm within this cluster, the distance to the generous benefits model diminished between 2005 and 2014. A similar trend occurred with regard to the private mode of coordination cluster, with the scope of institutional convergence being larger toward the latter model. It is far too early to tell if the similarity between Croatia and the generous benefits model is of a permanent or just a temporary nature. In other CEE11 countries, even if the distance to one of the clusters including the EU14 countries shortened, the similarity to the private mode of coordination cluster got larger. Worth mentioning is the case of Slovakia and Romania, with a different pattern emerging in the social protection area. In these two countries, the scope of the institutional convergence to the generous benefits model turned out substantially larger than the scale of a similar trend with regard to the private mode of coordination cluster.[11]

To sum up, the models of social protection system prevailing in CEE11 countries are in a state of flux, as their patchwork nature generates tensions between expectations of these countries' inhabitants who demand the same type of risk protection, as is the case in more advanced EU member states (EU14), and the capacity of the economies involved to finance these needs and the citizens' wariness or even aversion to the proliferation of a government-led (bureaucratic) mechanism of coordination in the economy (higher taxation, especially higher relative income taxes, combined with higher government spending). Finally, even if the relative level of public spending in CEE countries in core areas of the social safety net (healthcare, pensions and elderly people, sick and disabled persons, families with children and unemployed) catches up with the standards observed in the generous benefits or high taxes and public consumption clusters (which is not feasible without a substantial rise in the tax burden), the problem of unsatisfactory efficiency of public expenditures will remain a major challenge. The capacity of government administration to target the publicly financed assistance at the most economically handicapped social groups and the efficiency of public entities dealing with those funds (e.g. hospitals, bureaus and more broadly, publicly financed organizations) will be much harder to change.

Notes

1 As a quick reminder, in Chapter 2 we used the framework developed by Balassa and Samuelson (Balassa, 1964; Samuelson, 1964) to divide the six institutional areas concerned into two categories: "tradeables" (which emerged and then have evolved under at least a partial impact of non-domestic factors) and "non-tradeables" (in principle free of such influence).

2 It is a relatively straightforward task to measure the effectiveness of an institution through assessing the degree of achieving the goals set for this institution. Does the introduction of social transfers aimed at supporting families with many children translate into an

increase in the number of births and rising fertility of women (if this is the goal of this institution at all)? This is easy to check by comparing relevant indicators before and after the introduction of a new social policy instrument. However, the answer to the question about the efficiency of such an institution is much more difficult. Even if the fertility rate increased, it is difficult to assess whether alternative tools of a pro-natal policy (e.g. the development of state co-financed institutional forms of care for young children) would not ensure the same outcome at a lower cost. Clearly, one can use the tools of counter-factual analysis in this context, but it would be relatively simple to disprove the results of such an analysis. Hence, an objective assessment of the efficiency of specific institutions in the social protection area can turn out to be very difficult or even impossible.

3 As an example of such a scenario, one can use the fundamental switch in the institutional architecture of social protection in Poland, which took place after the last parliamentary elections in 2015. A new government program called *Rodzina 500 Plus* ("Family 500 Plus") was introduced. According to this program, all but the first children in a family are eligible for a public transfer payment equal to 500 zlotys a month (approximately 115 euros). A broadly shared consensus among sociologists and political scientists is that it was one of the key drivers of the electoral success of the PiS (Law and Justice) Party, and currently there is no major political party which would advocate terminating this program. The main reason for that was a widespread belief among the Polish society that the best type of policy that the government can launch in this area is a direct monetary transfer rather than a tax credit or increased public spending on nurseries or the educational infrastructure, for example. By the same token, the new public program (or a political project) assured complementarity between formal and informal institutions (i.e. laws and values). Simultaneously, the consensus among economists and demographers is that even if this new category of transfer payments positively affected the fertility rate (at least in the short run), the direct (ca. 25 billion zlotys or 5.8 billion euros) and indirect (e.g. a negative effect on the participation rate of women) costs of this program are far too high compared to its benefits. As a derivative, this substantial institutional change cannot be unequivocally assessed as the efficiency driver in that institutional area, even more so if its external complementarity with the "labor market and industrial relations" and "product market competition" areas is taken into account. On the other hand, it was efficient for both the political party that introduced this program and won the parliamentary elections and for the overwhelming majority of Polish households being the recipients of '500+' transfer payments. Given the reasonably good medium-run prospects of the Polish economy, winning the next parliamentary elections without maintaining this program seems impossible. In that way, an inefficient institutional change is likely to become a permanent component of Poland's social protection system.

4 If not specified otherwise, all data are taken from the Eurostat.

5 They are named using the etiquette introduced afterward by Amable.

6 See also Chapter 1 for a more general review of his approach and contribution to the field.

7 See Table A7.5 in the Appendix for a ranking of the most important characteristics of each model of social protection as identified by the ORCLUS algorithm.

8 Such a change is possible, as exemplified by an institutional switch that took place in Poland in 2016. It entailed a skyrocketing growth of transfer payments targeted at families under the "Family 500 Plus" program, which raised the ratio of this public expenditure line to both total expenditure and GDP to the level seen in the high taxes and public consumption cluster. See also endnote 3.

9 This category of tools includes, inter alia, active labor market policy, extending the age of professional activity and development of institutional forms of care for young children.

10 This is why these countries fit very well the category of "low-trust societies" developed by Fukuyama (1995).

11 It seems quite challenging to answer the question why the divergence trend in Romania and Slovakia was so strong compared to other countries representing the private mode of coordination model. One possible conjecture is that there was a significant proportion of the Roma minority in the total population in these two countries, which might have been a decisive explanatory variable for such an outcome. With the EU accession, this ethnic minority has become a recipient of growing financial transfers from the EU. Bearing in mind the fact that it is the relative level of transfers (as a share of GDP and total public expenditure) that determines the cohesion of the cluster encompassing nine CEE countries, their rising relative value in Romania and Slovakia may have determined the trend that differentiates these countries from the rest of the cluster involved.

References

Amable, B. (2003). *The diversity of modern capitalism*. Oxford: Oxford University Press.

Balassa, B. (1964). The purchasing power parity doctrine: A reappraisal. *The Journal of Political Economy*, 72.

Boeri, T. (2002). Let social policy models compete and Europe will win. *Paper presented at a conference hosted by the Kennedy School of Government*, Harvard University, 11–12 Apr.

Esping-Andersen, G. (1990). *The three worlds of welfare capitalism*. Princeton, NJ: Princeton University Press.

Estevez-Abe, M., Iversen, T. and Soskice, D. (1999). Social protection and the formation of skills: A reinterpretation of the Welfare State. *Paper presented during the 95th meeting of American Political Association*, Atlanta, 2–5 Sept.

Fenger, H.J.M. (2007). Welfare regimes in Central and Eastern Europe: Incorporating post-communist countries in a welfare regime Typology. *Contemporary Issues and Ideas in Social Sciences*, 3(2).

Fukuyama, F. (1995). *Trust. The social virtues and the creation of prosperity*. London: Penguin Books.

Rudra, N. (2007). Welfare states in developing countries: Unique or universal? *Journal of Politics*, 69(2), pp. 378–396.

Rudra, N. (2008). *Globalization and the race to the bottom in developing countries. Who really gets hurt?* Cambridge: Cambridge University Press.

Samuelson, P. (1964). Theoretical notes on trade problems. *Review of Economics and Statistics*, 46, pp. 145–154.

Sapir, A. (2006). Globalization and the reform of European social models. *Journal of Common Market Studies*, 44(2), pp. 369–390.

Wood, G. and Gough, I. (2006). A comparative welfare regime approach to global social policy. *World Development*, 34(10), pp. 1696–1712.

Appendix 7

Table A7.4 Distance from cluster in each subspace dimension (absolute, standardized values)

	Cluster 1 *Generous benefits*	*Cluster 2* *High taxes and public consumption*	*Cluster 3* *Private mode of coordination*
Austria	0	1.08	0.01
France	0	0.24	0.02
Greece	0	1.22	0.07
United Kingdom	0	1.55	0.30
Portugal	0	1.02	0.30
Italy	0	1.42	0.68
Slovenia	0	0.10	0.71
Croatia	0	1.48	0.79
Finland	0	0.55	0.91
Netherlands	0	0.18	1.17
Spain	0	0.56	1.41
Belgium	0	0.39	1.75
Ireland	0	1.00	2.41
Germany	0	1.08	3.65
Denmark	1.27	0	0.65
Sweden	0.71	0	1.42
Estonia	1.87	1.36	0
Hungary	0.63	0.61	0
Czech Republic	1.46	1.86	0
Poland	0.56	1.27	0
Latvia	1.97	1.78	0
Romania	3.67	2.66	0
Lithuania	1.59	1.89	0
Slovakia	0.47	0.50	0
Bulgaria	2.59	2.68	0

Source: Author's elaboration.

Table A7.5 Measures for cluster distinction in order of importance

Cluster 1 *Generous benefits*	*Cluster 2* *High taxes and public consumption*	*Cluster 3* *Private mode of coordination*
GOAtGDP	TRtGDP	BtE
GOAtE	ITtTR	BtGDP
TPIT	GOAtE	TRtGDP
BtE	GHtE	GOAtE
GHtGDP	GFtE	GSDtE
VATtTR	TPIT	VATtTR
BtGDP	GUtE	GHtGDP
GFtE	BtGDP	TPIT
TRtGDP	GHtGDP	GOAtGDP
GUtGDP	GPTGDP	GFtE
GSDtGDP	GFtGDP	GHtE
GUtE	GUtGDP	GUtE
GFtGDP	VATtTR	ITtTR
GHtE	GSDtE	GPTGDP
GSDtE	GSDtGDP	GSDtGDP
GPTGDP	GOAtGDP	GFtGDP
ITtTR	BtE	GUtGDP

Source: Author's elaboration.

Table A7.6 Change in value of variables between 2005 and 2014 (average for CEE11 countries)

	2005	*2014*	*Change between 2005 and 2014*
Benefits to total expenditures ratio	0.3	0.4	0.1
Benefits to GDP ratio	0.1	0.1	0.0
Public expenditures on healthcare to total expenditures ratio	0.1	0.1	0.0
Public expenditures on families to total expenditures ratio	0.0	0.0	0.0
Public expenditures on old age people to total expenditures ratio	0.2	0.2	0.0
Public expenditures on unemployed people to total expenditures ratio	0.0	0.0	0.0
Public expenditures on sick and disabled people to total expenditures ratio	0.1	0.1	0.0
Public expenditures on healthcare to GDP ratio	0.1	0.1	0.0
Public expenditures on families to GDP ratio	0.0	0.0	0.0
Public expenditures on old age people to GDP ratio	0.1	0.1	0.0
Public expenditures on pensions to GDP ratio	0.1	0.1	0.0
Public expenditures on sick and disabled people to GDP	0.0	0.0	0.0
Public expenditures on unemployed people to GDP	0.0	0.0	0.0
Income taxes revenue to total tax revenue ratio	0.2	0.2	0.0
Value-added taxes revenue to total tax revenue ratio	0.3	0.3	0.0
Total tax revenue to GDP ratio	0.2	0.2	0.0
Top personal income tax rate	0.3	0.3	−0.1

Source: Author's elaboration.

8 Knowledge system

Adam Karbowski

Introduction

According to Jackson and Deeg (2012), the knowledge system is one of the key institutional pillars that constitute each national political economy.[1] Knowledge systems encompass innovation, research and education components (Kearney, 2009; Farkas, 2011). In his Varieties of Capitalism (VoC) scheme, Amable (2003) considers the dynamic interactions between the education and research sector (the producer of ideas in the economy); the technology sector, which turns ideas into commercial opportunities; and the manufacturing sector, which transforms these commercial opportunities into marketable products and services (Edquist and Zabala, 2012; Karbowski, 2017). The education and research pillar is also oriented at supplying the national economy with an adaptable, mobile and well-trained labor force, as well as applicable knowledge. Certainly, the education and research pillar has to be properly supported by (1) the national financial system, which determines an implicit time horizon of innovation endeavors and plays an important role in selecting investment projects, and (2) the national system of labor relations, which shapes price competitiveness and cooperation in production relationships (Edquist and Zabala, 2012; Karbowski, 2017).

It is worth noting that in the Amablean (2003) concept, innovation considerations are present not only in the analysis of one of the five institutional domains (i.e. education system domain) of the national economy, but also as the ultimate goal of the social system (social system of innovation and production [SSIP]), that is, the ability of the social system to adapt and innovate (Amable et al., 1997; Karbowski, 2017).

The concept of the knowledge system underlines the relationships and synergies between innovation, research (and technology) and education as the main drivers of the knowledge economy (Veugelers and Mrak, 2009). It seems to be widely understood nowadays that progress in innovation, research (and technology) and education has to be looked for in a synchronized way – that is, the lack of progress in one domain can hinder advances in the other two areas. Further, careful attention should be paid to the links between the three aforementioned domains, because the absence of proper links between the components of the knowledge system can render advances in a single domain ineffective (Veugelers and Mrak, 2009; Soriano and Mulatero, 2010; Karbowski, 2017).

DOI: 10.4324/9780429056901-10

Over the last 20 years, knowledge systems worldwide have undergone profound transformation to emerge as the main drivers of industrial competitiveness, economic growth and socio-economic development (Amable, 2003; Kearney, 2009). It seems clear, then, why many countries in the world have shown increased readiness to strengthen their capacities for knowledge production. What is especially interesting is that this inclination has been rising across vastly different political, social, economic, technological and cultural contexts, each with their own capacity to respond (Karbowski, 2017).

Several official EU documents (for details, see Soriano and Mulatero, 2010) underline the importance of linking different institutional pillars of knowledge systems: innovation, research (and technology) and education. This need has been expressed and emphasized by the Swedish presidency of the European Union, for example, at the Lund conference (The Lund Declaration, 2009) and at the Gothenburg conference (Swedish Presidency of the European Union, 2009; Karbowski, 2015).

The three pillars of the knowledge system are peculiar from the economic and policy viewpoint due to the existence of externalities – both *intrinsic* externalities and externalities *between* the three domains considered (Romer, 1990; Grossman and Helpman, 1991; Aghion and Howitt, 1998; Soriano and Mulatero, 2010). Intrinsic externalities are derived from the differences between private and social returns to innovation, research and education, with the former being lower than the latter.[2] This results in underinvestment in the three discussed domains, giving rise to market failure and calling for public intervention (Hendrikse, 2003; Karbowski, 2015).

Externalities arise also between the innovation, research and education domains. According to Soriano and Mulatero (2010), the education sector produces skills that are indispensable inputs to research endeavors. Research activity, in turn, exerts pressure on education and that leads to education improvement (Soriano and Mulatero, 2009). Education plays the key role in fostering innovation in the economy. Following the arguments raised by Romer (1990), Grossman and Helpman (1991) and Aghion and Howitt (1998), innovation and economic growth are positive functions of the educational level of the labor force. Furthermore, proper education is required for the labor force to fully master new production techniques and organizational methods, as well as to easily adapt to innovative production and marketing solutions (Soriano and Mulatero, 2009; Karbowski, 2015).

Amable (2003) identified five clusters in the education and knowledge sector in his sample of countries (Rapacki et al., 2019). Amablean cluster 1 (Italy, Spain, Portugal, Greece and Austria) exhibits a relatively small number of graduates, a lagging educational system, a relatively high percentage of the labor force with only a primary education and relatively high unemployment among university graduates. Finland constitutes cluster 2, which can be characterized by a relatively strong public educational system and a very high share of science and technology students and graduates. Cluster 3 (the Netherlands, Belgium, France, Germany and Ireland) features a strong public education system with a special emphasis on secondary education. Denmark, Sweden and Norway constitute cluster 4. These countries display a very high level of public spending on education, which leads to high-quality education and high employment ratios both at the primary and secondary levels. Finally, cluster 5 (US, Japan, UK, Australia, Korea and Canada) is characterized by a tertiary education system with a relatively low level of public financing and rather low unemployment, especially for men.

When analyzing the field of knowledge production in Europe, Farkas (2011) identified four distinct groups of countries. According to this author, cluster 1 – the leading European innovators – consists of Finland, Sweden and Germany. In these countries, industry generates two-thirds of (high) total expenditures on research and development. This characteristic is accompanied by elevated employment levels in high-tech industries and knowledge-intensive services (Karbowski, 2017). Luxembourg constitutes a separate cluster. In that country, at a moderate level of research and development (R&D) expenditures overall, industry plays the dominant role in financing research and innovation. The export ratio of high-tech products is high, while knowledge-intensive services are at an average level (Karbowski, 2017). The third cluster comprises Ireland and the United Kingdom. Typical characteristics of this group include moderate levels of R&D expenditures and a significant role of the private sector in funding research and innovation. Moreover, the number of patents per capita is much smaller than in the leading innovating countries. The exports of high-tech products are high, similar to the share of employees in the knowledge-intensive services (Karbowski, 2017). A relatively low level of R&D expenditures is a typical feature of the fourth cluster, consisting of post-communist and Mediterranean countries. In terms of research and innovation financing, the share of government expenditure reaches 50%. This implies that the role of the private sector is relatively weak. The activities of multinational enterprises explain the smaller gap in the presence of high technologies compared with the remaining clusters (Karbowski, 2017; Rapacki et al., 2019).

According to Nölke and Vliegenthart (2009), decisions regarding R&D in CEE economies[3] are not dominated by concerns about the long-term innovation potential of the host country, but rather by their current profitability. In these economies, most R&D activity is conducted outside the region and then imported into the production process through transnational networks that bind together different places of production (Nölke and Vliegenthart, 2009; Karbowski, 2017). Innovation in CEE countries is predominantly imitative rather than creative (Hall and Soskice, 2001). Technological activities are skewed toward downstream non-analytical activities, like testing or standards (Karbowski, 2017; Rapacki et al., 2019).

The remainder of this chapter is organized as follows. In section 8.1, the set of institutional measures is presented that best describes the institutional environment of the knowledge systems in the CEE11 and EU14 countries. Based on the indicators selected, section 8.2 provides the empirical results of subspace clustering (cf., Czerniak, 2017) in the European Union in the institutional area involved. Section 8.3 discusses in more detail the pertinent results for Central and Eastern European economies. The chapter concludes with section 8.4, an analysis of institutional changes between 2005 and 2014 in CEE countries.

8.1 Measurement of institutions in the knowledge sector

The knowledge sector is embedded, in a sociological sense, in a broad set of institutions stretching from R&D organization and management through a national innovation system to a country's educational setup. These sets of institutions can be categorized into two groups: knowledge production institutions (e.g. R&D organization) and knowledge dissemination institutions (e.g. public education setup).

Based on the data provided by the OECD, Eurostat, the ECB and the World Bank, the following list of indicators has been used for analytical purposes in this chapter (see Table 8.1). Indicators 1–25 describe the knowledge production abilities of the sample economies, whereas indicators 26–42 describe these economies' knowledge dissemination abilities.

Table 8.1 Data sources

Variable name	*Variable description*	*Data source*
rd_exp_all	R&D expenditure (% of GDP, all sectors)	OECD
rd_exp_bes	R&D expenditure (% of GDP, business enterprise sector)	OECD
rd_exp_gs	R&D expenditure (% of GDP, government sector)	OECD
rd_exp_hes	R&D expenditure (% of GDP, higher education sector)	OECD
rd_pers_all	R&D personnel (% of the labor force, all sectors)	Eurostat
rd_pers_bes	R&D personnel (% of the labor force, business enterprise sector)	Eurostat
rd_pers_gs	R&D personnel (% of the labor force, government sector)	Eurostat
rd_pers_hes	R&D personnel (% of the labor force, higher education sector)	Eurostat
women_all	Share of women researchers (FTE, all sectors, %)	Eurostat
women_bes	Share of women researchers (business enterprise sector, %)	Eurostat
women_gs	Share of women researchers (government sector, %)	Eurostat
women_hes	Share of women researchers (higher education sector, %)	Eurostat
women_pns	Share of women researchers (private non-profit sector, %)	Eurostat
govern_rd_all	Share of government budget outlays on research and development (%)	OECD
govern_rd_civil	Share of government budget outlays on research and development in civil sector (%)	OECD
employ_know_serv	Employment in knowledge-intensive services (% of total employment)	Eurostat
employ_know_manu	Employment in high-tech manufacturing (% of total employment)	Eurostat
hr_st	Human resources in science and technology sector (% of active population)	Eurostat
turn_innov_all	Turnover (of enterprises) from innovation (% of total turnover) – total	Eurostat

(*Continued*)

Table 8.1 (Continued)

Variable name	*Variable description*	*Data source*
turn_innov_industry	Turnover (of enterprises) from innovation (% of total turnover) – industry sector	Eurostat
turn_innov_services	Turnover (of enterprises) from innovation (% of total turnover) – services sector	Eurostat
ht_exp	High-tech exports (% of total exports)	Eurostat
patents_epo	Patent applications to the European Patent Office (EPO) by priority year (per million inhabitants)	Eurostat
ht_patents_epo	High-tech patent applications to the EPO by priority year (per million inhabitants)	Eurostat
patents_uspto	Patents granted by the US Patent and Trademark Office by priority year (per million inhabitants)	Eurostat
pup_teach_rat	Pupil/teacher ratio in primary education	Eurostat
privat_exp_edu	Private expenditure on education (% of GDP)	World Bank
public_exp_edu	Public expenditure on education (% of GDP)	World Bank
house_broad_acc	Households with broadband (internet) access (% of households with at least one member aged 16 to 74)	Eurostat
school_expect	School expectancy (in years)	ECB
vocational_males	Pupils in upper secondary education enrolled in vocational stream (% of males)	Eurostat
vocational_females	Pupils in upper secondary education enrolled in vocational stream (% of females)	Eurostat
early_leavers	Early leavers from education and training (%)	ECB
young_peop	Young people neither in employment nor in education and training (15–24 years) – % of the total population in the same age group	Eurostat
employ_grad	Employment rates of recent graduates	Eurostat
st_grad	Science and technology graduates per 1,000 inhabitants aged 20–29	Eurostat
low_read_perf	Low reading literacy performance of pupils (share of 15-year-old pupils who are at level 1 or below of the PISA combined reading literacy scale)	Eurostat
foreign_lang	Foreign languages learned per pupil	Eurostat
comp_skill	Individuals' level of computer skills (individuals who have carried out one or two of six computer-related activities) – % of the total number of individuals aged 16–74	Eurostat
inter_skill	Individuals' level of internet skills (individuals who have carried out one or two of six internet-related activities) – % of the total number of individuals aged 16–74	Eurostat
atleast_upper	At least upper secondary educational attainment, age group 25–64, by sex (%)	Eurostat
tertiary	Tertiary educational attainment (age group 30–34), %	Eurostat

Source: Author's own compilation.

The dataset for the subspace clustering analysis covers 25 EU countries[4] (14 old member states and 11 CEE countries) and 42 institutional indicators, both input and output variables. The data were collected for the years 2005 and 2014 (or for the latest available record, but not prior to 2012).

It is worth pointing out that indicators 1–18 and 26–29 are, respectively, innovation and education input measures of institutional architecture in the knowledge sector, while indicators 19–25 and 30–42 constitute, respectively, innovation and education output measures of institutions concerned. It should also be noted that indicators 1–18 correspond to resources committed in innovation and R&D activities, that is, R&D expenditures on different assets, and human resources in R&D (allocated for various economic sectors). Indicators 19–25 correspond to outcomes of R&D activities, that is, patents and patent applications, turnover of business firms from innovation, and high-tech exports of enterprises. As regards the education subfield, measures 26–29 describe expenditures on education (both private and public), pupil/teacher structure in national education, and tangible assets basically important for high educational attainments of pupils (broadband internet access). Indicators 30–42 correspond to the outcomes or performance of an educational system, such as levels of skills (computer, internet, communication, comprehension, scientific and technological), labor market success (employment rates, participation in vocational streams) and educational attainment.

8.2 Models of capitalism in the European Union – knowledge system

As a result of the subspace clustering exercise, the following clusters in the area of knowledge creation (see Map 8.1) have been identified. Cluster 1, dubbed the *developed innovation-oriented* economies, comprises four EU countries (United Kingdom, Ireland, France and Belgium). Cluster 2, called *developed patent-oriented*, is formed of six other EU member states (Germany, Austria, Denmark, the Netherlands, Sweden and Finland). Cluster 3, labeled *stuck in the middle* countries, is formed by Italy and Slovenia. Cluster 4 is made up of 13 EU member states including 10 CEE countries as well as Greece, Portugal and Spain. Worth emphasizing is the fact that, based on the subspace clustering method and indicators selected, the overwhelming majority of CEE economies (10 out of 11) are found in the same cluster (4), while only Slovenia was "allocated" to cluster 3. Furthermore, it seems that almost all CEE countries share similar institutional traits in the field of knowledge creation with three Mediterranean economies: Greece, Spain and Portugal.

Table A8.5 in the Appendix provides the ranking of indicators that allowed to distinguish various clusters in the knowledge subsystem for all 25 EU economies concerned. Table A8.4 in the Appendix shows the distances from the identified clusters for all countries considered. *Developed innovation-oriented* countries fall into cluster 1. In contrast to other identified models of capitalism in the knowledge area, they are characterized by medium-high level of employment in knowledge-intensive services, a medium share of women researchers (full-time equivalent

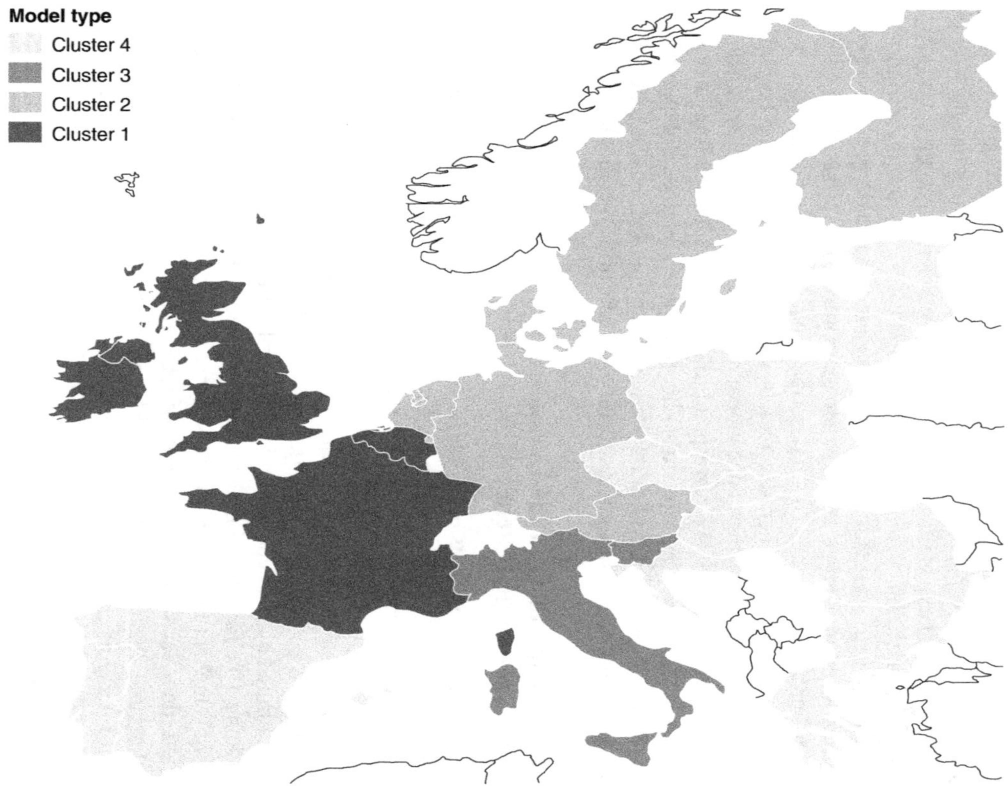

Map 8.1 Models of capitalism in the European Union: knowledge system

Source: Author's elaboration.

[FTE], all sectors), very high turnover from innovation in the industry sector, a medium level of patents granted by the US Patent and Trademark Office, a low or medium share of female pupils in upper secondary education enrolled in vocational stream, a medium level of patent applications to the European Patent Office, high turnover from innovation in all sectors, and a relatively low proportion of 15-year-old pupils who are at level 1 or below of the PISA combined reading literacy scale. According to Verspagen, Noben and Sluismans (2016), innovation in the countries classified in this cluster is policy-led. Innovation primarily becomes a public policy interest, and public policy initiatives raise both industrial and service-oriented firms' innovative actions to more elevated levels.

Cluster 2 embraces *developed patent-oriented* countries. They exhibit a relatively high level of patent applications to the European Patent Office, a relatively high level of patents granted by the US Patent and Trademark Office, high turnover from innovation in the industry sector, medium-high turnover in the services sector, a relatively low share of women researchers in business enterprise sector and a medium-high such share in private non-profit sector, a high proportion of households with broadband (internet) access, and very high individual levels of internet skills. According to Verspagen, Noben and Sluismans (2016), in Germany (i.e. the core country in this cluster) there is a strong emphasis on science-based innovation supported by public policy and industrial property law, entrepreneurial universities and secondary schools (with well-developed traineeship programs), and research institutes that work in close recognition of firm interests. All innovation actors are oriented at obtaining patents, also due to several strategic reasons (Boldrin and Levine, 2012). The key motives of strategic use of patents include improving the reputation of an enterprise, making operating costs of the enterprise's rivals higher and raising entry barriers in a market.

Cluster 3, dubbed *stuck in the middle*, reveals a number of distinctive traits compared to other models of capitalism identified in this area. It is characterized by a medium level of patents granted by the US Patent and Trademark Office, a medium level of patent applications to the European Patent Office, a medium level of employment in knowledge-intensive services, a medium share of female pupils in upper secondary education enrolled in a vocational stream, a medium share of women researchers in the business enterprise sector, private non-profit sector, and in all sectors (FTE), medium turnover from innovation in the industry sector, and a relatively high share of early leavers from education and training (especially for Italy). In brief, countries representing cluster 3 achieve average scores in terms of knowledge production and dissemination, with an exceptionally high share of early leavers from education and training.

As can be inferred from the foregoing description, cluster 3 is a mixture of institutional features of the German system (developed traineeship programs in secondary education, close cooperation of secondary schools with business firms, significant focus on patenting and patent protection) and those of the "aspiring" countries from cluster 4 (relatively weak universities, at best medium employment in knowledge-intensive services, relatively low high-tech exports). This cluster is characterized by the exceptionally high rate of early leavers from education and training. In future years, it may become a serious impediment to catching up with the developed clusters in the knowledge system. Therefore, this cluster seems to be trapped in the transitory setting (or "stuck in the middle") between developing and developed "knowledge clusters". Also, the output measures of institutions (the level of patents granted, share of pupils in upper secondary education enrolled in vocational stream, turnover from innovation) indicate that countries found in cluster 3 are only average performers, and there are no clear prospects for a speedy transition to a level prevalent in the developed knowledge production cluster (R&D expenditures, human resources in science and technology, and employment in high-tech manufacturing and knowledge-intensive services are lower than in the developed European knowledge clusters).

Cluster 4 can be labeled "aspiring" as (in contrast to other identified clusters) the constituting countries exhibit relatively low scores in terms of both knowledge creation and dissemination, the exception being comparatively high tertiary education attainments of citizens. Since this cluster is formed mostly by CEE countries, its more comprehensive and in-depth description is provided in the next section, devoted to Central and Eastern Europe.

Based on Table 8.2, we may identify two types of major innovation institutional setups. The first is a developed knowledge system with two variants (oriented at

Table 8.2 Cluster-average values for all variables

Variable name	*Cluster 1 Developed innovation oriented*	*Cluster 2 Developed patent oriented*	*Cluster 3 Stuck in the middle*	*Cluster 4 Aspiring*
rd_exp_all	2.0	2.9	1.8	1.1
rd_exp_bes	1.4	1.9	1.3	0.5
rd_exp_gs	0.2	0.2	0.2	0.2
rd_exp_hes	0.4	0.8	0.3	0.3
rd_pers_all	1.4	1.7	1.2	0.8
rd_pers_bes	0.8	1.1	0.7	0.3
rd_pers_gs	0.1	0.1	0.2	0.2
rd_pers_hes	0.5	0.5	0.3	0.3
women_all	32.4	28.4	35.5	41.5
women_bes	22.0	18.9	23.9	29.8
women_gs	36.9	40.8	47.4	50.1
women_hes	41.0	42.3	41.4	45.4
women_pns	43.4	48.9	41.1	43.7
govern_rd_all	1.1	1.7	0.9	1.1
govern_rd_civil	94.2	98.3	99.4	98.9
turn_innov_all	12.0	11.0	10.8	9.6
turn_innov_industry	17.9	15.4	13.2	12.0
turn_innov_services	10.2	7.0	7.8	6.3
ht_exp	7.7	7.8	6.4	8.4
employ_know_serv	46.7	45.0	34.8	34.1
employ_know_manu	4.5	5.5	7.8	5.0

Variable name	*Cluster 1 Developed innovation oriented*	*Cluster 2 Developed patent oriented*	*Cluster 3 Stuck in the middle*	*Cluster 4 Aspiring*
hr_st	52.6	53.2	40.3	38.9
patents_epo	107.9	271.5	67.7	15.5
ht_patents_epo	20.6	33.3	3.5	2.1
patents_uspto	62.1	110.9	21.2	6.7
school_expect	17.6	19.1	17.8	17.6
vocational_males	47.9	63.7	71.3	54.9
vocational_females	46.0	55.7	53.6	41.1
pup_teach_rat	17.2	13.5	14.0	13.5
privat_exp_edu	0.8	0.5	0.6	0.5
public_exp_edu	6.1	6.5	5.0	4.5
early_leavers	8.7	7.9	9.9	10.1
young_peop	11.5	6.8	15.5	13.2
employ_grad	79.6	85.9	60.0	73.3
st_grad	19.6	16.6	16.3	16.2
low_read_perf	15.3	16.1	20.3	21.4
foreign_lang	1.2	1.7	1.8	1.6
house_broad_acc	84.3	89.0	76.0	73.1
comp_skill	16.8	16.8	12.0	15.2
inter_skill	32.3	31.2	23.5	23.8
atleast_upper	78.3	83.6	73.4	80.8
tertiary	47.5	43.7	34.4	37.4

Source: Author's elaboration.

patenting and traineeships, as in Germany, or oriented at industry and services' innovation and tertiary education, as in the UK). The second type is a developing knowledge system with two variants (average in terms of patenting with a relatively strong traineeship program, such as in Slovenia, or relatively weak in all measures, seen in Bulgaria).

8.3 Models of capitalism in Central and Eastern Europe

As already indicated in the preceding section, 10 out of 11 CEE countries analyzed in this book (apart from Slovenia) form a separate cluster in the field of knowledge production and dissemination, together with Greece, Spain and Portugal (cluster 4).

Cluster 4 was dubbed "aspiring" as (unlike in the remaining three clusters) the countries involved exhibit a relatively low level of patent applications, comparatively small value of R&D expenditures, relatively low public and private expenditures on education, a smaller-than-average share of households with broadband internet access, and a relatively low individual level of internet skills. However, it is worth noting that citizens of the countries making up this cluster (especially in the CEE region) are relatively well-educated (medium-high levels of tertiary educational attainment).

Looking back, innovation, research and (higher) education in the 1990s were relatively low priorities in CEE countries, with chronic underfunding of their research institutions and universities as a permanent feature. The policymakers in the region strove to speedily catch up with the West and join the European Union, with its political standards and its levels of material affluence. At the outset of systemic transformation from a command-driven to a market-driven logic, knowledge systems in the CEE countries exhibited the following set of core characteristics as part of their command-economy legacy: (1) research and higher education heavily centralized as parts of the central planning system; (2) strong bureaucratic control over the knowledge production system; (3) research priorities and goals, curricula guidelines, and requirements for filling research and teaching positions defined and closely monitored by the government and communist party apparatus; (4) higher education as a unitary system that lacked short programs or bachelor's degrees; and (5) funding of research institutions and universities highly dependent on the government and based on incremental budgeting (Mateju et al., 2007; Kwiek, 2014).

The subsequent transformation of post-communist knowledge systems may be viewed as resulting from several interrelated and path-dependent pressures. First, there were pressures to continue with routines and organized practices inherited from the communist period. Second, there were pressures to survive the economic "shock therapies" of the early 1990s (particularly in Estonia, Slovakia, the Czech Republic and Poland). Third, there were pressures to design and employ new routines and practices, responding to the guiding principles of the reforms in the early 1990s (i.e. academic democracy, academic freedom and institutional autonomy) (Kwiek, 2014).

As noted by Nölke and Vliegenthart (2009), the 1990s brought significant cutbacks in government spending on research and education in CEE countries. The governments in these countries found it difficult to invest in public research and education given the fiscal constraints that went together with the intense competition for foreign direct investment (FDI) (Bohle and Greskovits, 2007). The system of vocational training in the early 1990s was practically the same in all CEE countries: large state-controlled enterprises cooperated with state-run technical schools (Buchen, 2004). This led to firm-specific and industry-specific skill formation. Along with the collapse of numerous state-owned enterprises at the beginning of transition, technical schools lost the opportunity to train pupils appropriately (Roberts, 2001; Buchen, 2004; Karbowski, 2017). Consequently, a new way of vocational training had to be found. Most CEE countries decided to re-orient their educational systems toward meeting the labor demands of transnational corporations (vocational training schemes have been restructured to meet those demands; see Roberts, 2001; Nölke and Vliegenthart, 2009). Further, the curricula of primary and secondary schools (and tertiary schools, to some extent) have been redesigned with a view to enhance the development of more versatile human capital which could be employed more broadly throughout the economy. This triggered a fundamental change in the system of education and training (i.e. a shift of emphasis toward producing general skills). Public vocational training dominated the system and not much vocational training occurred at the workplace (Nölke and Vliegenthart, 2009). Most CEE countries abandoned the "old" (socialist) system of vocational training and thereby moved in this respect into the direction of a liberal market economy (LME) pattern.

According to Verspagen, Noben and Sluismans (2016), CEE countries found in cluster 4 in our study generally tend to have innovation styles that are strongly dependent on external knowledge and competencies, such as supply chain-based innovation and external sourcing.

Slovenia turned out to be unique among CEE11 countries and chose a different direction. The "old" system of vocational training was put on a new basis by introducing a dual system of apprenticeships, very much like the German scheme (Buchen, 2004; Karbowski, 2017). Apprentices started to be trained both at business firms and in vocational schools, thereby acquiring both firm-specific and industry-specific skills (Geržina et al., 2000; Buchen, 2004; Karbowski, 2017). The development of company-specific skills is typical in the large and most advanced Slovenian firms. This is consistent with the Varieties of Capitalism (VoC) arguments regarding the generation of co-specific assets in CMEs (coordinated market economies) (for details, see Crowley and Stanojević, 2011).

Slovenia, in terms of its institutional architecture in the knowledge production domain, is reckoned close to the coordinated market economy benchmark, unique among the CEE11 countries. This country's uniqueness has been also confirmed by the subspace clustering method, since Slovenia turned out to be the only CEE economy that was not classified in the "aspiring" cluster. What, then, makes Slovenia so special?

According to Crowley and Stanojević (2011, p. 269), from the very outset of systemic transformation, Slovenia deliberately chose a gradualist rather than "shock therapy" approach to market reforms, with a relatively low level of FDI, a slow pace of privatization and adoption of seemingly rigid labor relations. As already mentioned, the standards of vocational education suffered a marked deterioration in Central and Eastern European countries, and these economies significantly moved toward more general skills training, as in the liberal capitalist model. Slovenia, in turn, implemented a dual system of apprenticeships, with a strong focus on the development of company-specific skills which were successfully used by large and most advanced Slovenian enterprises. This allowed for a relatively high innovativeness of Slovenian firms (in comparison with other CEE11 countries), reflected in the highest values of pertinent output measures of institutional architecture in the CEE11 group, including those showing in particular patenting activity, educational attainments and turnover from innovation.

To wrap up this part of the discussion, it may be argued that Slovenia, being part of cluster 3 in our study, embodies a mixture of institutional characteristics typical of the German system and those of the "aspiring" countries from cluster 4, described in more detail earlier in this section.

8.4 CEE countries' evolution in the period 2005–2014

Based on the data in Table 8.3 and Table A8.6 (see Appendix), one can trace the process of convergence or divergence of the institutional architectures inherent to

Table 8.3 Change in absolute distance from 2014 clusters for each CEE11 country and each subspace dimension between 2005 and 2014 (standardized values)

Country	*Cluster 1 Developed innovation oriented*	*Cluster 2 Developed patent oriented*	*Cluster 3 Stuck in the middle*	*Cluster 4 Aspiring*
Bulgaria	4.16	−1.07	1.96	0.38
Croatia	4.12	−0.06	3.13	0.21
Czech Republic	3.43	1.86	2.48	0.22
Estonia	3.68	−2.09	0.75	1.13
Hungary	2.76	0.08	0.96	0.22
Latvia	3.35	−1.00	1.44	0.52
Lithuania	3.74	−0.88	1.32	0.66
Poland	3.40	0.16	1.75	0.12
Romania	4.17	−1.88	1.81	0.18
Slovenia	4.01	2.05	3.27	0.27
Slovakia	4.03	1.82	3.93	0.11
Median change	***3.74***	***−0.06***	***1.81***	***0.22***

A positive value means moving closer to a given cluster; a negative value means moving farther from a given cluster.

Source: Author's elaboration.

the knowledge creation area in CEE11 countries between 2005 and 2014 relative to four European knowledge production clusters. In this period, the CEE economies shortened most remarkably (in terms of a median change) the institutional distance (moved closer) to cluster 1 or "developed innovation-oriented" countries. At the same time, they also revealed symptoms of a clear-cut institutional convergence, though about half the size of the former, to cluster 3 (i.e. the patterns prevailing in Italy and Slovenia). The distance to clusters 2 and 4 remained roughly unchanged.

The reduction of the institutional distance of CEE11 countries to cluster 1 occurred mainly across five dimensions: (1) a rapid increase in the share of households with broadband access to the internet, (2) a significant rise in the level of tertiary educational attainment, (3) a growing proportion of science and technology graduates, (4) an increase in the share of human resources in the science and technology sector, and (5) improved performance in the field of patent applications and patents granted.

These achievements resulted mainly from secondary and higher education reforms that took place in CEE11 countries from the early 2000s on. Reforms in education in the region were intended, implicitly or explicitly, to bring Central and Eastern European pupils, academics and students back into what was regarded the European academic community (Kwiek, 2014). Clearly, national reference points in education reforms were accompanied by European reference points, especially when the Bologna Process started and when this European initiative began to be used in national contexts in the CEE region as a justification for further reforms

(Kwiek, 2014). While in the transition period of the early 1990s models of reforming education were coming mostly from the World Bank, in the EU pre-accession period of the 2000s and in particular after the EU accession the role of both the Bologna Process and supranational European initiatives (e.g. the implementation of the Lisbon 2000 agenda) has been gradually growing (Kwiek, 2014). Today, the role of the European Union and various forms of EU funding, especially EU structural funds, is fundamental for national knowledge systems in the region (Kwiek, 2014). These institutional changes allow to explain a remarkable reduction of the institutional distance of CEE11 countries to the developed European knowledge production cluster (i.e. cluster 1 in our study) between 2005 and 2014.

The current state of the knowledge area in CEE11 countries is most likely transitory. The transformation that started in the early 1990s led to a liberalization of the knowledge subsystem and strong dependence on transnational corporations (Nölke and Vliegenthart, 2009) and foreign capital (Slovenia remained an exception). In the forthcoming years, a stronger focus on vocational training, development of company-specific skills, science and technology education, and higher patent activity of firms can be very beneficial to CEE economies. Simultaneously, a tighter industrial cooperation between countries of the CEE region would also be welcome.

Notes

1 Jackson and Deeg (2012) identify six institutional pillars of the national economy. Apart from the knowledge subsystem, they also include finance, corporate governance and responsibility, industrial relations, industrial policy and the welfare state.

2 This difference between private and social returns is one of the major constituents of endogenous growth theory (Romer, 1990). Under Romer's framework, innovations give rise to positive externalities in the national economy. Positive externalities imply that firms cannot fully capture the social benefits of their inventions, which, in effect, results in private underinvestment in R&D (Veugelers and Del Rey, 2014).

3 As a reminder, dubbed by these two authors the "dependent market economies" (DME) in their extended typology of the varieties of capitalism. For more details, see Chapter 2.

4 All current European Union members apart from Cyprus, Luxembourg and Malta.

References

Aghion, P. and Howitt, P. (1998). *Endogenous growth theory*. Cambridge, MA: MIT Press.

Amable, B. (2003). *The diversity of modern capitalism*. Oxford: Oxford University Press.

Amable, B., Barre, R. and Boyer, R. (1997). *Les Systemes d'innovation a l'ere de la globalisation*. Paris: Economica.

Bohle, D. and Greskovits, B. (2007). Neoliberalism, embedded neoliberalism, and neocorporatism: Paths towards transnational capitalism in Central-Eastern Europe. *West European Politics*, 30(3), pp. 443–466.

Boldrin, M. and Levine, D. (2012). *The case against patents*, Federal Reserve Bank of St. Louis Working Paper Series.

Buchen, C. (2004). What kind of capitalism is emerging in Eastern Europe? Varieties of capitalism in Estonia and Slovenia. *Paper presented at the 13th research seminar on managing the economic transition*, University of Cambridge, 12 Mar.

Crowley, S. and Stanojević, M. (2011). Varieties of capitalism, power resources, and historical legacies: Explaining the Slovenian exception. *Politics & Society*, 39, pp. 268–295.

Czerniak, A. (2017). Housing policies and varieties of residential capitalism in CEE countries. *Paper presented at the 3rd international conference on the role of state in varieties of capitalism (SVOC)* organized by the Hungarian Academy of Sciences and Central European University, Budapest, 30 Nov. – 1 Dec.

Edquist, C. and Zabala, J. (2012). Knowledge-intensive entrepreneurship, national systems of innovation and European varieties of capitalism: A conceptual framework. *AEGIS technical report.*

Farkas, B. (2011). The Central and Eastern European model of capitalism. *Post-Communist Economies*, 23, pp. 15–34.

Geržina, S, Vranješ, P. and Cek, M. (2000). Modernisation of vocational education and training in Slovenia 1999 – Final Report, National VET Observatory Slovenia.

Grossman, G. and Helpman, E. (1991). *Innovation and growth in the global economy.* Cambridge, MA: The MIT Press.

Hall, P. and Soskice, D. (2001). *Varieties of capitalism. The institutional foundations of comparative advantage.* Oxford: Oxford University Press.

Hendrikse, G. (2003). *Economics and management of organizations: Co-ordination, motivation and strategy.* London: McGraw – Hill.

Jackson, G. and Deeg, R. (2012). The Long-term trajectories of institutional change in European capitalism. *Journal of European Public Policy*, 19, pp. 1109–1125.

Karbowski, A. (2015). Set out EIT strategic agenda. Literature review and data collection. *Report accepted by the European Commission, project "Investigating the Impact of the Innovation Union"*, Horizon 2020, Brussels.

Karbowski, A. (2017). Institutional underpinnings of the development of knowledge subsystems in Central and Eastern Europe. *Ekonomista*, 1, pp. 30–46.

Kearney, M. (2009). Higher education, research and innovation: Charting the course of the changing dynamics of the knowledge society. In: V. Meek, U. Teichler and M. Kearney, eds., *Report on the UNESCO forum on higher education, research and knowledge 2001–2009*, Kassel: INCHER-Kassel.

Kwiek, M. (2014). Changing higher education and Welfare States in postcommunist Central Europe: New Contexts Leading to New Typologies? *CPP RPS*, 64.

The Lund Declaration (2009). *Europe must focus on the grand challenges of our time*, Lund, 8 July.

Mateju, P., Rehakova, B. and Simonova, N. (2007). The Czech Republic: Structural growth of inequality in access to higher education. In: Y. Shavit, R. Arum and A. Gamoran, eds., *Stratification in higher education. A comparative study.* Stanford: Stanford University Press.

Nölke, A. and Vliegenthart, A. (2009). Enlarging the varieties of capitalism: The emergence of dependent market economies in East Central Europe. *World Politics*, 61(4), pp. 670–702.

Rapacki, R., Gardawski, J., Czerniak, A., Horbaczewska, B., Karbowski, A., Maszczyk, P. and Próchniak, M. (2019). Emerging varieties of post-communist capitalism in Central and Eastern Europe: Where do we stand? *Europe-Asia Studies*, forthcoming.

Roberts, K. (2001). The new East European model of education, training, and youth employment. *Journal of Education and Work*, 14, pp. 315–328.

Romer, P. (1990). Endogenous technological change. *Journal of Political Economy*, XCVIII, pp. 71–102.

Soriano, F. and Mulatero, F. (2009). *Connecting the dots*, JRC European Commission, 55672 EN.

Soriano, F. and Mulatero, F. (2010). Knowledge policy in the EU: From the Lisbon strategy to Europe 2020. *Journal of Knowledge Economy*, 1, pp. 289–302.

Swedish Presidency of the European Union. (2009). *The knowledge triangle shaping the future of Europe*. Gothenburg, 31 Aug. – 2 Sept.

Verspagen, B., Noben, L. and Sluismans, R. (2016). Innovation systems and the role of public policy in the European innovation union, *I3U D9–3 preliminary report*, Maastricht, Submitted to the European Commission.

Veugelers, R. and Del Rey, E. (2014). The contribution of universities to innovation, (regional) growth and employment, *EENEE Analytical Report No. 18*, Leuven.

Veugelers, R. and Mrak, M. (2009). *The knowledge economy and catching up member states of the EU*, Knowledge Economists Policy Brief, 5, European Commission, Brussels.

Appendix 8

Table A8.4 Distance from cluster in each subspace dimension (absolute, standardized values)

Country	*Cluster 1 Developed innovation oriented*	*Cluster 2 Developed patent oriented*	*Cluster 3 Stuck in the middle*	*Cluster 4 Aspiring*
Belgium	0	0.05	1.73	1.04
Ireland	0	1.66	0.01	0.14
France	0	0.83	0.35	0.57
United Kingdom	0	0.86	0.70	1.24
Germany	1.50	0	0.73	1.06
Denmark	0.27	0	0.88	2.23
Austria	1.06	0	0.97	2.03
Sweden	0.91	0	1.11	1.77
Finland	0.46	0	1.46	3.30
Netherlands	0.73	0	1.55	1.81
Italy	1.80	0.09	0	1.01
Slovenia	1.29	0.36	0	0.64
Greece	1.53	0.15	0.03	0
Czech Republic	2.52	0.36	0.19	0
Slovakia	1.61	0.96	0.39	0
Spain	1.60	0.55	0.41	0
Croatia	1.55	1.03	0.60	0
Latvia	1.31	2.41	0.67	0
Lithuania	1.26	1.22	0.68	0
Poland	2.31	0.79	0.74	0
Portugal	0.18	0.63	1.01	0
Estonia	1.54	2.64	1.11	0
Hungary	2.30	0.49	1.29	0
Bulgaria	1.47	1.56	1.72	0
Romania	2.81	2.21	1.87	0

Source: Author's elaboration.

Table A8.5 Measures for cluster distinction in order of importance

Cluster 1 Developed innovation oriented	*Cluster 2 Developed patent oriented*	*Cluster 3 Stuck in the middle*	*Cluster 4 Aspiring*
employ_know_serv	patents_epo	patents_uspto	patents_epo
women_all	patents_uspto	employ_know_serv	patents_uspto
turn_innov_industry	turn_innov_industry	patents_epo	ht_patents_epo
patents_uspto	turn_innov_services	vocational_females	tertiary
vocational_females	women_bes	women_pns	women_bes
patents_epo	house_broad_acc	women_bes	house_broad_acc
turn_innov_all	women_pns	women_all	inter_skill
low_read_perf	inter_skill	turn_innov_industry	women_gs
house_broad_acc	employ_know_serv	early_leavers	employ_know_serv
comp_skill	tertiary	ht_exp	turn_innov_industry
turn_innov_services	vocational_males	vocational_males	hr_st
atleast_upper	employ_grad	employ_know_manu	ht_exp
st_grad	atleast_upper	inter_skill	govern_rd_civil
vocational_males	hr_st	tertiary	turn_innov_all
women_hes	women_all	women_gs	st_grad
women_bes	turn_innov_all	employ_grad	employ_grad
young_peop	women_gs	hr_st	comp_skill
ht_patents_epo	st_grad	atleast_upper	turn_innov_services
ht_exp	vocational_females	govern_rd_civil	employ_know_manu
pup_teach_rat	ht_patents_epo	turn_innov_all	women_all
employ_grad	low_read_perf	turn_innov_services	school_expect
tertiary	young_peop	low_read_perf	pup_teach_rat
women_gs	employ_know_manu	house_broad_acc	women_hes
govern_rd_civil	ht_exp	young_peop	young_peop
early_leavers	rd_pers_bes	st_grad	early_leavers
employ_know_manu	pup_teach_rat	ht_patents_epo	rd_pers_bes
rd_pers_bes	govern_rd_civil	women_hes	women_pns
inter_skill	rd_pers_all	rd_exp_hes	vocational_males
hr_st	women_hes	rd_pers_hes	low_read_perf
women_pns	early_leavers	govern_rd_all	public_exp_edu
rd_pers_hes	comp_skill	rd_exp_bes	atleast_upper
govern_rd_all	school_expect	public_exp_edu	rd_pers_all
rd_exp_bes	rd_exp_hes	rd_pers_bes	vocational_females
rd_exp_gs	rd_pers_hes	pup_teach_rat	rd_exp_hes
foreign_lang	rd_exp_bes	school_expect	rd_exp_bes
rd_pers_all	public_exp_edu	rd_pers_gs	rd_pers_hes
rd_exp_hes	foreign_lang	rd_exp_gs	govern_rd_all
rd_pers_gs	rd_pers_gs	foreign_lang	rd_exp_gs
public_exp_edu	privat_exp_edu	privat_exp_edu	privat_exp_edu
privat_exp_edu	govern_rd_all	rd_pers_all	foreign_lang
school_expect	rd_exp_gs	rd_exp_all	rd_pers_gs
rd_exp_all	rd_exp_all	comp_skill	rd_exp_all

Source: Author's elaboration.

Table A8.6 Change in value of variables between 2005 and 2014 (average for CEE11 countries)

Variable name	*2005*	*2014*	*Change between 2005 and 2014*
rd_exp_all	0.77	1.15	0.38
rd_exp_bes	0.34	0.63	0.29
rd_exp_gs	0.21	0.22	0.01
rd_exp_hes	0.22	0.30	0.09
rd_pers_all	0.59	0.76	0.18
rd_pers_bes	0.18	0.32	0.14
rd_pers_gs	0.17	0.17	0.00
rd_pers_hes	0.23	0.27	0.04
women_all	40.89	40.97	0.08
women_bes	32.06	29.46	−2.60
women_gs	47.59	49.30	1.71
women_hes	41.57	45.80	4.23
women_pns	37.64	40.38	2.75
govern_rd_all	0.93	0.97	0.04
govern_rd_civil	98.02	98.83	0.81
turn_innov_all	12.57	8.85	−3.72
turn_innov_industry	15.05	11.49	−3.56
turn_innov_services	9.13	4.97	−4.15
ht_exp	7.34	9.68	2.35
employ_know_serv	29.04	32.73	3.69
employ_know_manu	5.86	5.96	0.10
hr_st	32.76	39.48	6.72
patents_epo	10.43	19.28	8.85
ht_patents_epo	1.20	2.11	0.91
patents_uspto	5.39	7.37	1.98
school_expect	17.22	17.60	0.38
vocational_males	59.59	59.15	−0.44
vocational_females	44.98	44.16	−0.82
pup_teach_rat	14.83	14.30	−0.53
privat_exp_edu	0.54	0.53	−0.01
public_exp_edu	4.65	4.57	−0.08
early_leavers	10.74	8.81	−1.93
young_peop	13.95	12.70	−1.25
employ_grad	73.88	75.77	1.89
st_grad	10.23	16.40	6.17
low_read_perf	26.59	21.75	−4.85
foreign_lang	1.37	1.60	0.23
house_broad_acc	12.55	73.27	60.73
comp_skill	13.82	15.91	2.09
inter_skill	22.18	24.36	2.18
atleast_upper	81.69	87.30	5.61
tertiary	21.28	37.49	16.21

Source: Author's elaboration.

9 Housing market

Adam Czerniak

Introduction

The housing market is directly and very strongly embedded in its institutional environment, which is constructed both of formal laws or regulations and informal habits or preferences. These institutions constitute the allocation mechanisms of houses – how rental, social or owner-occupied residential estates are acquired, disposed and transferred from one market actor to another. The main driver of the institutional framework is the government's housing policy. It influences, more or less indirectly, market participants, shaping their actions, preferences and even valuation mechanisms, in particular as regards the tenure choice (Bourdieu, 2005).

Although institutions shaping housing markets are one of the key elements of the economic order of Western developed and post-socialist countries, they are not considered as separate institutional dimensions in standard classifications of the models of capitalism, such as the Diversity of Capitalism (Amable, 2003) or the Varieties of Capitalism (Hall and Soskice, 2001) frameworks. Only after the recent global financial crisis and the burst of the price bubble on the US real estate market (Shiller, 2009) did scholars begin to examine the institutional environment of the housing market, or as it is called in the literature, "varieties of residential capitalism" (Schwartz and Seabrooke, 2009). Schwartz and Seabrooke distinguish two dimensions by which countries can be classified in terms of their sets of housing institutions. The first, measured by the percentage of dwellings occupied by their owners in the total housing stock, allows to assess to what extent houses are commodified and treated as a means to wealth. The second dimension of their typology is measured by residential loan indebtedness in a given country. This variable allows to capture the scope of liberalization of mortgage markets and the stance of housing policy regarding ownership financing. Taking into account both dimensions, Schwartz and Seabrooke classify the sets of institutions in developed OECD countries into four models of residential capitalism: the liberal market model, the corporatist market model, the Catholic-familial model and the statist-developmentalist model.

The available research on residential capitalism in emerging economies is, however, still quite scarce, and the methodology put forward by Schwartz and Seabrooke is not fully suited to deal with housing markets in such countries. The most comprehensive attempt to classify the institutional environment of the

DOI: 10.4324/9780429056901-11

housing market in the European post-socialist countries has been made by Stephens et al. (2015). The authors discuss the transformation of the housing market, providing an in-depth institutional and sociological analysis of various models of social security prevailing in the CEE region. In turn, more light on the privatization process and changes in the supply of social housing during the systemic transformation period has been shed in two monographs authored by Scanlon, Whitehead and Fernández Arrigoitia (2014) and by Fearn (2004), respectively. The former discusses the supply of social housing in Europe, with a particular focus on all post-communist countries, while the latter analyzes the situation only in the housing market in the Czech Republic, Serbia and Hungary. Good supplements to this last study are the work of Lux (2001), which describes the supply of social housing in Poland, Slovakia and the Czech Republic, and two crosscutting papers presenting a review of real estate privatization reforms in CEE countries (Pichler-Milanovich, 2001) and characteristics of housing markets and policies in six countries from across the region (Lux, 2003). The common conclusion of these studies is that CEE countries lack uniform, coherent and effective housing policies and that the region is characterized by a large variation of residential capitalism models. Moreover, the results of these scholarly endeavors indicate that the most effective support for housing market development, understood as the reduction of dwelling shortages, has been achieved by countries that pursued policies aimed at the development and deregulation of the rental market.

Finally, two works focused on the institutional environment of the mortgage market in CEE countries are worth mentioning. In the first one, Aalbers (2009) analyzes the reasons for the persistently high regionalization and diversification of mortgage lending in the EU. He points out that despite the far-reaching unification of banking regulation, the domination of national financial institutions in many countries has been conducive to the diversification of mortgage lending conditions. The second paper by Bohle (2014) argues that the institutional differences between Estonia and Hungary did not have a significant impact on the development of the housing boom and bust in either of these countries. The institutional setting was only important in the aftermath of the mortgage crisis – affecting the pace of recovery and socio-economic consequences of the boom itself.

This short overview of literature on the diversity of residential capitalism in the CEE countries indicates that notwithstanding a large variety of housing policies that have been pursued, they have had only a limited influence on the features of the housing market itself. Second, the studies concerned provide some evidence in favor of the hypothesis that the model of residential capitalism in CEE countries is substantially different from those that are prevalent in Western European countries. However, in none of these works has an attempt been made to provide a clear classification of the institutional surrounding of housing markets across the CEE region.

9.1 Measurement of institutions

Before one can categorize the models of capitalism in the housing market dimension, it is necessary to define the scope of the analysis, as the housing market (in a sociological sense) is embedded in a wide set of institutions stretching from financial market regulations through taxation systems to social housing provision and ownership protection laws. These sets of institutions can be classified into four groups that affect (1) housing financial affordability, (2) housing equity management, (3) rental housing affordability and availability and (4) social housing availability. Next we briefly analyze[1] each group, dividing the factors constituting each of these sets into input and output measures of institutions (i.e. variables directly dependent on housing policies and those describing the characteristics of the housing market they embrace) (Próchniak et al., 2016).

Housing financial affordability ranks among the vastest institutional dimensions as it consists of a large variety of factors. Regarding input measures, one can distinguish between those related to fiscal policies and those linked to financial market regulations. The government can influence the financial affordability of dwellings through the taxation of real estate owners, regulating transaction costs for both buyers and sellers of residential estates, granting subsidies or tax deduction schemes for homebuyers, especially first-time buyers and those buying dwellings on credit, as well as through granting credits on preferential terms and conditions, subsidies and credit guarantees for housing constructors or through imposing zoning laws (Poterba, 1984; Catte et al., 2004; Girouard, Kennedy and Noord, 2005; van den Noord, 2005; Glaeser, Gyourko and Saiz, 2008; Imbs and Favara, 2015). These policies can be measured by the share of general government expenditures on housing development and taxes on land and buildings. The government has at hand an even larger set of instruments when it comes to financial market regulation. It can impose restrictions from mortgage interest, loan-to-value and debt-to-income caps through regulating mortgage-backed securities issuance or foreign currency (FX) loans offers to altering banks' risk-weighted-assets calculation methods (Chiuri and Jappelli, 2003; Catte et al., 2004; Scanlon et al., 2004; Arce and López-Salido, 2008; Bini, 2010; Andrews, Caldera Sánchez and Johansson, 2011). All of them influence credit supply – their costs and conditions.

Output measures of housing financial affordability are to a large degree path dependent, as the ownership structure, housing market liquidity, or even credit availability are influenced by many factors that alter only very slowly (e.g. household preferences, stock of dwellings, income inequality). Hence, the translation of housing policies into changes in this dimension of residential capitalism takes a long time. One might measure it by looking at the share of owner-occupied dwellings; the share of the population living in overcrowded, deprived estates; the share of young adults living with their parents; the share of housing costs in disposable income; the ratio of house prices to annual incomes; and the surface of a house that can be bought on credit by a household with average income.

The second set of institutions affecting housing equity management possibilities stays in a recurrent relationship with the first one: the availability of housing equity withdrawal instruments is dependent on the affordability of residential estates and the demand for dwellings depends on the future profitability of equity invested in housing. However, the government can use some specific instruments to influence housing equity management that to a large extent do not influence affordability of residential estates. The most important one regards the protection of property laws – from protection of housing buyers and tenants, through inheritance and foreclosure regulations to efficiency of re-privatization policies, which are of highest importance to post-communist countries (Henderson and Ioannides, 1983; Englund et al., 2005; Greenspan and Kennedy, 2008; Augustyniak et al., 2013; Bohle, 2014). These policies influence the ability and willingness of people to buy, sell and rent houses. Without effective protection of property laws, the allocation of dwellings becomes ineffective and a large share of housing stock is endangered with deprivation.

Apart from that, transaction costs of housing equity management (e.g. inheritance taxes, taxation of close in time transactions of buying and selling the same estate) can also be used by the government to alter the institutional environment of the housing market as they induce frictions in residential transactions (Ommeren, 2008; Caldera Sánchez and Andrews, 2011). The last subset of input measures in this dimension of capitalism regards the financial regulation of housing equity withdrawal possibilities, that is, whether fixed-rate mortgages and HEL[2] or HELOC[3] types of loans are allowed and reasonably priced, as well as whether households can use refinancing instruments with regard to housing loans (Sowell, 2010). Effects of these policies on the institutional setting can be measured with output variables such as the share of houses occupied by owners with mortgages, the share of variable-rate mortgages in the amount of outstanding credits, and the occupation rate of dwellings.

The third and fourth set of institutional factors influence the availability of other ways of satisfying housing needs than owning a dwelling. In the case of renting, the government can impact supply and prices in this market segment. The most common instruments used are those regulating tenant-landlord agreements, especially regarding rent controls and eviction laws (Cuerpo, Kalantaryan and Pontuch, 2014). On the fiscal side, the government can manage the institutional surroundings of the rental market through setting taxes on rent incomes, subsidizing investors in affordable rental houses or allowing tenants to fully or partially deduct rents from their tax base (Mills, 1990; Haurin, Hendershott and Wachter, 1996; Ditch, Lewis and Wilcox, 2001; Englund et al., 2005; Andrews and Caldera Sánchez, 2011). As one might notice, this set of input institutional factors overlaps with both sets of measures described above, as eviction laws influence at the same time the ease of housing equity management for landlords, and fiscal regulations affect the optimal tenure choice of households and profitability of investing in dwellings for rent, translating into demand for residential estates and, eventually, their prices (Mills, 1990). Effects of these housing policies manifest themselves through such output measures as the availability of dwellings rented at a market price and the cost of rents relative to household incomes.

The availability of social dwellings[4] is that dimension of residential capitalism that can be fully managed by state's housing policy. However, this set of institutions is also subject to some path-dependence mechanisms as the increase in social housing supply is very costly and time-consuming, and the control of the state over social dwellings is therefore also limited. Governments can influence the availability of social dwellings twofold, either through constructing, buying and maintaining residential estates or through subsidizing privately owned properties, like housing cooperatives (Ditch, Lewis and Wilcox, 2001; Whitehead and Scanlon, 2007; Andrews, Caldera Sánchez and Johansson, 2011; Kemeny, 2011). The effects of these policies can be measured through the share of dwellings rented at below-market prices and the share of residential estate owned by state entities – from local government unities to state agencies.

Based on the foregoing analysis, a dataset of 23 institutional measures was created encompassing both input and output variables. The data were collected for 2005 (i.e. the initial year of this study) and for 2014 (i.e. the final year or the latest available record, but not prior to 2010). In several cases, some expert estimates had to be made to ensure comparability of records across different data sources (e.g. census versus Hypostat and Eurostat data on housing stock). A description of all these measures together with data sources are presented in Table 9.1.

Table 9.1 Data sources

Variable name	*Variable description*	*Data source*
affordability_i	Loan affordability index as computed by numbeo.com	numbeo.com
Cities	Share of population living in cities	Eurostat
DTI	Average (hypothetical) mortgage installment as a percentage of average monthly salary	numbeo.com
gg_housing	General government expenditure on housing as a share of GDP	Eurostat
gg_housing_dev	General government expenditure on housing development as a share of GDP	Eurostat
houses	Share of population living in houses (freely standing or detached)	Eurostat
housing_costs	Share of housing costs in disposable household income	Eurostat
housing_depr	Share of population living in a dwelling that is considered as overcrowded, while also exhibiting at least one of the housing deprivation measures	Eurostat
living_w_parents	Share of young adults aged 25–34 living with their parents	Eurostat
LTV_typical	Typical loan-to-value (LTV) ratio for new mortgage loans	ESRB, Hypostat and information gathered from various internet sources
mortg_rest	An index measuring the restrictiveness of housing finance regulations, i.e. existence of LTV, maturity and debt-to-income (DTI) limits, covered bonds and mortgage-backed securities financing availability, average maturity of mortgage credit, foreign exchange	Own calculations based on ESRB and Hypostat data as well as information gathered from TenLaw (Kuttner and Shim, 2016), PWC, EPRA and various internet sources

(*Continued*)

Table 9.1 (Continued)

Variable name	*Variable description*	*Data source*
	mortgage loan prohibition and possibility of listing real estate investment trusts (REIT) (0–1; higher value means more restrictive regulations)	
occupation_rate	Dwellings occupied permanently as a share of total dwellings	Own calculations based on Hypostat and Eurostat census data
overcrowding	Share of population living in a dwelling that is considered as overcrowded	Eurostat
owner	Share of population living in owner-occupied dwellings	Eurostat
owner_m	Share of population living in owner-occupied dwellings with mortgage or housing loan	Eurostat
price_income_ratio	Average flat prices in big cities to median equivalized net income	Own calculations based on numbeo.com and Eurostat data
rent_control_i	An index measuring the restrictiveness of rent control (0–2; higher value means higher rent control)	Own recoding based on answers to questions 1–3 from the Cuerpo, Kalantaryan and Pontuch (2014) questionnaire
rent_income_ratio	Average rent prices in big cities to median equivalized net income	Own calculations based on numbeo.com and Eurostat data
residential_loans	Total outstanding residential loans as a share of GDP	Hypostat
social_dwellings	Share of dwellings owned by municipalities or state	Own estimations based on housingeurope.eu, TenLaw, national statistical offices and OECD data
taxes_re_gdp	Taxes on land, buildings and other structures as a share of GDP	Eurostat
tenant_mrkt	Share of population living in rented dwellings with a rent at market price	Eurostat
vrm	An index measuring the prevalence of variable rate mortgages (0 – minority; 1 – large share, but less than half; 2 – medium prevalence; 3 – predominantly; 4 – only variable)	Own recoding based on Hypostat data as well as information gathered from various internet sources

Source: Author's elaboration.

9.2 Models of residential capitalism in EU member states

While examining the data gathered on institutional measures with the ORCLUS subspace clustering algorithm, four distinct groups of countries that share a similar set of institutions were identified. In line with earlier research, especially the classification of Schwartz and Seabrooke (2009), the three sets of institutions that constitute models of residential capitalism prevailing mainly in old EU member states were dubbed as follows: the *liberal-corporatist model* found among Northern European countries (cluster 1), the *statist model* that is prevalent in most core eurozone member states (cluster 2), and the *commodified-familial model* in the south of Europe (cluster 3). Apart from these three models, that were already described in the literature, a new, distinct model predominant in CEE countries (cluster 4) was identified and named the *non-commodified model* of residential capitalism. Only one old EU member state (Italy) shares a similar set of institutions with the non-commodified model. The spatial distribution of these four models across the European Union is depicted on Map 9.1, while their institutional characteristics are provided in Table 9.2, followed by a short description of all the typical Western European models of residential capitalism.

The *liberal-corporatist model* is present in the Anglo-Saxon (United Kingdom, Ireland), Nordic (Sweden, Finland, Denmark) and Benelux countries (Belgium, the Netherlands). It is characterized by high indebtedness of the population, reflected by the highest average share of households living in an owned dwelling with a mortgage (46.8% in comparison to around 25% in other old EU countries; for the exact values for each measure and each country group, see Table 9.2). This is closely connected with high financial affordability of housing (2.1 pts vs 1.3 pts in other incumbent EU member countries) driven by financial market deregulation, which manifests itself in high LTV levels (80% on average) and a large market for securitization instruments, as well as by the lowest levels of house prices in relation to income (1.7 compared to over 2 in other countries).

In contrast to the classification put forward by Schwartz and Seabrooke, our approach does not necessitate a distinction between the liberal and the corporatist model of residential capitalism as countries that exhibit financial deregulation, low house prices and high indebtedness of households – that is, they have a market-based (or liberal) system of housing allocation and are at the same time characterized by the highest share of social housing (17.5% of dwelling stock on average), relatively high rent controls and the largest public spending on housing policies (0.8% of GDP) among all EU countries. The latter features imply a wide margin of state interventions in the housing market, which is characteristic for the corporatist model of Schwartz and Seabrooke. These interventions are motivated by the need to provide security for those who are excluded from a liberal system of dwelling allocation and cannot satisfy their housing needs through the market. As a result, countries that embody the liberal-corporatist model of residential capitalism have a set of institutions that is on average most akin to the statist model among other varieties of residential capitalism in the European Union (see Table A9.4 in the Appendix).

In the liberal-corporatist model, houses are treated as a means to wealth, hence the tenure choice and housing investment decisions are problems solved with optimal portfolio allocation methods. This is reflected by the highest occupation rate of dwellings (on average 90% in comparison to around 80% in other EU

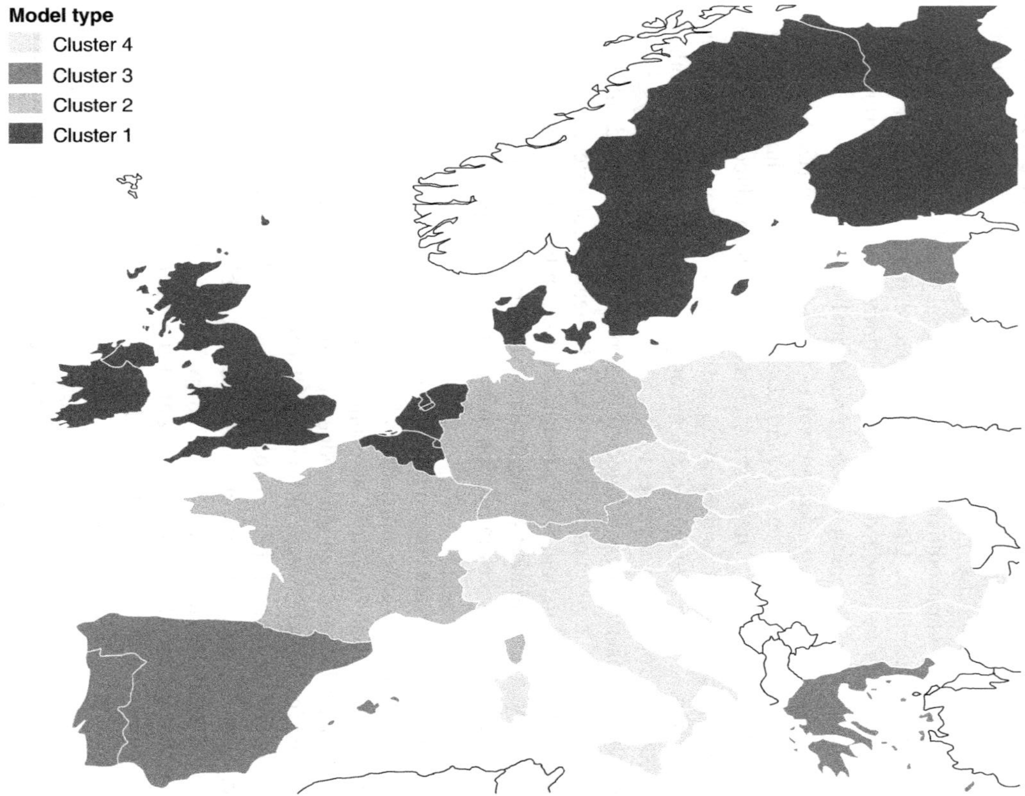

Map 9.1 Models of capitalism in the European Union: housing market

Source: Author's elaboration.

Table 9.2 Cluster-average values for all variables

	Cluster 1 Liberal-corporatist	*Cluster 2 Statist*	*Cluster 3 Commodified-familial*	*Cluster 4 Non-commodified*
affordability_i	2.1	1.3	1.4	1.2
cities (%)	39.2	36.8	44.2	33.0
DTI (%)	49.7	80.1	73.4	89.1
gg_housing (%)	0.6	0.5	0.0	0.1
gg_housing_dev (%)	0.2	0.2	0.1	0.3
houses (%)	74.9	55.2	42.0	55.7
housing_costs (%)	23.1	21.3	24.8	21.3
housing_depr (%)	1.4	2.6	4.3	10.7
living_w_parents (%)	10.6	16.6	39.7	43.8
LTV_typical	0.8	0.7	0.6	0.7
mortg_rest	0.3	0.1	0.4	0.6
occupation_rate (%)	89.5	83.7	71.6	81.4
overcrowding (%)	6.0	9.7	14.3	35.4
owner (%)	68.3	58.2	77.3	84.7
owner_m (%)	46.8	27.7	25.1	10.0
price_income_ratio	1.7	2.0	2.3	3.0
rent_control_i	0.7	1.1	0.4	0.3
rent_income_ratio	0.4	0.3	0.5	0.6
residential_loans (%)	72.2	37.7	46.1	16.6
social_dwellings (%)	17.5	13.7	1.5	3.1
taxes_re_gdp (%)	1.0	1.0	1.0	0.6
tenant_mrkt (%)	23.3	28.7	12.1	6.2
vrm	1.6	1.3	2.5	2.7

Source: Author's elaboration.

countries) as residential estate owners are driven purely by rent-seeking motives, and equity needs to provide interest or is withdrawn as quickly as possible. Moreover, in contrast to some works on the myth of ownership (Kemeny, 1981, 2011) arguing that in countries like the United Kingdom or the Netherlands the main goal of households was to purchase a home to live in, in the liberal-corporatist model the average share of rental housing is almost equal to one-fourth of the dwelling stock. This is because people very often decide to rent rather than to buy, if they are not interested in investing their capital in housing.

The most salient features of the *statist model*, present only in Germany, Austria and France, include the lowest share of owner-occupied houses in the dwelling stock among all EU member states (58.2% on average in comparison to three quarters in other EU countries). This is a result of a high provision of cheap rental dwellings (rent-to-income ratio is equal to 0.3 in comparison to 0.5 in other member states) and high availability of social housing (13.7% of the dwelling stock is owned by municipalities). Another distinctive feature of this model of residential capitalism is a low rate of household indebtedness – the amount of outstanding residential loans relative to GDP is equal to 37.7% and is lower than in other incumbent EU member states. This comes despite a very deregulated financial market (the mortgage restriction index equals 0.1 pts) as households do not desire to buy residential dwellings for themselves. On the contrary, a deregulated financial market is favorable for corporate market actors who finance rental housing investments with cheap capital borrowed from banks or trusts.

Security in the statist model is provided through an extended control of tenant-landlord relations with restrictive eviction procedures and high rent controls (the rent control index stands on average at 1.1 pts, whereas in other EU countries it is well below 1 pt). In this model of residential capitalism, the state intervenes also directly through a variety of subsidies and allowance schemes for private investments in cheap rental housing (general government spending on housing amounts to 0.7% of GDP, almost as high as in liberal-corporatist countries). As a result, the share of households that occupy a rented dwelling and pay a below-market price for it is the highest among all EU countries and totals on average 13.1%. These two tools of state intervention – restrictive rental market regulations and large subsidies for developers – are highly complementary. The former institutions increase the risk of renting and, hence, lead to crowding out of private landlords as well as to increases in risk premiums built in to the rents. The latter institutions compensate for these effects through reducing the cost of capital being part of rents and at the same time attracting to the housing market more corporate investors that can better securitize the risk stemming from restrictive rental market regulations.

The statist model is the only one occurring in the EU countries in which houses are perceived as a social right – households' main desire is to have a decent place to live in, which is of a required quality and of affordable cost, regardless of the tenure mode. This goes in line with high household mobility, as dwellings are changed as often as the preferences of households are changed due to family or labor market reasons. As a derivative, statist countries have the least commodified housing markets among old EU member states. This is reflected in their proximity to the non-commodified model of residential capitalism mostly embodied in CEE countries.

The *commodified-familial model*, which prevails in Spain, Portugal, Greece and among CEE countries also in Estonia, features a large share of owner-occupied dwellings (on average 77% compared to below 70% in other old EU member states). That is a result of the ownership myth prevalent in countries with this set of institutions (i.e. a pervasive belief that owning a dwelling is by far the best way to satisfy one's housing needs and the safest asset in a household portfolio). Buying a home is also seen as the main constituent of establishing a family and is usually treated as a necessary condition for having children. Another important feature of this model is a very low occupation rate (only 71% of all residential estates are permanently used) that co-exists with an overcrowding rate twice as high as in other incumbent EU member states (14.3%). Moreover, residential estates are already to a large extent commodified, especially regarding new dwellings, which is reflected in a high level of residential loans (46.1%, which is higher compared to statist countries and lower than in liberal-corporatist EU member states). All the aforementioned characteristics indicate that the market-based system of dwelling allocation is present but not working effectively in the commodified-familial model.

In this model of residential capitalism, the ineffective market-based system of dwelling allocation is to a large extent replaced by a family-based system, as parents are expected to satisfy the housing needs of their kids. Hence, the share of young adults living with parents is the highest among all old EU member states (39.7%) and the private rental market is just slightly more than half the size of its counterparts in liberal-corporatist or statist countries. In such a situation the role of the state is confined to protecting borrowers – the mortgage market is highly restrictive and LTV ratios are the lowest in the whole EU25 (typically 60% for new loans). Government does not provide any social housing or subsidies for private provision of dwellings for rent – expenditures on housing policies are the lowest in the entire EU25 and amount on average to 0.1% of GDP. Government usually also refrains from subsidizing housing purchases for first-time buyers, as families are usually socially obliged to transfer savings for residential estate investments to younger generations.

The current state of the model of residential capitalism prevalent in southern EU countries is most likely transitory. The transformation that started with the demographic boom in the 1990s, which was directly followed by a cultural conversion, echoed in the weakening of familial ties and the abandonment of Catholic values by young adults. This was fueled by the creation of the eurozone, which facilitated the inflow of cheap capital to housing markets in southern European countries and was conducive to a liberalization of the housing market, which was followed by a large commodification of dwellings (Italy remains still an exception). As a result, one cannot speak anymore of the Catholic-familial model of residential capitalism (along the lines of the Schwartz and Seabrooke typology), which ceased to exist in these countries. However, due to path-dependence restrictions the real estate markets concerned were not transformed yet into liberal ones and plenty of features of the old model remain in place. Hence, the set of institutions in these countries was dubbed "familial" so as to better describe the current model of residential capitalism that prevails in the south of the EU. In the years to come, a further weakening of familial ties will erode the security foundations of the current model of residential capitalism and will trigger further changes in the institutional surrounding of the housing market. The most likely scenario entails a gradual shift to the liberal-corporatist model as an increasing demand for new owner-occupied housing will be financed through residential loans, which eventually will require more state interventions to provide security for those excluded from the housing market. Ireland already chose this path of transformation: its institutional model was classified in the Schwartz and Seabrooke framework as Catholic-familial at the beginning of the 21st century and now it can be classified as liberal-corporatist, but still with a very high proximity to the commodified-familial model (0.05 standard deviation distance; see Table A9.4 in the Appendix).

9.3 Models of residential capitalism in CEE countries

The CEE region differs largely from the rest of the European Union in terms of housing market institutions. Despite many between-country dissimilarities, the governments across the region developed a distinct model of residential capitalism that can be found nowhere else in Europe but Italy, which resembles many of housing market characteristics to be found in CEE countries. We dubbed it the *non-commodified model* of residential capitalism, as low commodification of dwellings is the common thread to all highly diversified institutional setups in CEE countries – a vast majority of residential estates across the region were never bought or sold in the market or even appraised by banks, individuals or public entities. This model is prevalent in all CEE countries but Estonia, whose set of institutions was classified as familial.

According to the subspace clustering results, the three most important characteristics (see Table A9.5 in the Appendix) of the institutional architecture that constitute the non-commodified model of residential capitalism are (1) a low supply of social housing (only 3.5% of dwellings are state-owned); (2) a small private rental market (6.2% of dwellings are rented for a market price); and (3) a large proportion of young adults living with parents (43.8%). This translates into the highest share of owner-occupied houses in the dwelling stock among all EU countries. Another important feature of this model is a very low indebtedness of households: outstanding residential loans amount on average to only 16.6% of GDP, which is less than a quarter of the levels featured in liberal-corporatist countries. Moreover, the market for consumption mortgage credits or reversed mortgages is almost non-existent in this model of residential capitalism.

The foregoing characteristics of the non-commodified model coincide with the prevailing perception of dwellings, which are seen as family goods – their worth is usually not included in the subjectively assessed wealth of households, they are passed on from generation to generation and people are not very eager to sell them or withdraw equity allocated in housing. As a result, the secondary market for houses is shallow, the prices of dwellings are the highest relative to incomes among all EU members and, hence, housing financial affordability is much lower than in the rest of the EU25. Furthermore, the market for reasonably priced rented dwellings of average standard is almost non-existent, as is the rental market in small towns and rural areas. This leads to the conclusion that the market-based system of dwelling allocation is present only in big cities but largely ineffective and almost non-existent in rural areas.

The prevailing system of dwelling allocation is family-based and is even wider spread than in the commodified-familial model, as the mortgage market is highly restrictive and household savings are much lower, which is reflected in only a 10% share of households living in real estate with a mortgage. As a derivative, the non-commodified model of residential capitalism is characterized by a very high overcrowding rate: 35.4% of occupied dwellings are not sufficiently large to provide a decent standard of living for the inhabitants. Moreover, the housing stock is old, over 10% of occupied dwellings are deprived and almost 20% of the residential estates are left unoccupied. This indicates that the equity allocated in housing is used inefficiently in this system, which brings about large housing shortages in CEE countries.

As dwellings are overcrowded and of low quality, families are excited to live on their own in estates of a decent standard that are located in proximity to their work, school or other places of their socio-economic activity. This desire is a mixture of the ownership myth and the statist approach to houses as a social right. It manifests itself in people's attitude that can be dubbed "owner-occupied houses as a social right". This attitude and the excitement it generates are most likely effects of path dependence. On the one hand, houses were never commodified during the communist era and were treated as a social right both by the state and by households. On the other hand, the rapid privatization process in the laissez-faire spirit of libertarian economy gave birth to a massive desire for ownership and lack of alternative methods of satisfying housing needs. Social dwellings that remained in the hands of the state after privatization were mostly deprived and aimed at satisfying the housing needs of a small proportion of people who were not able to get along in a market economy (Lux, 2001). At the same time, rental markets are still very unstable and fragmented across the region, with dwellings provided mainly by private non-corporate owners, which induces low levels of tenant protection and high rents (Rubaszek and Czerniak, 2017), making this tenure choice detrimental for a large number of households that search for a long-term mode to satisfy their housing needs.

The role of the state in the non-commodified model of residential capitalism remains limited. After the mass privatization period, governments withdrew their involvement in the housing market with a short interlude before the global financial crisis, when the mortgage market was liberalized and housing purchases were stimulated through public subsidies. After 2008, governments decided to restrict access to residential loans with a view to reduce the exposure of borrowers to financial distress. The provision of social dwellings is small in comparison to liberal-corporatist or statist countries, similar to public spending on housing policies (0.4% of GDP on average). As the private rental market is small and confined mainly to high-end dwellings, governments across the region do not engage in regulating tenant-landlord relations (the rent control index is on average at the lowest level among all EU countries and is equal to 0.3 pts).

The non-commodified model of residential capitalism exhibits many similarities to the commodified-familial model: they share a similar system of family-based allocation of dwellings, insignificant scope of state intervention, small rental market and low levels of household indebtedness. Bulgaria and Poland (see Table A9.4 in the Appendix) are the two countries whose institutional architectures most resemble the commodified-familial model of residential capitalism in the south of the EU. Only institutions in Hungary are more akin to the liberal-corporatist model than to the commodified-familial one. The most diverse sets of institutions were traced in Romania and Slovakia: they do not even to a small degree approximate those prevailing in any of the incumbent EU member states.

As was noted above, out of all 11 CEE countries, only Estonia was classified as a commodified-familial model, which was a derivative of a higher household indebtedness and much smaller housing shortages in this Baltic state, compared to the regional average. At the same time, Estonia is to a very large extent akin to non-commodified countries (only 0.14 standard deviation in the institutional similarity distance).

9.4 Evolving models of residential capitalism in CEE countries between 2005 and 2014

The non-commodified model of residential capitalism reveals in many respects a patchwork nature and hence is highly unstable. Various institutions in which the housing market is embedded are non-complementary – for example, a liberal approach of the state to housing co-exists with large housing deficiencies, as does a vast group of people who are excluded from the market-based system of housing allocation with high demand for state intervention among the society. This system generates tensions between housing market participants: home buyers vs. banks, tenants vs. landlords, social dwelling occupants vs. the state – naming only some of the fault lines. This immanent patchwork nature of the non-commodified model can be attributed to a high path dependence of the housing market structure and to inadequate housing policies pursued across the region since the beginning of the 21st century. These policies were aimed at combining institutions from the liberal-corporatist model with a family allocation system of dwellings and statist approach to housing typical for a post-communist society (Czerniak, 2017). One can observe this process by analyzing the changes in institution measures, both in the case of input and output variables throughout the region since the enlargement of the European Union (see Table 9.3 and Table A9.6 in the Appendix).

Between 2005 and 2014, the institutions encompassing the housing market in CEE11 countries evolved in the direction of residential capitalism models typical

Table 9.3 Change in absolute distance from 2014 clusters for each CEE11 country and each subspace dimension between 2005 and 2014 (standardized values)

	Cluster 1 Liberal-corporatist	*Cluster 2 Statist*	*Cluster 3 Commodified-familial*	*Cluster 4 Non-commodified*
Bulgaria	1.01	0.19	2.40	0.09
Croatia	0.13	−0.09	0.44	0.51
Czech Republic	0.42	0.44	1.59	0.59
Estonia	0.70	0.54	0.55	−0.01
Hungary	0.57	0.37	−0.22	0.34
Latvia	0.33	0.48	−0.15	0.32
Lithuania	0.75	0.22	1.00	0.09
Poland	1.33	0.11	3.57	0.25
Romania	2.72	0.55	5.99	0.45
Slovakia	1.27	0.15	0.12	0.25
Slovenia	0.69	0.50	0.31	0.35
Median change	***0.70***	***0.37***	***0.55***	***0.32***

Source: Author's elaboration.

for the incumbent EU member states, especially the liberal-corporatist one – the median change in institutional similarity, as measured in the liberal-corporatist dimension designated by the ORCLUS algorithm, equaled 0.70 standard deviation and was the highest recorded for all four dimensions (see Table 9.3). This can be explained mainly by a housing policy common across the region before the global financial crisis that was aimed at increasing financial affordability of owner-occupied houses, especially through providing cheap mortgage credit and government subsidies for first-time buyers. The average DTI in CEE11 countries was almost halved between 2005 and 2014 – from 147.1% to 87.0% of income – which led to an increase in household indebtedness (the level of outstanding residential loans grew from 9.0% to 17.4% of GDP) and a twice as large share of households living in a dwelling with a mortgage (from 5.0% to 10.2%, respectively). This policy helped to tackle some of the problems in the housing market: it reduced the overcrowding rate by almost one-third and halved the share of deprived houses in the occupied dwelling stock. As a result, housing shortages diminished and the general quality of residential estates across the region improved. However, at the same time even more people, especially young couples, became excluded from the housing market, which is reflected in a 10% increase of the share of young adults living with parents. Moreover, the shift in CEE governments' priorities from satisfying the housing needs of citizens to support first-time buyers reduced the amount of available social dwellings by a quarter.

The above-described evolution path of residential capitalism in the CEE region resembles the one taken a decade earlier by southern European countries, which ended up with a boom-bust episode that hampered their long-term economic growth and brought social unrest after the global financial crisis. This is indicated by the change in institutional similarity between the CEE region and those EU14 states that exhibit the commodified-familial model of residential capitalism – between 2005 and 2014 institutional measures for 9 out of 11 CEE countries became more similar to those in the south of Europe (see Table 9.3), and in some cases (Romania, Bulgaria and Poland) the change exceeded even 2 standard deviations. This was mainly caused by mass privatization of social dwellings, abolition of co-operatives and the slowest reduction in housing shortages in these countries due to a high cost of taking up mortgage credits. Simultaneously, the institutional environment of the housing market in Hungary and Latvia slightly diverged from the commodified-familial model, but no single housing policy change can be made responsible for that.

More evidence that the CEE11 countries have in general followed the evolution path of Greece, Spain or Portugal is seen in the case of Estonia. As shown on Map 9.1, this Baltic state is the only one in the region that in 2014 had a largely commodified housing market with no dwelling shortages (i.e. it exhibited the institutional proximity to the model of residential capitalism prevalent in southern Europe). However, if one takes a closer look at the institutional environment in this country in 2005, right after the EU enlargement it was much more akin to the non-commodified model than to any other model identified in our analysis. In the following years Estonia evolved into the liberal-corporatist direction, in line with the trend prevailing in all other CEE countries, but to such an extent that it diverged from the non-commodified model and became classified as a commodified-familial one. This can be attributed to the housing policy pursued in this country that combined subsidies for house buyers with restrictive macro prudential policy and low mortgage interest rates. This policy resulted in a large increase in residential loans to the highest level among CEE countries, which helped to finance housing investment on such a scale that allowed for an almost full disappearance of overcrowded and deprived houses in Estonia.

It is also worth noting that from 2005 to 2014, the similarity between housing market institutions in CEE countries and in countries with a statist model of residential capitalism slightly augmented. This is only a statistical effect, however, because none of the housing policies pursued across the region was aimed at introducing institutions typical for the statist model. One might attribute this increase in similarity to the surge in household indebtedness, which is on average higher in all incumbent EU member states irrespective of the prevailing model of residential capitalism, and to a fast hike in incomes that surpassed in most countries the rise in rents, resulting in an increased financial availability of rental houses. The latter process was largely an effect of underdeveloped rental markets that did not change largely (both in terms of real prices and supply) in CEE countries over the last decade, the only exception being the Czech Republic.

The model of residential capitalism in CEE countries is in a state of flux, as its patchwork-like structure generates tensions between housing market participants and does not allow to fully tackle the dwelling shortage problem. Eventually, this system needs to change, either through an institutional drift in the direction of a liberal-corporatist model similar to that seen in commodified-familial countries or through an active housing policy that would create a distinct and stable model of residential capitalism similar to the statist one present in Germany or Austria, but with a larger share of owner-occupied dwellings. The latter option is more desired from a social planner perspective, as it will minimize the imbalances generated on the tangent point of social desire for state interventions and an increasingly commodified approach to dwellings.

Notes

1 An extended analysis can be found in Czerniak (2017).
2 Home equity loan.
3 Home equity line of credit.
4 In this chapter, social housing is understood as all the dwellings that are offered to households at below-market rents; they are either state-owned or privately owned (e.g. cooperatives) and subsidized.

References

Aalbers, M. B. (2009). The globalization and europeanization of mortgage markets. *International Journal of Urban and Regional Research*, 33(2), pp. 389–410.

Amable, B. (2003). *The diversity of modern capitalism*. Oxford: Oxford University Press. doi: 10.1093/019926113X.001.0001.

Andrews, D. and Caldera Sánchez, A. (2011). Drivers of homeownership rates in selected OECD countries. *OECD Economics Department Working Papers*, 849.

Andrews, D., Caldera Sánchez, A. and Johansson, Å. (2011). Housing markets and structural policies in OECD countries, *OECD Economics Department Working Papers*, 836, p. 85.

Arce, O. and López-Salido, D. (2008). Housing bubbles. *American Economic Journal*, 3(January), pp. 212–241.

Augustyniak, H. et al. (2013). To rent or to buy – Analysis of housing tenure choice determined by housing policy. *NBP Working Paper*, 164(33).

Bini, L. (2010). ECB : From boom to bust: Towards a new equilibrium in bank credit. Ernst & Young Business School Seminar, Milan, 29 Jan.

Bohle, D. (2014). Post-socialist housing meets transnational finance: Foreign banks, mortgage lending, and the privatization of welfare in Hungary and Estonia. *Review of International Political Economy*, 21(4), pp. 913–948.

Bourdieu, P. (2005). *The social structures of the economy*. Cambridge, UK: Polity Press.

Caldera Sánchez, A. and Andrews, D. (2011). To move or not to move : What drives residential mobility rates in the OECD ? *OECD Economics Department Working Papers*, 846, p. 40.

Catte, P. et al. (2004). Housing markets, wealth and the business cycle. *OECD Economics Department Working Papers*, 394, pp. 4–42.

Chiuri, M. C. and Jappelli, T. (2003). Financial market imperfections and home ownership: A comparative study. *European Economic Review*, 47(5), pp. 857–875.

Cuerpo, C., Kalantaryan, S. and Pontuch, P. (2014). Rental market regulation in the European Union. *European Economy Economic Papers*, 515.

Czerniak, A. (2017). Housing policies and varieties of residential capitalism in CEE countries. In: *3rd conference on the role of state in varieties of capitalism (SVOC)*, Central European University, Budapest, 30 Nov – 1 Dec.

Ditch, J., Lewis, A. and Wilcox, S. (2001). *Social housing, tenure and housing allowance: An international review*. Edited by Department for Work and Pensions. London: Crown.

Englund, P. Kim, K. H., Malpezzi, S. and Turner, B. (2005). Housing tenure across countries: The effects of regulations and institutions. *American Real Estate and Urban Economics Association International Meeting*, Los Cabos, Mexico, Aug.

Fearn, J. (2004). Too poor to move, to poor to stay: a report on housing in the Czech Republic, Hungary and Serbia. Available at: http://pdc.ceu.hu/archive/00002871/ [Accessed 12 Nov. 2017].

Girouard, N., Kennedy, M. and Noord, P. Van Den. (2005). Recent house price developments: The role of fundamentals. *OECD Economic Outlook*, pp. 123–154.

Glaeser, E. L., Gyourko, J. and Saiz, A. (2008). Housing supply and housing bubbles. *Journal of Urban Economics*, 64(2), pp. 198–217.

Greenspan, A. and Kennedy, J. (2008). Sources and uses of equity extracted from homes. *Oxford Review of Economic Policy*, 24(1), pp. 120–144.

Hall, P. A. and Soskice, D. (2001). *Varieties of capitalism*. Oxford: Oxford University Press. doi: 10.1093/0199247757.001.0001.

Haurin, D. R., Hendershott, P. H. and Wachter, S. M. (1996). Borrowing constraints and the tenure choice of young households. *National Bureau of Economic Research*, 5630.

Henderson, J. V. and Ioannides, Y. M. (1983). A model of housing tenure choice. *American Economic Review*, 73(1), pp. 98–113.

Imbs, J. M. and Favara, G. (2015). Credit supply and the price of housing. *American Economic Review*, 105(3), pp. 958–992.

Kemeny, J. (1981). *The myth of home-ownership: Private versus public choices in housing tenure*. London: Routledge and Kegan Paul.

Kemeny, J. (2011). The ideology of home ownership: Homeownership societies and the role of housing. *Housing, Theory and Society,* 28(1), pp. 100–101.

Kuttner, K. N. and Shim, I. (2016). Can non-interest rate policies stabilize housing markets? evidence from a panel of 57 economies. *Journal of Financial Stability*, 26, pp. 31–44.

Lux, M. (2001). Social housing in the Czech republic, Poland and Slovakia. *International Journal of Housing Policy*, 1(2), pp. 189–209.

Lux, M. (2003). Efficiency and effectiveness of housing policies in the Central and Eastern Europe countries. *International Journal of Housing Policy*, 3(3), pp. 243–265.

Mills, E. S. (1990). Housing tenure choice. *The Journal of Real Estate Finance and Economics,* 3(4), pp. 323–331.

Pichler-Milanovich, N. (2001). Urban housing in Central and Eastern Europe: Convergence, divergence or policy “collapse”. *International Journal of Housing Policy*, 1(2), pp. 145–187.

Poterba, J. M. (1984). Tax subsidies to owner-occupied housing: An asset-market approach. *The Quarterly Journal of Economics*, 99(4), pp. 729–752.

Próchniak, M. et al. (2016). The emerging models of capitalism in CEE11 countries – A tentative comparison with Western Europe. *Warsaw Forum of Economic Sociology*, 7(2), pp. 7–70.

Rubaszek, M. and Czerniak, A. (2017). Preferencje Polaków dotyczące struktury własnościowej mieszkań: opis wyników ankiety. *[Housing Tenure Preferences of Poles: Survey Results] Bank i Kredyt*, 48(2), pp. 197–234.

Scanlon, K., Whitehead, C.M.E. and Fernández Arrigoitia, M. (2014). *Social housing in Europe*. Chichester: John Wiley & Sons.

Scanlon, K., Whitehead, C.M.E., Pichler-Milanović, N. and Cirman, A. (2004). *International trends in housing tenure and mortgage finance*. London: London School of Economics.

Schwartz, H. M. and Seabrooke, L., eds. (2009). *The politics of housing booms and busts*. London: Palgrave Macmillan UK.

Shiller, R. J. (2009). *Irrational exuberance*. Princeton: Princeton University Press.

Sowell, T. (2010). *The housing boom and bust*. Philadelphia: Basic Books.

Stephens, M., Lux, M. and Sunega, P. (2015). Post-socialist housing systems in Europe: Housing welfare regimes by default? *Housing Studies*, 30(8), pp. 1210–1234. Routledge.

van den Noord, P. (2005). Tax incentives and house price volatility in the euro area: Theory and evidence. *Economie Internationale*, 1(101), pp. 29–45.

van Ommeren, J. (2008). *Transaction costs in housing markets*. Available at: http://papers.ssrn.com/sol3/papers.cfm?abstract_id=1285971 [Accessed 6 Oct. 2017).

Whitehead, C. M. and Scanlon, K. (2007). *Social housing in Europe*. London: London School of Economics and Political Sciences.

Appendix 9

Table A9.4 Distance from cluster in each subspace dimension (absolute, standardized values)

	Cluster 1 Liberal-corporatist	*Cluster 2 Statist*	*Cluster 3 Commodified-familial*	*Cluster 4 Non-commodified*
Belgium	0	0.53	0.72	0.67
Finland	0	0.27	1.09	1.10
Netherlands	0	1.22	0.26	3.02
Denmark	0	0.84	1.26	2.62
Ireland	0	0.35	0.05	0.86
Sweden	0	1.15	2.10	2.49
United Kingdom	0	0.28	0.72	0.92
Germany	2.29	0	2.64	0.44
France	1.09	0	1.28	1.59
Austria	1.99	0	2.26	1.95
Portugal	0.24	0.13	0	0.35
Greece	2.44	1.12	0	0.42
Spain	0.86	0.64	0	0.31
Estonia	1.35	1.27	0	0.14
Hungary	0.86	0.98	0.93	0
Czech Republic	1.95	0.95	0.72	0
Poland	1.91	1.43	0.08	0
Latvia	2.16	1.61	0.47	0
Lithuania	2.15	1.95	0.44	0
Slovenia	2.07	1.10	0.56	0
Slovakia	1.95	1.52	1.11	0
Bulgaria	2.34	1.76	0.06	0
Romania	2.65	2.08	1.80	0
Croatia	2.31	1.62	0.20	0
Italy	1.85	0.87	1.15	0

Source: Author's elaboration.

Table A9.5 Measures for cluster distinction in order of importance

Cluster 1 Liberal-corporatist	*Cluster 2 Statist*	*Cluster 3 Commodified-familial*	*Cluster 4 Non-commodified*
owner_m	owner_m	owner_m	social_dwellings
tenant_mrkt	owner	residential_loans	tenant_mrkt
DTI	houses	owner	living_w_parents
residential_loans	tenant_mrkt	DTI	owner
social_dwellings	residential_loans	houses	occupation_rate
Houses	DTI	living_w_parents	overcrowding
Owner	living_w_parents	cities	owner_m
overcrowding	overcrowding	occupation_rate	housing_costs
housing_costs	cities	overcrowding	DTI
cities	occupation_rate	social_dwellings	cities
occupation_rate	housing_costs	housing_costs	houses
housing_depr	social_dwellings	tenant_mrkt	vrm
living_w_parents	housing_depr	housing_depr	housing_depr
rent_control_i	vrm	price_income_ratio	residential_loans
gg_housing	taxes_re_gdp	rent_control_i	taxes_re_gdp
vrm	rent_control_i	vrm	price_income_ratio
taxes_re_gdp	affordability_i	affordability_i	affordability_i
rent_income_ratio	price_income_ratio	taxes_re_gdp	gg_housing_dev
affordability_i	gg_housing	rent_income_ratio	rent_control_i
mortg_rest	mortg_rest	mortg_rest	rent_income_ratio
price_income_ratio	LTV_typical	LTV_typical	mortg_rest
LTV_typical	rent_income_ratio	gg_housing_dev	gg_housing
gg_housing_dev	gg_housing_dev	gg_housing	LTV_typical

Source: Author's elaboration.

Table A9.6 Change in value of variables between 2005 and 2014 (average for CEE11 countries)

Variable name	*2005*	*2014*	*Change between 2005 and 2014*
affordability_i	0.8	1.2	0.5
cities (%)	36.0	33.0	−3.0
DTI (%)	147.1	87.0	−60.1
gg_housing (%)	0.2	0.1	−0.1
gg_housing_dev (%)	0.3	0.3	0.0
houses (%)	53.9	54.6	0.7
housing_costs (%)	23.3	21.4	−1.9
housing_depr (%)	20.7	10.2	−10.5
living_w_parents (%)	37.7	41.5	3.8
LTV_typical	0.6	0.7	0.1
mortg_rest	0.4	0.6	0.3
occupation_rate (%)	84.1	82.0	−2.1
overcrowding (%)	48.6	34.2	−14.4
owner (%)	83.2	85.5	2.3
owner_m (%)	5.0	10.2	5.2
price_income_ratio	3.8	3.0	−0.8
rent_control_i	0.4	0.4	0.0
rent_income_ratio	0.7	0.6	−0.1
residential_loans (%)	9.0	17.4	8.3
social_dwellings (%)	3.8	2.7	−1.1
taxes_re_gdp (%)	0.4	0.5	0.1
tenant_mrkt (%)	4.3	5.2	1.0
vrm	3.0	2.7	−0.3

Source: Author's elaboration.

10 The empirical results of subspace clustering – a summary

Ryszard Rapacki and Adam Czerniak

Introduction

The main aim of this chapter is to shed new empirical light on the nature and most salient features of the evolving post-communist capitalism in 11 Central and Eastern European countries (CEE11) which joined the European Union between 2004 and 2013, against the backdrop of Western European models of capitalism. To this end, we summarize the empirical results of the subspace clustering exercise conducted in Chapters 4 through 9.

Simultaneously, we pursue four specific objectives. First, in this chapter we make an endeavor to identify the current models of Western European capitalism co-existing in the European Union and to confront the results with the original typology developed by Amable 15 years earlier (Amable, 2003). Second, we strive to verify the hypothesis that CEE11 countries have formed their own model(s) of post-communist capitalism, distinct from the patterns established in Western Europe. Third, we seek to explain the evolution of post-communist capitalism in CEE11 economies between 2005 and 2014 and to check if their institutional architectures were subject to convergence or divergence trends vis-à-vis Western European counterparts. Fourth, based on the findings of our empirical study, we also aim to substantiate the proposal of using the notion of "patchwork capitalism" as the most adequate term that denotes the unique nature and most salient features of the model of post-communist capitalism that has emerged in CEE11 countries.

The research approach adopted in this study capitalizes on the conceptual framework and typology put forward by Bruno Amable (2003) and originally designed for Western market economies. With a view to account for transition-specific characteristics of the evolving institutional setups in CEE11 countries and the peculiarities rooted in their command-economy legacy, we extended and modified the original Amablean analytical framework. Departing from this approach, we applied a new advanced analytical tool (the subspace clustering machine-learning method) that enables quantification of the results of our comparisons.

The chapter is structured as follows. In section 10.1, we synthesize the empirical results of our exercise, broken down into six institutional areas singled out for the purpose of this research. In section 10.2 we discuss and interpret major findings aggregated for the whole sample. In section 10.3, we derive and justify the

DOI: 10.4324/9780429056901-12

notion of "patchwork capitalism" as the most emblematic term highlighting the peculiar nature of post-communist capitalism in Central and Eastern Europe. In section 10.4 we wrap up with main conclusions of the discussion.

10.1 Empirical results

This section provides a brief overview of the empirical results of our study for each of the six institutional areas scrutinized, including in particular the number and composition of clusters identified in each area, based on the application of the subspace clustering machine-learning method with the ORCLUS algorithm (for details, see Chapter 3).

Product market competition

The subspace clustering analysis in this area was based on 23 indicators, representing the determinants of competition (for details, see Chapter 4), mainly input measures of institutions. The analysis carried out for 2014 allowed to distinguish two clusters (labeled liberal and a regulation-driven) among the 25 EU countries. The liberal cluster includes almost all EU members while the regulation-driven cluster embraces three neighboring southern European states: Greece, Italy and Slovenia. Such outcomes result from the fact that Western European countries are relatively similar in the area of product market competition. Long-lasting membership in the EU forced the Western European countries to adopt many regulations enhancing competition. These countries had enough time to adjust their institutional environment to the EU requirements.

Two indices in particular – time required to enforce a contract, and time to prepare and pay taxes – range among the most important variables that determine the liberal cluster. It turns out that there are large between-cluster discrepancies regarding judicial efficiency and the efficiency of the tax system. The best performers in terms of these two yardsticks are gathered in the liberal cluster, as the majority of EU25 countries have efficient market institutions that entail lower transaction costs in countries from this cluster than those from the regulation-driven cluster. As a result, in Mediterranean countries product market competition is less intense because the institutional environment features higher regulations and greater administrative burden, and hence, it is more aggravating to start and run private businesses.

The CEE region does not constitute its own cluster in the institutional area of product market competition. Ten out of 11 CEE countries in our sample were classified into the liberal cluster while the outlier (Slovenia) exhibits similar institutions to Italy and Greece. The relative homogeneity of the region was achieved thanks to the EU integration process, as between 2005 and 2014 all CEE11 countries converged institutionally to their Western peers. New EU member states were obliged to introduce many reforms to make their product markets more competitive and to safeguard common standards in the single European market. The fact that they belong to the EU implies that many aspects of product market competition (e.g. prohibition of favoring domestic companies or restrictions on the level of public aid) tend to be unified across the analyzed group due to the EU competition policy aimed at promoting competition.

Labor market and industrial relations

The empirical analysis in this part of the study was based on 17 measures of institutional architecture in the labor market and industrial relations area, including both input and output variables (see Chapter 5).

As a result of subspace clustering, four distinct groups among the EU25 countries were identified as the continental, Anglo-Saxon, statist and deregulated models. The Anglo-Saxon cluster includes the United Kingdom and Ireland. It is characterized by decentralized bargaining systems, where bargaining takes place at the company level and government interventions are limited to providing the conflict resolution mechanisms linked to the wage disputes settlements. In this cluster, pro-competitive and pro-quality factors in the workplace play a dominant role. Relations between management and employees are mostly confined to information sharing and consultations, thus bypassing the collective bargaining mechanism, which is conducive to a decentralized and voluntary nature of industrial relations.

The continental model can be found in almost all EU14 countries, with the exceptions being the UK, Ireland, Greece and Portugal. Countries in this model exhibit a relatively low share of long-term unemployed among all jobless persons. Another distinctive feature of this model is a small percentage of young people who neither study nor work (NEETs). The "solidaristic" face of the labor market becomes even more pronounced if we take account of a high proportion of employees with the lowest qualifications and a small share of precarious workers in total employment, which are characteristic for this model.

The statist cluster is made up of Greece, Portugal, and four CEE countries (Croatia, the Czech Republic, Poland and Slovenia). These countries are characterized by a low employment rate, which may result from the difficulties faced by low-skilled workers in finding a job. Another salient feature of this cluster is low quality of employment. The rationale behind such outcomes should be sought in a relatively high employment rate among precarious workers, a relatively large share of people working on fixed-term contracts in total employment and labor costs that are lower than in other clusters. "Statist" countries exhibit weak mechanisms of "industrial democracy", as seen in low unionization and undeveloped forms of employee representation, which are accompanied by a slightly lower coverage of collective agreements than in the continental cluster. The key to understanding why four CEE economies joined Greece and Portugal in this cluster seems to be the "state". If one wants to put these countries in a coherent picture, a growing importance of government (socio-economic) policies should be stressed. There are multiple examples of unilateral government decisions in individual countries, which led to unfavorable changes in the labor market and to a weakening of industrial democracy mechanisms.

Finally, the *deregulated* cluster comprises decentralized and deregulated economies, namely Bulgaria, Estonia, Hungary, Latvia, Lithuania, Romania and Slovakia – solely CEE countries. The most characteristic institutional properties of this cluster include undeveloped "industrial democracy" mechanisms coupled with a limited scope of employee representation and limited coverage of collective agreements, which altogether result in low work quality. They embrace in particular a low employment rate and a small proportion of low-skilled workers in total employment as well as a high share of precarious workers. What distinguishes this cluster from the statist one is a larger significance of limited state intervention in labor relations and a smaller share of self-employed people.

When analyzing how institutions in the CEE region changed over time, it can be observed that most countries followed the path of decentralization in the sphere of industrial relations and deregulation in the labor market (i.e. a consistent shift of the burden of collective bargaining down the system of industrial relations to the level of organizations). This was to make the collective negotiations more flexible and to better match their results to the current economic situation. The trade unions and single employers were increasingly expected to bargain and bilaterally regulate working and wage conditions. Therefore, these conditions are now to a large extent dependent upon the decision of the employer, whose position tends to be constrained by more or less extensive labor law. The exceptions to this pattern include Poland, Lithuania and Latvia. The first two countries have pursued policies aimed at tightening the state's grip on the labor market and strengthening government's decision-making monopoly in the domain of labor relations, with varying degrees of success. Latvia has undertaken the ambitious challenge of building a system close to the Anglo-Saxon benchmark, which is likely to increase the country's competitiveness in the labor market dimension.

Financial intermediation

This part of the empirical study was based on ten indicators describing the institutional architecture in the financial intermediation area, including both input and output variables (see Chapter 6).

The subspace clustering exercise allowed to detect only two asymmetric clusters within the EU25 (i.e. countries where financial intermediation relies on banks and those in which it is based on capital markets). A bank-based model is present in 20 countries including nine EU14 states and all CEE11 economies. The common factor to all countries in this cluster is the role of banks as a major provider of capital to the corporate sector. Compared to the market-based model, they exhibit a relatively lower (even by three-fourths) indices of capital market capitalization and turnover, as well as the value of assets in pension funds. Simultaneously, these countries are characterized by a relatively higher amount of outstanding loans and banking sector assets.

Financial intermediation institutions in Denmark, Netherlands, Spain, Sweden and the United Kingdom were classified into the market-based cluster, in which the capital market is the most important source of funds. These countries, apart from having a more developed capital market, also excel in the protection of property rights and are characterized by a fiercer competition in the banking sector. It should be emphasized that countries making up the market-based cluster have in fact more developed institutions of both the capital market and the banking sector than other EU25 states.

It is worth noting that "bank-based countries" do not form a homogenous cluster in terms of the prevailing patterns of institutional architecture. It can be even claimed that what makes the countries concerned to be classified in this cluster is mainly underdevelopment of their capital markets. As a result, it appears reasonable to further disaggregate this cluster and to distinguish three subclusters: 2A (Ireland, Belgium, France, Portugal and Greece), in which the institutional distance from the market-based cluster is relatively small; 2B (Finland, Germany, Italy and Austria as well as Croatia), displaying a moderate distance; and 2C (all CEE11 countries except Croatia), with a relatively large institutional gap.

Against this background it should be noted that CEE countries do not form a coherent group, either, as they differ in the degree of development of both segments of their financial systems and institutional arrangements adopted. Relative similarities among them occur in the field of property rights protection and concentration of banking sector assets. Another significant factor of similarity is the important role of the state as the owner of enterprises. All in all, they do not embody any single institutional pattern, distinct from Western European benchmarks.

It may be concluded that the financial systems of the CEE countries compared to the old EU members tend to lag behind. The largest gap can be traced in the development of capital market institutions. Such institutions have been established in every CEE country but their significance largely differs across the region – from noticeable and even significant (as in Poland and Croatia) to quite symbolic (Slovakia). The banking sector, whose level of development and significance used to be much higher in these countries, is also underdeveloped compared to Western European economies. The institutional distance, however, in the latter area is not so large, and the diversity within the CEE11 group in this regard is much smaller. Moreover, all countries from the region except Latvia tend to converge to the financial intermediation models predominant in the EU14, which can be attributed to financial market integration and standardization of the regulatory environment, especially when it comes down to banking supervision, right after the EU accession and then in the aftermath of the global financial crisis.

Social protection system

The empirical analysis in this part of the study relied on a dataset comprising 17 measures of institutional architecture in the area of social protection, including mostly input variables (for details, see Chapter 7).

As a result of subspace clustering in the social protection system, three distinct clusters of countries featuring similar sets of institutions were identified: a high taxes and public consumption model found in Denmark and Sweden; a generous benefits model prevalent in the rest of the EU14 member states as well as in Slovenia and Croatia; and a private mode of coordination model predominant in other CEE11 countries.

The main differences between the two models present in EU14 countries are concentrated mostly in the architecture of the tax system. High taxation, both in relative and absolute terms, distinguishes Denmark and Sweden from the rest of the incumbent EU members, but the ratio of benefits to total public expenditure in these countries is lower not only compared to the other EU14 states but also to the CEE11 region. Thus the protection from different risks in these Nordic countries is assured through collective consumption rather than by means of direct financial help.

The generous benefits model is characterized mostly by the up-close ratio of public expenditures on elderly people to both total public expenditures and GDP. Another important feature of this model, relative to other identified clusters, is the highest ratio of benefits to both total expenditures and GDP. Hence, this model is based mostly on transfer payments or redistributive allocation of public expenditure among members of the society rather than on a direct provision of public goods and services needed by particular social groups. Nevertheless, public resources are directed mostly to elderly people and only in a limited proportion to families and sick and disabled persons. The relative tax burden in this model is substantially lower than in other EU14 countries. The major source of general government revenue is indirect taxes, mostly the value-added tax.

The private mode of coordination model differs considerably from other types of social protection systems prevalent in the European Union, mainly due to two factors: a much lower benefits-to-GDP ratio and a lower share of total tax revenue in GDP, being collected mainly from consumption taxes, which puts a larger burden on households with relatively low incomes.

The model of social protection prevailing in most CEE11 countries lacks necessary complementarities, the existing mechanisms do not protect society from major risks and – what is more important in the long run – they do not provide enough positive externalities to the economy. Between 2005 and 2014 the institutional architecture in this area, despite being largely unstable and haunted by U-turns in government policy paradigms across the region, was subject to only limited changes of a more fundamental nature. This shows its resistance to the effects of both the EU membership and the global economic crisis.

Knowledge sector

The set of indicators employed in this part of the research included 42 measures, both input and output variables, of the institutional infrastructure in the knowledge sector (for details, see Chapter 8).

Based on the application of the subspace clustering method, four clusters of countries have been identified in this area: developed patent-oriented economies (Germany, Austria, Denmark, the Netherlands, Sweden and Finland); developed innovation-oriented economies (UK, Ireland, France and Belgium); stuck in the middle countries (Slovenia and Italy); and aspiring countries (the remaining ten CEE member states together with Greece, Spain and Portugal). Worth noting is the fact that all but one of the CEE11 countries (Slovenia) are classified in the same cluster, sharing similar institutional patterns with three Mediterranean economies.

The most salient institutional traits of developed patent-oriented economies include a relatively high level of patenting activities, a high turnover of enterprises in innovative products and a high share of households with broadband internet access and elevated individual level of internet skills.

In turn, developed innovation-oriented economies are characterized by a medium-high level of employment in knowledge-intensive services, a very high turnover (higher than in the first cluster) in innovative products and a medium level of patenting activity.

The two stuck in the middle countries exhibit a medium level of patent achievements, medium level of employment in knowledge-intensive services, medium turnover of enterprises from innovation and a relatively high share of early leavers from education and training.

The remaining EU25 or aspiring countries can be best described by a relatively low level of patenting and medium-high level of tertiary educational attainment coinciding with a relatively low share of households with broadband internet access and a low level of internet skills.

Between 2005 and 2014, the CEE economies experienced the largest institutional convergence in this area toward developed innovation-oriented economies and – to a smaller extent – to the stuck-in-the-middle countries like Italy, which also converged to the top notch of EU25 states. Simultaneously, the institutional distance of the CEE11 group from the developed patent-oriented cluster remained roughly the same. The institutional convergence occurred mainly due to (1) a rapid increase in the share of households with broadband internet access in CEE countries, (2) a significant rise in the level of tertiary educational attainment, (3) a growing number of science and technology graduates per 1,000 inhabitants, (4) an upward trend in the share of human resources in science and technology sector and (5) a sizeable growth of patent applications and patents granted to entities from CEE countries.

The current state of the knowledge system in CEE11 countries is most likely transitory. The transformation that started in the early 1990s led to a liberalization of the system and strong dependence on transnational corporations and foreign capital (Slovenia remained an exception).

Housing market

The empirical analysis in this area relied on 23 institutional measures, both input and output variables, divided into six groups (see Chapter 9).

While examining the data with the subspace clustering algorithm, four distinct groups of countries that share a similar set of institutions, which represent four models of residential capitalism, have been identified: the liberal-corporatist model found among Northern European countries (Ireland, the United Kingdom,

Belgium, the Netherlands, Denmark, Sweden and Finland); the statist model that is prevalent in most core eurozone member states (France, Germany, Austria); the commodified-familial model in the south of Europe (Portugal, Spain, Greece) and in Estonia; and the non-commodified model predominant in Italy and all CEE countries but Estonia.

The liberal-corporatist model is characterized by high mortgage indebtedness of the population, high financial affordability of housing driven by financial market deregulation and by low house prices relative to income. These characteristics reflect a market-based system of housing allocation. However, at the same time countries with a liberal-corporatist model of institutions feature a wide margin of state interventions in the housing market – the share of social housing is the highest among all EU25 economies, rent controls are relatively rigid, and the government spends the biggest sums on housing policies.

The most salient feature of the statist model is the lowest share of owner-occupied houses in the dwelling stock among all EU member states. This is an outcome of a large-scale provision of cheap rental dwellings and high availability of social housing. Another distinctive property of this model is a low rate of household indebtedness, which comes despite a very deregulated financial market that provides cheap capital from banks or trusts for rental housing investments. State interventions in the statist model are visible in an extended control of tenant-landlord relations with restrictive eviction procedures, high rent controls and a variety of subsidies and allowance schemes for private investments in cheap rental housing.

The commodified-familial model features a high share of owner-occupied dwellings. That is a result of the ownership myth prevalent in countries with this set of institutions (i.e. a pervasive belief that owning a dwelling is by far the best way to satisfy one's housing needs and the safest asset in a household portfolio). Buying a home is also seen as the main constituent of establishing a family and is usually treated as a necessary condition for having children. Another important trait of this model is a very low occupation rate that co-exists with an overcrowding rate twice as high as in other EU14 countries. Moreover, residential estates are already to a large extent commodified, especially regarding new dwellings, which is reflected in a high level of residential loans. All the aforementioned characteristics indicate that the market-based system of dwelling allocation is present but not working effectively and in many aspects it is complemented by a family-based system, as parents are expected to satisfy housing needs of their children. Hence, the share of young adults living with parents is the highest among all EU14 member states. The government refrains from market interventions. The state does not provide any social housing or subsidies for private provision of dwellings for rent and usually also does not subsidize housing purchases for first-time buyers.

The CEE region differs largely from the rest of the European Union in terms of housing market institutions. Despite many between-country discrepancies, the governments across the region developed a distinct model of residential capitalism that can be found nowhere else in Europe but Italy. It is most of all characterized by a low commodification of dwellings, low supply of social housing, an underdeveloped rental market and a large proportion of young adults living with parents. This translates into the highest share of owner-occupied houses in the dwelling stock among all EU countries. Another distinctive feature of this model is a very low indebtedness of households.

The foregoing characteristics of the non-commodified model coincide with the prevailing perception of dwellings, which are seen as family goods – their worth was never appraised and is usually not included in the subjectively assessed wealth of households. Dwellings are passed on from generation to generation and people are not very eager to sell them or withdraw equity allocated in housing. As a result, the secondary market for houses is shallow, the prices of dwellings are the highest relative to incomes among all EU members and, hence, housing financial affordability is much lower than in the rest of Europe. This leads to the conclusion that the market-based system of dwelling allocation is present only in big cities but largely ineffective and almost non-existent in rural areas. Hence, the prevailing system of dwelling allocation is family-based and is even more widespread than in the commodified-familial model. As a derivative, the non-commodified model is characterized by a very high overcrowding rate, a low occupation rate and a large share of deprived dwellings. This indicates that the equity allocated in housing is used ineffectively in this system, which brings about large housing shortages in CEE countries.

Between 2005 and 2014, the institutions encompassing the housing market in CEE countries evolved in the direction of residential capitalism models typical for incumbent EU member states, especially the liberal-corporatist one. This can be explained mainly by a housing policy common across the region before the global financial crisis that was aimed at increasing financial affordability of owner-occupied houses, especially through providing cheap mortgage credit and government subsidies for first-time buyers, which led to an increase in household indebtedness.

This evolution path resembles the one taken a decade earlier by southern European countries, which ended up with a boom-bust episode that hampered their long-term economic growth and brought social unrest after the global financial crisis. This is indicated by the change in institutional similarity between the CEE region and those incumbent EU states that host the commodified-familial model: between 2005 and 2014, institutional measures for 9 out of 11 CEE countries became more similar to these countries. This was mainly caused by mass privatization of social dwellings, abolition of co-operatives and the slowest reduction in housing shortages in these countries due to a high cost of taking up mortgage credits.

10.2 Discussion

As a summary of the foregoing descriptive characteristic of empirical results broken down into six institutional areas, in this section we embark on a more general discussion of major findings of the present study. Table 10.1 provides a stylized, comparative picture of the number and composition of clusters identified among

Table 10.1 Clusters identified in the EU25 countries in six institutional areas, 2014

Institutional area	*Cluster 1*	*Cluster 2*	*Cluster 3*	*Cluster 4*
Product market competition	IT, GR, SI	AT, BE, BG, CZ, DE, DK, EE, ES, FI, FR, HR, HU, IE, LT, LV, NL, PL, PT, RO, SE, SK, UK		
Labor market and industrial relations	IE, UK	AT, BE, DE, DK, ES, FI, FR, IT, NL, SE	CZ, GR, HR, PL, PT, SI	BG, EE, HU, LT, LV, RO, SK
Financial intermediation	DK, ES, NL, SE, UK	AT, BE, BG, CZ, DE, EE, FI, FR, GR, HR, HU, IE, IT, LT, LV, PL, PT, RO, SI, SK		
Social protection	AT, BE, DE, ES, FI, FR, GR, HR, IE, IT, NL, PT, SI, UK	DK, SE	BG, CZ, EE, HU, LT, LV, PL, RO, SK	
Knowledge sector	BE, FR, IE, UK	AT, DE, DK, FI, NL, SE	IT, SI	BG, CZ, EE, ES, GR, HR, HU, LT, LV, PL, PT, RO, SK
Housing market	BE, DK, FI, IE, NL, SE, UK	AT, DE, FR	EE, ES, GR, PT	BG, CZ, HR, HU, IT, LT, LV, PL, RO, SI, SK

Source: Authors' elaboration.

the 25 EU member countries in the final year of our empirical exercise. The picture involved is further sharpened in Tables 10.2 through 10.5, which are shown in the subsequent parts of this section (see also Rapacki and Czerniak, 2018).

A more in-depth analysis of the data in Table 10.1, as well as those in Tables 10.2 through 10.5, allows to come up with several interesting insights. They may be synthesized as follows.

1 The number of clusters identified across the six institutional domains ranges between two and four, including the new EU members from Central and Eastern Europe (CEE11). This result may be interpreted as a confirmation – at the most aggregate level – of the general conclusion made by Amable (i.e. the co-existence of diverse models of capitalism in the European Union).
2 Notwithstanding this fundamental similarity, our findings point to a number of essential differences compared to the results established by Amable (2003). The key differences to be emphasized include in particular the following:

Table 10.2 The status of the Amablean models of capitalism in the light of subspace clustering results

Institutional area	*Anglo-Saxon cluster (with UK)*	*Nordic cluster (with Sweden)*	*Mediterranean cluster (with Italy)*	*Continental European cluster (not internally coherent)*
Product market competition	No	No	Yes	Yes
Labor market and industrial relations	Yes	No	No	Yes
Financial intermediation	Yes	No	No	Yes
Social protection	No	Yes	No	Yes
Knowledge sector	Yes	No	Yes	Yes
Housing market	Not applicable			

Source: Authors' elaboration.

i The clusters identified in this study (let alone for Western European EU members) differ depending on the institutional domain involved, both in terms of their number and makeup. Hence, the claim made by Amable that the diversity of Western European capitalism in each institutional area is the same among the EU countries seems ungrounded on the basis of up-to-date data.

ii The composition of particular clusters identified in our study differs from the Amablean benchmarks dubbed the Anglo-Saxon, Continental European, Nordic and Mediterranean models of capitalism:

- In some areas (product market competition and financial intermediation), the ongoing Europeanization of markets and their institutional unification caused some clusters to disappear.
- In almost all institutional areas, the Nordic model merged with either of two models (the Continental or the Anglo-Saxon model), the exception being the social protection system.
- Moreover, the makeup of clusters identified differs considerably from one institutional area to another (a country may be classified in distinct clusters depending on the area involved), which makes the overall picture quite ambiguous and impedes the task of coming up with a viable general typology of the co-existing models of contemporary capitalism in the European Union.

A more detailed comparative breakdown of our results is provided in Table 10.2. The main message they convey is that by 2014, the original typology developed by Amable did not hold for almost a half of the cells specified in the table (9 out of 20). This was particularly the case of the Nordic and Mediterranean models of capitalism. On the other hand, the opposite was true for the Continental model and, to a lesser degree, the Anglo-Saxon model.

3 Given the results of the subspace clustering exercise, it can be contended that CEE11 countries developed their own distinct model of capitalism. This outcome corroborates – at least at the most aggregate level – the findings of a recent study on comparative capitalism in the EU by Farkas (2016). The only two institutional areas in which these countries do not significantly differ from their Western European peers are those that are highly unified across the EU: the product market competition and financial intermediation. Interestingly, the results of the present study have also confirmed our earlier findings (see Próchniak et al., 2016), that post-communist EU member states exhibit many similarities with Mediterranean countries. As shown in Table 10.3, only these incumbent EU members are sometimes classified as a part of the CEE11 cluster.

4 The model of post-communist capitalism identified in CEE11 countries exhibits in many respects a patchwork nature which is due – in the most general terms – to the heterogeneity or institutional ambiguity[1] inherent in the design and operation of this model. While we will delve into the theme of patchwork capitalism in the CEE region in more detail and justify the use of this term in the subsequent section, here we focus on the empirical findings alone.

Thus, in the light of the empirical results of subspace clustering, the patchwork essence of the evolving capitalism in the CEE11 countries manifests itself particularly at two levels of their institutional architecture:

- *Inter-area patchwork*

  In each country, the elements of the institutional matrix that were adopted and amended in the course of systemic transformation have a different heritage for various areas (i.e. they are derived from different established Western European models of capitalism). Most of these elements have been transplanted from countries like Germany, which embody the most common Continental European model, but some parts are of Mediterranean (mostly from Spain or Italy), Nordic (mostly Sweden) or Anglo-Saxon heritage (see Table 10.4). This frequently makes

Table 10.3 Stylized picture of CEE11 capitalism, 2014

Institutional area	*Distinct cluster for CEE11 countries*	*Number of outliers*	*Number of EU14 countries in the CEE11 cluster*
Product market competition	No	N/A	N/A
Labor market and industrial relations	**Yes**	**4 (HR, CZ, PL, SI)**	**2 (GR, PT)**
Financial intermediation	No	N/A	N/A
Social protection	**Yes**	**2 (HR, SI)**	**0**
Knowledge sector	**Yes**	**1 (SI)**	**3 (GR, PT, ES)**
Housing market	**Yes**	**1 (EE)**	**1 (IT)**

Source: Authors' elaboration.

Table 10.4 Closest models of Western European capitalism for CEE11 countries

Institutional area	*Bulgaria*	*Croatia*	*Czechia*	*Estonia*	*Hungary*	*Latvia*	*Lithuania*	*Poland*	*Romania*	*Slovakia*	*Slovenia*
Product market competition	DE	DE	DE	**DE**	**DE**	**DE**	**DE**	DE	**DE**	DE	**IT**
Labor market and industrial relations	DE	DE	DE	DE	DE	DE	DE	DE	DE	DE	DE
Financial intermediation	**DE**	**DE**	**DE**	**DE**	**DE**	**DE**	**DE**	**DE**	**DE**	**DE**	**DE**
Social protection	DE	**DE**	DE	SE	SE	SE	DE	DE	SE	DE	DE
Knowledge sector	UK	IT	IT	IT	DE	IT	IT	IT	IT	IT	**IT**
Housing market	IT	IT	IT	**IT**	UK	IT	IT	IT	IT	IT	IT

DE – Continental European cluster (with Germany) identified with the ORCLUS algorithm.
IT – Mediterranean cluster (with Italy or Spain but not Germany) identified with the ORCLUS algorithm.
UK – Anglo-Saxon cluster (with UK but not Germany) identified with the ORCLUS algorithm.
SE – Nordic cluster (with Sweden but not Germany and UK) identified with the ORCLUS algorithm.
Cluster acronyms for countries that are actually classified into that cluster are shown in bold type.

Source: Authors' elaboration.

individual institutional areas incompatible, as they represent divergent inner logic and are often not complementary to each other, which hampers economic development and generates social tensions among various groups of vested interests in the CEE countries.

- *Intra-area patchwork*

  There also exists a systemic mismatch within the respective areas, particularly between input and output characteristics of the institutional architectures involved, which has been clearly shown in one of our earlier empirical studies (Próchniak et al., 2016). It originates from a clear deficit of institutional complementarities within these areas, especially between formal and informal institutions. Such a patchwork can be traced back to the systemic transformation period, when CEE countries adopted policies and elements of the institutional orders that proved to be efficient in the incumbent EU member states without taking proper account of the peculiarity of their own institutional endowment (its economic, political, social and cultural characteristics) in which these elements of Western-type capitalism would be embedded. This was conducive to a lack of complementarities between the path-dependent institutional matrix existing in a country (measured mainly by output variables) and the newly adopted policies (measured mostly by input variables). These effects can be most vividly seen in such institutional areas as the social protection system and the housing market, where the current institutional environment is subject to a strong path dependence.

5 Notwithstanding the fact that we identified one single model of post-communist capitalism prevalent in CEE11 countries, our subspace clustering exercise has also shown that the CEE group is quite heterogeneous. This is in particular due to three factors:

   i The empirical evidence points to a considerable differentiation of institutional characteristics or institutional architectures among CEE11 countries.
   ii In all but two institutional areas concerned (product market competition and financial intermediation), some CEE11 economies have been outlying from the Central and Eastern European cluster (see Table 10.3). The number of outliers ranges between one and four, depending on the area involved.
   iii Capitalism in Central and Eastern Europe has evolved over time, as the CEE11 countries experienced both convergence and divergence trends of their institutional architectures vis-à-vis their Western European peers between 2005 and 2014. Moreover, each of the countries followed its own distinct vector of institutional changes (see Table 10.5).

From the aforementioned findings, it may be inferred that the CEE region hosts a diversity of patchwork capitalism. In other words, each of the CEE11 countries

Table 10.5 Convergence of CEE11 countries to Western European models across six institutional areas, 2005–2014

Clusters as identified with the ORCLUS algorithm / *Institutional area*	*Continental cluster (with Germany)*	*Mediterranean cluster (with Italy or Spain but not Germany)*	*Anglo-Saxon cluster (with UK but not Germany)*	*Nordic cluster (with Sweden but not Germany and UK)*
Product market competition	convergence: 10 divergence: 1	convergence: 7 divergence: 4		
Labor market and industrial relations	convergence: 6 divergence: 5		convergence: 5 divergence: 6	
Financial intermediation	convergence: 9 divergence: 2		convergence: 7 divergence: 4	
Social protection	convergence: 5 divergence: 6			convergence: 5 divergence: 6
Knowledge sector	convergence: 5 divergence: 6	convergence: 11 divergence: 0	convergence: 11 divergence: 0	
Housing market	convergence: 10 divergence: 1	convergence: 9 divergence: 2	convergence: 11 divergence: 0	

Source: Authors' elaboration.

followed its own distinct vector of changes, which eventually led to a unique patchwork of institutions in each of these countries. Yet, the institutional variance within the CEE11 region is smaller than the differences between those countries and other models of capitalism identified among EU member states.

10.3 Patchwork nature of post-communist capitalism in Central and Eastern Europe

In this section we will capitalize on the empirical findings of subspace clustering discussed above and will endeavor to embark on some generalizations and to justify the use of the term "patchwork capitalism" as the most adequate descriptor of the essence of post-communist political economies that have evolved in Central and Eastern Europe since the outset of systemic transformation.

The notion of patchwork capitalism prevalent in CEE11 countries can be best comprehended as an institutional matrix incorporating components or building blocks transplanted from various institutional orders, with special emphasis on the co-existing models of contemporary Western-type capitalism. Simultaneously, what makes patchwork capitalism even more "patchy" and incoherent is a significant component of path dependence in each CEE country.

The latter factor can be further split into two interdependent parts of a country's historical heritage, that is, (1) embedded in the proto-capitalist past (before World War II) and (2) the command-economy legacy. As a result, the institutional architecture in a CEE country may be depicted as a structure made up of three layers:

(1) a proto-capitalist legacy, (2) a socialist heritage, and (3) imprints of diverse models of contemporary Western-type capitalism,[2] with a predominant role of the last layer.

Seen in a broader, social science perspective, the very word "patchwork" was – independent of our own research and terminology – first used over 30 years ago by a Hungarian historian, Jenö Szücs (1983, 1988), who applied the terms "patchwork feudalism" and "patchwork capitalism" to describe historical developments in Hungary and other Central Eastern European countries in the 19th century and the first half of the 20th century. In his view, institutions imported to these countries from more advanced Western European states used to be redefined in the importer countries and often served different purposes compared to their original functions.

His basic idea was that the area stretching from the Baltic Sea to the Adriatic Sea was a region between West and East which always tried to follow Western developmental and cultural patterns. However, the CEE region tended to lag behind the Western standards and its development was on many occasions interrupted. Thus, the economic, social and political institutions in Central Eastern Europe were always (at least partially) distorted imitations of their Western counterparts. With a view to make his arguments even more persuasive, Szücs extended the historical perspective beyond the past two centuries and brought many examples supporting his idea of "patchwork feudalism" and "patchwork capitalism" from the Middle Ages.

As the concept of patchwork capitalism highlights heterogeneity of post-communist political economies in CEE countries, it is worthwhile to contrast this term with some "rival" notions that at first glance may seem similar or even synonymous. In the ongoing scholarly debate on the diversity of emerging capitalism in the former socialist countries, three such notions are particularly worth comparing with our proposal: "cocktail capitalism", "hybrid capitalism" and "mixed capitalism".

The term "cocktail capitalism" was coined by a Romanian scholar, Lucian Cernat (Cernat, 2006). In his book, Cernat claimed that the diversity of national forms of capitalism can be organized into three basic types: Anglo-Saxon capitalism, Continental capitalism and developmental capitalism. His analysis also showed that incomplete institutional frameworks borrowed from several existing models of capitalism, coupled with the important component of command-economy legacy, were conducive to the emergence of "cocktail capitalism" as a distorted form of developmental capitalism.

Notwithstanding some similarities to the very idea of "patchwork capitalism", we would argue that the concept of "cocktail capitalism" significantly differs from the former in terms of both content and coverage. This is due to two factors. In the first place, while the notion of "cocktail capitalism" is confined to one country (i.e. Romania), "patchwork capitalism" is meant to denote the nature of post-communist capitalism in a broader group of countries, that is new member states of the European Union from Central and Eastern Europe including Romania. The second difference boils down to the ingredients of cocktail vs. patchwork capitalism. While the former implies a blend of elements that constitute both the command-economy legacy and new building blocks of a market economy, the term patchwork capitalism describes a type of institutional architecture that reconciles components and parts transplanted from various models of Western European capitalism. In other words, whereas cocktail capitalism reconciles elements inherent to different economic systems, patchwork capitalism comprises components of different varieties of the same system.

Moreover, it may be also argued that the two notions being compared imply two opposite types of synergies inherent to post-communist capitalism. Whereas "cocktail capitalism" implicitly suggests mostly positive synergies between the building blocks of the political economy concerned (a cocktail's good taste results from putting the right ingredients in the right proportions and in the right sequence), the term "patchwork capitalism" hints at negative synergies within an institutional architecture being a derivative of its incoherence and deficit of institutional complementarities.

The notion of patchwork capitalism may be also confronted with the concepts of *hybrid capitalism* and *mixed economies*. The latter terms were introduced earlier in this book and discussed as part of a survey of most representative research on comparative capitalism in former socialist countries carried out in Chapter 2 (see, e.g., King and Szelenyi, 2005; Mykhnenko, 2007). The common thread of all three concepts concerned is their stress on heterogeneity of the emerging capitalism in former socialist countries, which is due to the fact that the institutional architectures in these countries reconcile building blocks coming from various institutional orders or models of capitalism.

On the other hand, the names "hybrid capitalism" and "mixed economies" are fairly general as they point solely to a well-known fact of the co-existence of different parts under one roof or institutional matrix without defining more precisely their number and implications. The concept of "patchwork capitalism" goes further, as it starts where the two notions in question have stopped. In this sense it is an extension and complement of these two general concepts. It digs deeper into the core of the evolving post-communist capitalism and reveals those features and intricacies of its institutional matrix which are not seen under the emblems of hybrid capitalism or mixed economies. In particular, it points to such peculiar traits of the political economies prevalent in 11 Central and Eastern European countries as:

- Institutional ambiguity (which is more than just heterogeneity);
- Divergent inner logic of the respective institutional areas and constituents of pertinent political economies, which explains institutional incoherence and deficit of institutional complementarities;
- Different levels of institutional incoherence;
- Mismatch between formal and informal institutions;
- Similarly, a misfit of input and output measures of institutional architecture;
- Possible frictions and idle capacity (or systemic entropy) of the political economies involved as a result of institutional incoherence which may give rise to inefficiencies.[3]

10.4 Concluding remarks

To wrap up the foregoing discussion, it may be argued that the results of the subspace clustering exercise corroborate a substantial part of our starting conjectures and allow a positive verification of our hypotheses. In particular, they seem to support four of our claims:

1 The present study provides a new empirical evidence confirming the co-existence of diverse models of capitalism in the European Union – and even more so if the new EU member countries from Central and Eastern Europe are included in the research sample.
2 The number and composition of particular clusters identified in this research differ from the Amablean benchmarks dubbed the Anglo-Saxon, Continental European, Nordic and Mediterranean models of capitalism.
3 The CEE11 countries developed their own distinct model of capitalism, compared to Western European benchmarks.
4 The model of post-communist capitalism identified in CEE11 countries exhibits in many respects a patchwork nature. This is due to the institutional ambiguity inherent in its design, including a clear deficit of complementarities in their institutional architectures, both within particular areas and between them.

Yet the empirical results of the present study do not yield an unequivocal picture of the diversity of contemporary capitalism co-existing in the European Union. Despite some common patterns, the variance of institutional architecture across the EU member states reveals many faces depending on the institutional area analyzed. Moreover, in a number of areas institutional disparities between some countries ceased to exist in the last decade as the European integration has moved onward.

Hence, a further in-depth and interdisciplinary research on comparative post-communist capitalism is required, including more refined applications of the subspace clustering method coupled with a comprehensive case study analysis in different institutional areas.

Notes

1 We use this term, which was originally coined by Mykhnenko (2005), in a broader sense which incorporates, inter alia, the notions of incoherence and deficit of institutional complementarities in various dimensions.
2 Here a seeming analogy may be found to a well-known concept of Octavio Paz developed in his Nobel Prize–winning novel *The Labyrinth of Solitude* (Paz, 1961). He found the key to understanding the identity of contemporary Mexico as a derivative of the reminiscences in the collective consciousness of three distinct stages (or temporal layers) in country's history: the pre-Colombian past, the colonial era, and the contemporary stage following the Mexican Revolution of 1917.
3 In our earlier studies (see, e.g., Próchniak et al., 2016) we found multiple examples of such inefficiencies or underperformance. At the most aggregate level, while the whole

CEE11 group and most individual countries exhibited the highest relative institutional similarity to the Continental model of capitalism (represented by Germany) in terms of input variables or measures of institutions, they simultaneously proved much more akin to the Mediterranean model (Spain or Italy) in terms of output variables or economic performance.

References

Amable, B. (2003). *The diversity of modern capitalism*. Oxford: Oxford University Press.

Cernat, L. (2006). Domestic institutions and economic performance: 'Cocktail Capitalism'. In: *Europeanization, varieties of capitalism and economic performance in Central and Eastern Europe. Studies in economic transition*. London: Palgrave Macmillan.

Farkas, B. (2016). *Models of capitalism in the European Union. Post-crisis perspective*. London: Palgrave Macmillan.

King, L.P. and Szelenyi, I. (2005). Post-communist economic systems. In: N.J. Smelser and R. Swedberg, eds. *The handbook of economic sociology*. Princeton: Princeton University Press.

Mykhnenko, V. (2005). *What type of capitalism in Eastern Europe? Institutional structures, revealed comparative advantage, and performance of Poland and Ukraine*. Discussion Paper 6. Glasgow: Centre for Public Policy and Regions, University of Glasgow.

Mykhnenko, V. (2007). Strengths and weaknesses of 'weak' coordination: economic institutions, revealed comparative advantages, and socio-economic performance of mixed market economies in Poland and Ukraine. In: B. Hancké, M. Rhodes and M. Thatcher, eds., *Beyond varieties of capitalism. Conflict, contradictions, and complementarities in the European economy*. Oxford: Oxford University Press.

Paz, O. (1961). *The labyrinth of solitude*. New York: Grove Press.

Próchniak, M., Rapacki, R., Gardawski, J., Czerniak, A., Horbaczewska, B., Karbowski, A., Maszczyk, P. and Towalski, R. (2016). The emerging models of capitalism in CEE11 countries – A tentative comparison with Western Europe. *Warsaw Forum of Economic Sociology*, 7:2(14), Autumn, pp. 7–70.

Rapacki, R. and Czerniak, A. (2018). Emerging models of patchwork capitalism in Central and Eastern Europe: Empirical results of subspace clustering. *International Journal of Management and Economics*, 54(4), pp. 251–268.

Szücs, J. (1983). The three historical regions of Europe: An outline. *Acta Historica Academiae Scientiarum Hungaricae*, 29(2–4), pp. 131–184.

Szücs, J. (1988). Three historical regions of Europe. In: J. Keane, ed., *Civil society and the state*. London: Verso.

Concluding remarks

Ryszard Rapacki

The results of our research project and their discussion carried out in this book prompt a number of general conclusions, which may be seen as a self-assessment of the suitability of the conceptual and methodological framework and the very approach adopted in this research.

First and foremost, in our view the analytical framework applied in this study and recapitulated below proved to be an appropriate research tool, as it enabled achieving most of the research goals set at the outset of this project. Moreover, we would also argue that, due to its versatility, it may serve the purpose of more comprehensive studies on comparative capitalism in the European Union as a tool capable of coping with new research challenges, including new phenomena and processes unfolding in Europe. The framework, developed originally by Bruno Amable in 2003 (see Chapter 2 for a reference), was subject to essential extensions and amendments by the present authors. As a reminder, the following extensions and amendments to the original Amablean methodology were introduced (Chapter 3):

- We combined the macroeconomic analytical perspective with selected components of the microeconomic foundations derived from Hall and Soskice (2001) – apart from a country clustering exercise, we also scrutinized the coordination mechanisms prevalent in each cluster and assessed their complementarity with both formal and informal institutions.
- We discarded the tacit assumption made by Amable that the number of models/varieties of capitalism in the European Union is finite and predetermined by the typology crafted 15 years earlier for a distinct group of countries. Similarly, we did not assume an a priori continuity of the four models of Western European capitalism singled out by Amable in 2003.
- Unlike in Amable's original exercise, which boiled down to a snapshot of various models of capitalism prevailing in the Western developed world during the 1990s and 2000s, the major focus in our study was placed on the dynamics of institutional architecture in the CEE region, which enabled capturing the evolution of the emerging capitalism in the CEE11 countries.
- Another important extension of the original analytical framework consisted in the inclusion of the housing market as the sixth institutional area in the set of basic research categories.

- The present empirical study relied on a vast dataset encompassing more than 130 institutional measures; they covered both the "input" and "output" sides of the institutional architecture in the CEE11 countries and enabled capturing both formal and informal institutions, which added to the versatility of our approach, as the role of the latter in former socialist countries is particularly important.
- In our study, more complex and advanced quantitative methods (i.e. subspace clustering) were employed, as compared to the original DoC approach. They enabled identifying the common traits and differences between the CEE11 economies and Western European models of capitalism and allowed the analysis of a larger, and hence more comprehensive, set of indicators.

Second, as expected, the subspace clustering machine-learning research method (i.e. the ORCLUS algorithm) turned out to be an appropriate quantitative technique for the purpose of the present study, as it combined – at a higher level of technical sophistication – the virtues of the principal component analysis and the traditional clustering technique (see Chapter 3). It enabled discriminating between various clusters of countries sharing similar sets of institutional arrangements in a multidimensional space while at the same time ranking the institutional indicators involved in line with their order of importance as determinants of each cluster in each institutional area.

Finally, due to its comprehensive coverage, the empirical study on comparative capitalism in the European Union carried out in this book made it possible to accommodate in one broad typology all the EU member countries in the research sample, both the newcomers (CEE11) and the incumbents (EU14), which enhances the versatility of this research approach and the applicability of the adjusted conceptual and methodological framework concerned.

In the concluding part of the book, it is also worthwhile to synthesize the major empirical findings of our research (Chapters 4 through 9 and Chapter 10). They may be summarized as follows.

1 Our research corroborated in most general terms the co-existence of diverse models of capitalism in the European Union by 2014, which enhances and adds validity to the conclusion arrived at by Bruno Amable at the beginning of the previous decade.
2 Notwithstanding this general similarity, however, our findings point to several key discrepancies compared to the results established by Amable (2003). They include in particular the following: (1) the clusters identified in this study differ depending on the institutional area involved, both in terms of their number and makeup; (2) the composition of particular clusters identified in our study exhibits clear dissimilarities with regard to the Amablean points of reference, dubbed the Anglo-Saxon, Continental European, Nordic and Mediterranean models of capitalism; moreover, (3) in all but one institutional area, the Nordic model merged with either of two models – the Continental or the Anglo-Saxon one.

Further, the makeup of clusters identified differs considerably from one institutional area to another (a country may be classified to distinct clusters depending on the area involved), which makes the overall picture quite ambiguous and impedes the task of coming up with a viable general typology of the co-existing models of contemporary capitalism in the European Union.

3 The results of subspace clustering have shown that CEE11 countries developed their own distinct model of capitalism, the only exceptions being the product market competition and financial intermediation (i.e. those institutional areas that are highly unified across the EU). This result is consistent with another finding: the existence of a few outliers from the CEE11 group in particular areas which were found in Western European clusters.

4 Parallel to the findings described under the previous heading, the results of the present study have also confirmed that the new EU member states from the CEE region exhibit in many respects visible similarities to Mediterranean countries.

5 Seen in the light of the empirical evidence gathered in our study, the model of post-communist capitalism identified in CEE11 countries exhibits in many respects a patchwork nature which is due – in the most general terms – to the heterogeneity or institutional ambiguity inherent in the design and operation of the institutional matrix prevalent in these countries.

The notion of patchwork capitalism prevalent in CEE11 countries can be best comprehended as an institutional matrix incorporating building blocks transplanted from various institutional orders, and in particular from the co-existing models of contemporary, Western-type capitalism. This gives rise to a clear deficit of institutional complementarities (both within particular institutional areas and between them) and makes the whole structure incoherent. Simultaneously, what makes patchwork capitalism even more "patchy" and incoherent is a significant component of path dependence in each CEE country.

6 Capitalism in Central and Eastern Europe has evolved over time, as the CEE11 countries experienced both convergence and divergence trends of their institutional architectures vis-à-vis their Western European peers between 2005 and 2014.

7 The present research also provided unequivocal empirical evidence that the CEE region hosts a diversity of patchwork capitalism. This is a derivative of the fact that each of the CEE11 countries followed its own distinct vector of changes, which eventually led to a unique patchwork of institutions in each of these countries. Yet, the institutional variance within the CEE11 region is smaller than the differences between those countries and other models of capitalism identified among the incumbent EU member states.

To wrap up this part of the concluding remarks, we are inclined to argue that the results of the subspace clustering exercise presented in this book seem to corroborate a substantial part of our starting conjectures and allow a positive verification of most of our hypotheses. Simultaneously, it sounds like a plausible assertion that the results of our study, interpreted in terms of a general picture of patchwork capitalism in CEE11 countries and its reference to the established models of Western European capitalism, are relatively resilient to changes in the individual components and parts of the institutional architecture taking place in the CEE countries after 2014, the final year of our empirical study.

Still, with the benefit of hindsight, we realize that we have not succeeded in achieving all research objectives set for our project or in answering all research questions and in confirming each and every initial conjecture. Moreover, the new phenomena and processes unfolding both in the CEE region and in the European Union after 2014 may to some extent blur the present picture of the co-existing models of capitalism, which entails new challenges for comparative capitalism studies and calls for appropriate updates to the research agenda and for possible refinements in the dataset of institutional measures and quantitative techniques employed. These new trends may have materialized at the level of individual institutional areas (such as the labor market and industrial relations; see Chapter 5) or the entire political economy in single countries or their entirety.

Looking forward, one of the key challenges facing the prospective research on comparative capitalism in former socialist countries in Central and Eastern Europe (which is also consistent with the findings established in our study) stems from the fact that patchwork capitalism in these countries has continued to be in a state of flux. This is equivalent to saying that, in contrast to developed market economies, the process of systemic transformation in CEE countries entailed a high degree of discontinuity and volatility. Even today, it is hard to predict therefore which institutional characteristics existing in former socialist countries are permanent and are likely to have lasting consequences and which are only of a temporary nature.

This problem has become even more pronounced with the anti-liberal counterrevolutions that began in two CEE11 countries: Hungary in 2010 and Poland in 2015. They both effectively entailed a fully-fledged departure from the institutional orders that had been established in these countries since 1990. Moreover, the turnarounds that occurred in Hungary and Poland came as a surprise to many scholars in the field of comparative political economies who believed that the institutional architectures in these two countries have been quite well established and tentatively coined the category of "embedded neoliberal" type of capitalism (e.g. Bohle and Greskovits, 2012; see also Chapter 2).

In their recent article, Ivan Krastev and Stephen Holmes (2018) interpret the underlying reasons for this abrupt institutional switch as a derivative of an increased social discontent resulting from an excessive reliance of both Hungary and Poland (and the CEE countries in general) on Western institutional solutions, and by the same token, the predominant imitative pattern of economic and institutional development of these countries. The side effect of imitation is the complex of inferiority coupled with a feeling of lost national identity, non-authenticity or even humiliation. This is paralleled by a pervasive perception of being monitored and assessed by the benchmark Western countries, which may be interpreted in terms of excessive dependence on Western norms and standards or a constrained national sovereignty. According to these authors, an equally important source of social frustration and disenchantment that may explain the anti-liberal counter-revolutions in these countries has been the libertarian trends observed in the West since the EU Eastern enlargement in 2004, which remodeled the prevailing value systems and cultural norms in Western societies. These changes have been conceived by a growing proportion of Poles and Hungarians as incompatible with national traditions and own cultural patterns, which fed the rising electoral support for "euroskeptical" and conservative political parties like Fidesz in Hungary and PiS in Poland (Krastev and Holmes, 2018).[1] Another key factor that compounds the foregoing trends is economic migration and the problem of refugees which combined to prompt the question of the genuine cultural identity of many Western societies and, as a derivative, another fundamental question of the right developmental and axiological "European" role model to be followed by the latecomer EU countries in the future.

These questions and the corresponding dilemmas become even more acute in view of the recent changes unfolding in the "core" EU member countries. These include in particular the case of Brexit in the UK, the "yellow jacket" unrests in France and a rising electoral support for "euroskeptical" and populist political parties, including the extreme right, in most incumbent EU countries, which culminated with the takeover of power by the Movement of Five Stars and the Northern League in Italy. They all appear to be a symptom of much deeper cultural, economic, social and political processes reflecting, inter alia, profound changes in social stratification, a shrinking middle class and a growing gap or social polarization between the elites in big cities and the "popular class" elsewhere. All these new trends combined are likely to alter the hitherto "European identity". At the same time, they cast serious doubts over the future of the European Union and overshadow its ability to undertake concerted actions and policies in the global environment.

Summing up, in the light of the foregoing discussion, such factors as the role of imitation, and similarly the significance of the dependent patterns of development and peripheral position of the CEE region in the European Union and the global economic order, should be added to the future research agenda on comparative capitalism in Central and Eastern European countries as new dimensions and essential determinants of their evolving model(s) of patchwork capitalism. Simultaneously, the prospective studies on comparative capitalism should be ready to abandon the assumption that the present models of capitalism co-existing in the European Union and identified in our research are engraved in stone.

Note

1 On the other hand, however, we should not forget that in the case of Poland the electoral support for the ruling PiS party in the 2015 parliamentary elections amounted to only some 37%, and the proportion of Poles who support the idea of country's EU membership consistently exceeds 60% in public opinion polls and ranks among the highest in the European Union.

References

Amable, B. (2003). *The diversity of modern capitalism*. Oxford: Oxford University Press.

Bohle, D. and Greskovits, B. (2012). *Capitalist diversity on Europe's periphery*. Ithaca and London: Cornell University Press.

Hall, P. and Soskice, D. (2001). *Varieties of capitalism. The institutional foundations of comparative advantage*. Oxford: Oxford University Press.

Krastev, I. and Holmes, S. (2018). Explaining Eastern Europe: Imitation and its discontents. *Journal of Democracy*, 29(3), July, pp. 117–128.

Index

Note: Page numbers in **bold** indicate a table on the corresponding page.

www.ingramcontent.com/pod-product-compliance
Lightning Source LLC
LaVergne TN
LVHW011127300926
849160LV00008B/539

* 9 7 8 0 3 6 7 7 2 7 2 0 8 *